VISIONARIES AND MYSTICS

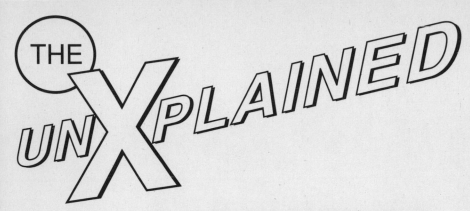

THE unXPLAINED

VISIONARIES
AND MYSTICS

JAMIE STOKES

p

First published in 2000 by Parragon

Parragon
Queen Street House
4 Queen Street
Bath BA1 1HE, UK

Produced by Magpie Books, an imprint of
Constable Robinson Ltd, London

ISBN 0-75253-596-X

Illustrations courtesy of Fortean Picture Library and Popperfoto

Page design by Sandie Boccacci

A copy of the British Library Cataloguing-in-Publication Data
is available from the British Library

Printed and bound in the EC

For Mum and Dad

Contents

Contents •

Introduction

• •

Assuming you are reading this book and not burning it to keep you warm in a post-apocalyptic nuclear winter you should be basking in the knowledge that the many prophecies of doom that placed the end of the world at the end of the second millennium have not come true. It's a safe bet that a new generation of prophets will adjust the date of their predictions so that they coincide with the next row of noughts to be thrown up by the Western calendar.

Prophecy is a notoriously tricky business, especially if the date of the prophecy falls within the lifetime of the prophet. The greats, like Nostradamus, avoided this difficulty assiduously by not giving dates or by giving numbers that could be interpreted as almost any date.

Modern prophecy and astrology are the only healthy survivors of a raft of schemes and systems by which our ancestors tried to make sense of the world. In this book you will discover what these systems were, what they led to and how they have survived in warped and transmuted forms into the modern era.

The first section deals with the central mystery of the human condition, the soul. Where did it come from, where is it going and what is it for? Today we are obsessed by the twin ideas of creating an artificial mind or soul and of attaining immortality through science. The ancients did not see themselves as having these options and had to rely on their visions of the universe to answer these questions. Each culture evolved its own story about the nature of the soul and the journey that they expected it to make through time. We have similar stories today.

In the next section we enter the world of prophecy. This is the story of humanity's quest to glimpse the unknowable future and to divine the ultimate fate of the universe. Inevitably these visions are largely apocalyptic. Stories from the Hopi peoples of North America to villagers of twentieth-century Portugal demonstrate that nobody expects the end of the world to be rosy. Prophecy is as alive today as it ever was and it has the same problems that it always had.

From time to time in the long history of the world peoples and civilizations have come and gone and left no more than the faintest trace of their existence. Other peoples have vanished from the face of the earth and left behind monuments that are among the most powerful mysteries that there are. Places like Stonehenge or the Pyramids of Giza clearly played a central role in the spiritual lives of these peoples but we are left with the tantalizing mystery of exactly what role. These sites are charged with significance and spiritual meaning that is just beyond our grasp but which draws us ever deeper into them. Some of them are explored in the third section.

The fourth section investigates the intimate and age-old relationship between humans and the world they live in. All cultures have had to come to terms with certain unalterable facts about the world. Among these are the turning of the seasons and the cycles of birth and death in nature. In this section we discover how observation of these phenomena lead to the development of attempts to read meaning into them. A key aspect of this search became the reading of the sky and the movement of the heavenly bodies across it. One aspect of this obsession became astrology, another noted the connection between these cycles and the seasons and made a mystic calendar out of them. Traces of both of these traditions are enshrined in modern culture in surprising ways.

The last section ties all these themes together by examining the myths and legends that people have been telling each other ever since they learned how to use language. Some of the best-known myths of the ancient world can be found here, along with some that are rather less well known in the West. In all of these tales we see how the mysteries of life and the universe were transformed into understandable symbols and related to human experience. Within these tales are the roots of modern culture and the key to understanding humanity's unique view of creation.

Search for the Soul

The Story of the Soul

The notion of the soul is inextricably linked with the human instinct for religion; without one there is little point in the other. As civilizations have emerged and collapsed the key concept of the soul has passed through many incarnations and the religions it has been associated with have evolved highly complex theologies. Anthropologists have long speculated that the origins of religion were based on a primitive concept of the soul that may have emerged very near the beginning of the human story.

It is difficult to estimate when human beings began to manifest religious beliefs. The very earliest evidence for cultural importance being attached to death comes from fifty-thousand-year-old Neanderthal burials. Close examination of some sites has suggested that the dead were placed in pits and decorated with garlands of flowers. Whether these findings are just coincidence or whether they indicate the first stirrings of religious feeling even before modern man as a species had emerged remains a matter of fraught speculation.

The earliest certain evidence of religious activity comes with the sudden explosion of European cave art between thirty-five and twenty thousand years ago. Among the representations of game animals and hunters there are half-human half-animal figures that surely represent gods or shamans. Tiny figurines of grossly exaggerated female forms from the same period also seem to indicate a cult associated with a fertility goddess. These primitive religions are simply too distant for us to ever achieve a detailed understanding of what they involved but, by studying primitive religions that have survived in other parts of the world into modern times, we can perhaps make close guesses.

In 1871 the Oxford anthropologist Sir Edward Taylor, advanced his theory of "animism" which he believed was the very earliest model of the soul in human thinking. Taylor argued that early humans probably believed that almost everything had a distinct soul as well as a "body" or physical form. People, animals, trees, rivers, mountains and anything else that could be seen as changeable and in some sense "alive" were probably credited with an animating force. Taylor's views were based on the observation that primitive cultures tend to have vast numbers of petty gods; there is a god of the deer, a god of the home, a god of the river and, of course, a god of the sun and of the moon.

The key to understanding this primitive philosophy is to understand the perception of death. When a person or animal dies they stop moving, they stop breathing and the heart stops beating – obvious statements, but these were the only clues early humans had as to what was going on. Death was understood as the parting of two distinct elements, the physical body and the force that made the physical body move. It seemed clear that the "make it go" force had somehow left the body, which implied that this force was still out there somewhere, wandering around without a body. From this it is a short step to the notion of a disembodied soul.

This basic statement of the process of death is the cornerstone on which all subsequent religions were based – according to the theories of the anthropologists. Armed with this understanding early humans were able to make guesses about the nature and location of this animating force in the living body.

For many cultures the obvious suspect was the breath. Living people tend to breathe more or less constantly, the dead hardly ever do. Also, when death occurs, the breath can be seen and heard escaping from the body – it looks like an open-and-shut case. Among the Eskimo peoples it was traditional for people to block up their nostrils after somebody had died to prevent their own souls getting any ideas and trying to escape. Peoples of the South Pacific sometimes held the nose and mouth of a dying person closed so that the soul could not escape – a somewhat radical solution that probably killed more than it cured.

Another favourite choice for the location of the soul was the blood or the heart. Blood flows like a river as long as a person is alive and the heart is a mysterious force buried inside the body that seems to act of its own accord. The soul–blood belief is the root of the widespread practice of drinking the blood of defeated enemies. To the primitive mind, if the soul is the blood then it should be possible to top up the strength of your own soul by drinking the soul of somebody else. In Africa and Asia the concept lies at the heart of rituals of blood-brothership. By sharing each other's blood the souls are mingled ensuring trust and loyalty.

In some traditions the notion of the soul took a quite

different form. Particularly among shamanistic religions of the East the soul is seen as a kind of invisible shadow of the body that follows it around during life. According to this view sickness was an affliction of the soul "reflected" back onto the body. The mirror image plays an important part in these traditions. Pools of water were presumably the earliest mirrors but when man-made mirrors came along these took over the religious function. Mongolian shaman wore nine mirrors as part of their ceremonial dress which they used to cure the sick. In some parts of the world the mirror image is seen as extremely dangerous because it exposes the soul. People who have a fear of photographic images are largely influenced by the mirror-soul concept.

A natural development from attempts to locate and identify the soul is the emergence of a model of what happens to the soul after it leaves the body. Originally, disembodied souls were probably thought to wander about the landscape much like the living but, as patterns of human civilization became more complex, so did the need to find a home for the disembodied soul. Probably the most elaborate expression of the soul and its place during and after life was developed by the ancient Egyptians.

The Egyptians' notion of what makes up a human being was extremely complex. Every person was thought to consist of several vital "body" parts and "soul" parts. These include the natural body, the spirit body, the heart, the shadow and the body casing. The heart-soul, or *ka*, comes closest to the modern concept of the soul and was usually represented in Egyptian art as a bird with a human head.

Egyptian civilization is something of a paradox. They

were a highly artistic and creative people capable of incredible expressions of beauty. Essentially they loved life and had a horror of death, and yet death came to dominate their culture. As the centuries passed much of the Egyptians' skill and inventiveness went into preparations for death; their most enduring monuments, the pyramids, are essentially tombs. Exactly how this paradox came about is something of a mystery, but a clue lies in the ancient tale of Osiris, god of eternity and a kind of Egyptian Christ.

According to the legend, Osiris had once been the ruler of Egypt. It was he who had established Egyptian civilization; he was the original lawgiver – a common figure in ancient mythologies. Regarded as a god by his people, Osiris became the victim of his brother, Seth's, envy. One day Seth constructed a magnificent chest made of beautifully decorated wood and ivory. At a feast he promised that he would give the chest to anyone who could lie down comfortably inside it. Guest after guest tried to win the prize but it didn't fit any of them properly. Finally Osiris came forward. Seth had cleverly constructed the chest to fit his brother exactly and, when he lay down inside it, he rushed forward and nailed down the lid. The chest, which had become a coffin, was then thrown into the Nile with Osiris still inside.

Seth took over the kingdom. Isis, Osiris' winged wife, searched the river until she found the chest and recovered the body of her husband. Seth was enraged. He stole the body and hacked it into fourteen pieces, which he scattered across the kingdom. Once again, Isis recovered the parts of her husband's body and reassembled them. Following instructions given to her by the gods she swathed the body in bandages and

Osiris, King of the Dead, attended on by Egyptian goddesses
Isis and Nepthys.

performed a series of sacred rituals. She then fanned the corpse with her wings and Osiris was resurrected to take his place as the lord of eternity. Isis later gave birth to Horus, the son of Osiris, who challenged Seth and reclaimed the kingdom.

The legend of the resurrection of Osiris became the model for all Egyptians' hope of resurrection after life. A key element in this belief was that the dead body must be preserved whole in order for it to be raised again in the next life. From this came the Egyptians' obsession with the preservation of the body through mummification. The sacred rites imparted to Isis by the gods became the basis for the elaborate burial procedures recorded in the Egyptian Book of the Dead. Compiled over many centuries the Book of the Dead became the Egyptians' sacred text. Among its instructions is a prayer offered up by a mortal in the hope of resurrection:

> *Do not let my body become words, but deliver me as you did yourself. I pray to you, do not let me fall into rottenness . . . when the soul departs a man sees corruption and the bones of his body rot and become wholly stinkingness, the members decay piecemeal, the bones crumble into a helpless mass, and the flesh becomes a fetid liquid, and he becomes a brother to the decay that comes upon him, and he turns into a multitude of worms, and an end is made of him.*

The vital importance of preserving the physical body, or *kbat*, and providing for its success in the afterlife became central to Egyptian society. Over centuries the mummification process was refined and improved to the degree that the bodies of Pharaohs entombed thousands of years ago can still be unwrapped and examined today. The vast array of possessions and provisions found with ancient Egyptian burials clearly indicate that the next life was expected to be very much like this life. Burial chambers were lined with kegs of wine and bushels of wheat. Weapons and chariots ensured that the resurrected Pharaoh could fight with honour and sometimes hundreds of servants were killed and preserved so that they could continue to serve their master through eternity.

In the East the development of the idea of the soul took a separate path. The dominant religion of the region, Hinduism, taught that the afterlife is just a temporary resting place before the soul is reborn back on Earth in a new body. Unlike the Egyptians, Hindus saw reincarnation or resurrection as something to be avoided. To be reborn meant only that the trials and hardships of life would have to be lived through all over again. The Tibetan Book of the Dead, in direct contrast to the Egyptian version, contains instructions on how to avoid being resurrected.

The Book warns that, after death, the soul will find itself tossed about in the universe by the wind of karma which, having no body, it will find impossible to resist. In this state the thought will inevitably occur to the soul to long to have a body again. The most dangerous point comes when the soul is enticed by visions of humans and animals enjoying the physical pleasures of sex. Drawn towards these ecstatic visions and longing to feel sensations again the soul must nevertheless resist the urge to try and take the place of one of the participants. If the urge is not resisted "The feeling which you would then experience would make you faint away . . . and afterwards you will find that you have been conceived as a human being or an animal."

The next major development in the story of the soul came with the ancient Greeks. In Greek mythology the afterlife is represented as an unremittingly awful place of greyness and suffering. There is no hint of reward for a life well lived, only punishment for those who have offended the gods and stagnation for the rest. A classic illustration of this joyless philosophy comes in part of Homer's *Odyssey*. At one point in his wandering the hero of the tale, Odysseus, visits the edge of the underworld. There he digs a pit and fills it with animals' blood. One by one the dead file past – some Odysseus allows to drink from the pit, which gives them some temporary life force and enables them to speak. Odysseus sees once-mighty heroes, including the great Achilles whom he had fought beside at Troy, reduced to insubstantial wraiths.

The vast majority of ancient Greek mythology originated in a period long before the era known as Classical Greece when great thinkers like Plato and Pythagoras laid the foundations for much of modern Western civilization. It was during this period that notions of the soul began to take on a more modern appearance. One particularly telling tale that points to the beginnings of this process is the story of Aristeas recorded by the chronicler Herodotus.

Aristeas collapsed suddenly one day and was assumed to be dead. When his family came to claim his body, however, it was nowhere to be found. Several years later Aristeas turned up and told a fantastic tale; his soul had left his body and gone on a fabulous journey all over the world where he had seen and heard many wonderful things. It's a simple story and rather easy to pick holes in – the absence of the body seems to suggest that Aristeas was still using it – but it has an upbeat feel that is different from the usual Greek notion of the disembodied soul.

The next step in the development of the Greek soul story takes the rather unlikely form of the cult of Dionysus. Famed for their wild and drunken orgies the Dionysians celebrated the story of Dionysus the god of wine and ecstasy. According to the legend Dionysus had been torn apart by his enemies while in the form of a bull.

The rituals of the cultists involved getting very drunk on wine, whipping themselves into an ecstatic frenzy and then tearing a live bull to pieces. The purpose of this wild ritual was to achieve a moment of liberation from the body. The cultists hoped to reach a moment of identification with the spirit of their god. This "ecstasy", which in Greek means "outside the body", was known as *enthusiasmos*, which means "inside the god". It was really the first time that the notion of the soul becoming part of a divine whole entered religious thought.

Orpheus developed the Dionysian cult into a more refined form. He rejected the ecstatic element but retained the idea of the soul as divine. According to the followers of Orpheus the soul was a god-like entity imprisoned in an earthly body and destined to return to an afterlife where it would receive punishment or reward according to the purity of the life it had led. Pythagoras, who is remembered today mostly for his mathematical theories, spent much of his life refining and developing the Orphean vision of the soul. Pythagoras introduced the idea that the soul not only survived death but could migrate to another body. This was probably the first time that the theory of reincarnation had been put forward in the West.

Many of these Greek developments later found a place in Christian theology. Greece became an important centre for the development of Christian thought many centuries later when it was part of the Roman Empire. The earliest widely accepted copies of the Christian bible are Greek copies and inevitably contain elements of Greek thought in the translation.

Since the earliest times in cultures all over the world the spiral has been a symbol of the soul. This representation can be seen etched on a vast scale in the Nazca Plain of Peru, in twenty-thousand-year-old cave paintings in France and in modern-day sand paintings created by Australian aborigines.

Of course there have been other symbols but the spiral seems to express something basic about the human perception of the soul. It has been interpreted as a representation of a sacred cave, the womb or the dizziness of spiritual experience. All of these may be true but the symbol really needs no interpretation, it is as clear today as it has always been. It is simply the winding path, the journey ever inwards and ever outwards that is our experience and understanding of the human soul.

The Soul Journey

The notion of the soul is common to virtually every religion that has arisen throughout history. Its description and purpose varies enormously but two essential elements are found in every account; the soul survives death and it is the essence of the person. In the

Western tradition the journey through life is seen as a one-off. This is not so in the Eastern tradition.

The central strand of Christian thinking sees this journey as a kind of test with the afterlife as a reward or punishment for the degree of success the individual has achieved in living according to the will of God. Other strands describe life as a punishment, a sort of dream or a chance to prove one's worth. Almost all agree that death is the last stage in the life journey and that the soul spends the rest of its eternal existence in a separate spiritual realm.

An interesting philosophical consequence of this tradition is that souls are not really immortal in the sense that they last for all time. The soul comes into existence from the moment the person is created and continues from that point throughout the rest of eternity – in the period before the person is created there is no disembodied soul waiting around for a body to occupy. In the Eastern spiritual tradition the soul is seen rather differently.

The oldest surviving branch of Eastern religious thought is embodied in Hinduism. In the West the best-known aspect of this very ancient religion is the notion that individual souls are reborn many times into many different bodies; that they undergo constant reincarnation. The *jiva*, or soul, is as central to Hinduism as it is to Christianity but it is seen as playing quite a different role in the universe.

By comparing the cultural history of the two regions where these distinct views of the soul originated it is easier to understand the difference in concepts. The major religions of the West, Judaism, Christianity and Islam, in order of conception, are all based around the idea of a single all-powerful god who has a special relationship with humans as opposed to any of the other creatures that live on Earth. The idea of this special relationship is a manifestation of people's observation that we differ from other animals in fundamental ways.

The main thrust of the Western religious tradition is to see humanity as designated masters of the world. It's possible that this view comes from the fact that these religions arose in a part of the world where survival is a considerable struggle – the semi-desert of the Middle East. Whatever the reason, the basic vision of human life in this tradition can be expressed as starting in innocence or ignorance, progressing through a world full of spiritual and physical peril and finally achieving paradise and knowledge.

This model is so deeply rooted in Western culture that it has become the template by which we express almost every aspect of our civilization. The latest form of the idea can be clearly seen in the current belief in technological progress.

Having all but abandoned the idea of a creator-god we instead describe human evolution as a journey from primitive ignorance and innocence, through aeons of slow and painful development to a future state in which all will be happiness and light. The old belief in the linear, one-way progress of the soul epito-mized by Christian texts such as *Pilgrim's Progress* has been replaced by the belief in the linear, one-way development of the human race from tree-dwelling simian to technologically advanced future-man.

The journey of the soul, according to the Western tradition, follows a single, irrevocable path. This journey is symbolically represented in numerous mythological accounts. At their simplest these accounts see the soul progressing from the everyday world to a kind of super-world where the pleasures or pains of Earth are magnified and stretched over eternity. A classic example is the old Norse myth of Valhalla. In this vision the souls of individuals who have lived good and brave lives are transferred to a kind of endless banquet in the realm of the gods where the pleasures of food, drink and fighting are prolonged indefinitely and stripped of their consequences.

The most basic and popular vision of the afterlife in Islam and Christianity are similar; Paradise is seen as an endless succession of physical and spiritual pleasures. Theologians down the centuries have tried in vain to dislodge this essentially hedonistic view and replace it with one in which the pleasure of Paradise is the total presence of God. In most people's minds however the idea always remained firmly entrenched that the reward for living a good life was never having to worry about the things that constantly worry us on Earth: rejection, poverty and disease.

The great pagan religions of the Romans and the Greeks included very clear and detailed accounts of the journey of the soul. Both cultures pretty much shared the same gods and beliefs and their accounts of the journey of the soul after death were also very similar. In classical thought the afterlife was rarely an attractive place, it was seen essentially as an underworld of shadows and forgetfulness. The realm of the underworld is typically described as guarded by fierce monsters, such as the three-headed dog Cerberus, and inhabited by dark lords and beasts.

The great fourteenth-century poet Dante used many elements of Greek and Roman myth in his epic poem *Divine Comedy*. It describes an imaginary journey made by Dante into the Christian afterlife and gives a detailed account of the medieval vision of heaven, hell and purgatory. Guided by the Roman poet Virgil, Dante is first led into the descending circles of the pit of hell which, he learns, is situated directly beneath the city of Jerusalem. On each level different classes of sinner are tormented through eternity with highly specific and vividly described tortures. He sees heretics condemned to spend everlastingness in burning graves, faithless priests head down in sulphurous pits and "sowers of discord" doomed to be perpetually slashed and hacked by sword-wielding demons.

After visiting the very bottom of the pit of hell, where Dante sees Satan himself gnawing on the head of Judas Iscariot, the poet is taken through purgatory and stands on the banks of the River Lethe. A symbolic river that separates the world of the living from the world of the dead is a common element in ancient mythology. Dante uses the Lethe, the Greek river of forgetfulness, to symbolize this passage. Souls that wade across the river are washed clean of all sin and the memory of their sin before entering the kingdom of heaven.

Dante's description of heaven is far less interesting than his description of hell but two elements stand out. The poet is reunited with his lost love, Beatrice, who died young, and he witnesses the ultimate fate of souls that have achieved the pinnacle of heaven; they become incorporeal, shining forms that circle the radiance of God forever. Such is the power of Dante's epic work, one of the greatest classics of Western literature, that his images have passed into popular folklore – ask anyone to describe heaven or hell and their account will sound a lot like Dante's.

In the East the basic vision developed in a different way. The classic Eastern model is of a never-ending cycle in which progress through the world and ultimately the world itself are illusions. The soul begins in the lowest of creatures – which presumably means the simplest – and is reborn into the bodies of progressively higher creatures over many millennia until it is finally born into a human body. From this stage the process ceases to be one of automatic progression. Depending on the life that the now self-aware soul leads it may be born into a another human of a higher caste, into a similar life or may even descend a level again and be reborn as an animal.

The final destination of the soul is believed to be a state of oneness with God and escape from the cycle of perpetual reincarnation. This can only be achieved once the soul has become purified and has come to realize the limitations of the finite universe. In Hindu theology there are many minor gods who are essentially seen as embodiments of aspects of life but the ultimate god is unknowable and has no name. The great god of the Hindus is beyond the finite universe and can only be perceived by a soul after thousands of years spent on the great wheel of reincarnation. This vision is expressed in one of the best-known Hindu sacred texts, the *Bhagavad Gita*:

> *Worn-out clothes*
> *Are shed by the body:*
> *Worn-out bodies*
> *Are shed by the dweller*
> *Within the body:*
> *New bodies are put on*
> *By the dweller, like clothes*

The progress of the soul according to Hindu beliefs moves through four stages on its way to final freedom. These are the four "wants". The first two, pleasure and worldly success, form the Path of Desire. Every soul is destined to spend many lifetimes exploring this path before it realizes its futility. Hinduism actively encourages people to pursue worldly pleasures and ambitions since the desire to do so indicates that the soul has not yet worked through enough of them before its current incarnation.

Once the soul has satiated its appetites on the Path of Desire and realizes that they can never bring lasting happiness it is able to move onto the Path of Renunciation which is made up of the want for duty and for liberation from the world. The obstacles that must be overcome before a soul can proceed down the Path of Renunciation are joy, ignorance and finally the finiteness of being. Methods of overcoming these obstacles are the main teaching of Hinduism. They include meditation, yoga and the art of living a good life.

The mechanism that drives the Hindu vision of perpetual rebirth is known as *karma*. Originating from a Sanskrit word meaning "action" or "deed" karma is essentially a philosophy of moral causality. Simply stated it teaches that all actions have an effect on the future destiny of the soul; evil actions or intentions result in exactly equal evil events befalling the soul in its next incarnation; good actions or intentions result in a new incarnation full of happiness and good fortune. One ancient Hindu text, the *Upanishad*, describes the process:

> *According as were his works and walks in life, so he become. He that does righteously become*

righteous. He that does evil become evil. He become holy through holy works and evil through evil.

The notion of the karmic balance-sheet is directly linked with the Hindu notion of the world as physical and therefore finite. As long as the soul is subject to karma it will never be free because its actions will always have consequences that must be played out in another incarnation. Because of this, the world is sometimes referred to as the *karma-bhumi* or karma-sphere. Only by escaping the physical can the soul hope to break the karmic chain.

Since the introduction of Eastern religious thought to the West many people have found the idea of karmic reincarnation attractive because it offers a solution to the so-called problem of evil. Christianity has always had a problem in satisfactorily explaining why God allows some people to be born into lives of misery and ill-fortune. Why should one person be born into a good family, never suffer ill health and become effortlessly successful while another person is born into poverty, suffers appalling disease and dies without having the opportunity to achieve anything? Hinduism allows the belief that the apparent random nature of good or bad fortune is actually driven by karma – bad lives are simply the result of evil done in a past life and good lives are the result of evil endured in a previous incarnation.

Hinduism offers a solution to one of the most compelling arguments against God, but it also creates its own problem. The idea of karma essentially leaves the individual powerless to effect his or her own life – if you have acted badly in a previous life that you don't even remember then you can do nothing to avoid ill-fortune in your current life. No matter how well you live the benefits will only come in a subsequent incarnation. It is partly this philosophy that underpins the traditional Indian caste system.

For centuries, Indian society was dominated by a rigid system of social distinctions that classed people according to the family they were born into. Ranging from the "untouchable" caste, who were considered the lowest form of humanity, to the Brahmin caste, who were believed to be the highest, the caste system enshrined a tradition of brutal discrimination. It was impossible for an individual to move outside of his or her caste; if you were born an untouchable then you could never hope to do anything but the most menial work. Brahmins on the other hand could look forward to a life of limitless opportunity. Hinduism justified the system by encouraging the belief that only souls that had acted badly would be born as untouchables and only those that had acted well would be reincarnated as Brahmins.

One man who spoke out against this system and created a new religion in the process was the sixth-century Indian prince Siddhartha Gautama, otherwise known as Buddha. Buddhist beliefs are clearly a development from Hinduism but the vision of the soul is much less personal. Buddha firmly moved the burden of responsibility back onto the individual in his or her current lifetime.

The Buddhist idea of the soul journey is often compared to a wave. As a wave moves towards the shore it has power and identity for a time. This ends when the wave hits the shore and breaks up. The wave, or at least the potential of the wave, returns to the sea. Later the wave returns but this time it has different characteristics and is made up of different water molecules – but it is still the same wave in some sense. In Buddhism the soul is like the wave – it has a temporary, personal and unique identity which ends in death. The soul itself does not end with death, just its identity. When the wave returns it has a new and different identity. The physical universe is like the sea; full of potential waves or souls that appear again and again in temporary guises.

In this philosophy actions do not have consequences in later incarnations because each incarnation is only a temporary form of the wave and has no lasting causal effect. As in Hinduism, the ultimate aim of the Buddhist soul is to escape from the endless cycle of crashing against the shore but this must be achieved in the course of one lifetime. If the soul fails to escape before death then it must start all over again in the next life.

Buddha called this ultimate goal *nirvana*, which means something like "to extinguish". He saw it as a state in which the soul is able to renounce the physical universe and the illusions of its own joys and sufferings. The Buddhist vision of the soul has become very popular in modern society because it allows the belief that we have eternal souls without requiring any belief in a supernatural afterlife or a guiding, omnipotent God. Buddhism is essentially atheistic – it denies the existence of deities or other beings that exist beyond the compass of human experience. At the same time it offers a path that promises freedom from the worries that have motivated belief in an afterlife.

It is clearly a fundamental part of human thought to see life as a journey – a journey of the soul. Whether that journey continues after the stage we know as death, whether it doubles back on itself or continues on to ever greater heights or depths are questions that lie at the heart of the world's great religions.

Near Death Experiences

Death is not what it was. In the good old days you could rely on the dead to stay that way, barring encounters with wandering messiahs – an embarrassment the Lazarus family probably never lived down. Shakespeare called it "the undiscovered country from which no traveller returns", which sounds as good as ever, but just isn't true anymore. Medical science has advanced to such an extent that death is no longer permanently fatal. When the body gives up and all its systems shut down there are a whole range of machines that can take over and drag the person back from the other side. For the first time in our history we can actually ask the question "what is it like to die?" and get an informed and precise answer.

Amazingly, the answer given by more and more people who have experienced this short round-trip bears startling similarities to what priests and other mystics have been telling us for years. Like all the most important phenomena of our age the return-from-death experience has its own abbreviation: Near Death Experience or NDE. Rather misleading in the sense that it implies a person has experienced being near to dying – as if they narrowly missed being hit by a bus. In fact these people have actually and technically died and then returned to life; the "nearness" is more a question of events in proximity to death – both before and after.

The modern phenomenon of NDE first came to light in the early 1970s when Dr Elisabeth Kubler-Ross studied the psychology and physiology of dying. Since her pioneering work the subject has been intensively studied by a number of scientists who have shown that people's experiences tend to have a remarkable degree of similarity. In other words the NDE passes the so-called invariance hypothesis; there are enough common features in each different case for it to be regarded as a real and distinct phenomenon. In addition, these studies have demonstrated that NDEs are becoming almost epidemic. In a 1981 Gallup Poll about twelve million American citizens were found to have been resuscitated or in some other way to have clinically died and "come back". Of these, thirty-five to forty per cent reported an NDE.

So, what is it like to die? The testimonies of the thirty-five to forty per cent of resucitees who reported NDEs have a remarkable degree of similarity. The experience is generally described as taking part in five distinct stages. Most people who have NDEs do not get beyond the first or second stage. A few miss some of the stages out, although the stages they do experience happen in the same order. A very few experience all five stages with varying degrees of detail.

The first and most common stage of an NDE is a sudden and unexpected sense of bliss or total calm. This often comes over a person in the midst of pain or extreme discomfort. It is described as a kind of release; as if the mind of the person is suddenly no longer connected to the labouring body. The sensation is described variously as "euphoric", "calm" or as a kind of deliverance. For many, this is as far as the NDE goes, for others the sensation continues throughout the rest of the experience.

The second and most well-known stage of an NDE is known as the out-of-body experience (or OBE). In many ways this is similar to so-called astral-body dreams in which an individual finds him or her self somehow "outside" their own body. Often the person finds themselves floating above the scene of their own death and looking down at the frantic efforts of doctors trying to revive them.

Experiencers tend to report a sudden sharpening of their senses and mental processes in this state. They are able to hear and understand exactly what everybody is saying and the scene appears bathed in the brightest, clearest light so that every detail is visible. For some, this stage seems to last a considerable time. Once they become used to their new state experiencers often try to communicate with people they see, only to be disappointed when they look or walk right through them. Others find that they feel absolutely unconcerned by the drama being played out below them and take to wandering about the hospital or scene of the accident in their new ethereal bodies:

> *I could see people all around and I could understand what they were saying. I didn't hear them audibly . . . It was more like knowing what they were thinking, exactly what they were thinking, but only in my mind, not in their actual vocabulary. I would catch it the second before they opened their mouths to speak.*

People returning from OBEs are often able to tell medical staff exactly what was said and done in the emergency room or even in other parts of the hospital at a time when monitors showed that they had no brain activity at all. For most, the OBE is the end of the experience, but for some they proceed to a deeper and more disturbing phase – the "dark tunnel" or "transition" phase:

> *Going through a tunnel, a very, very dark tunnel . . . It started at a narrow point and became wider and wider. But I remember it being very, very black. But even though it was black, I wasn't afraid because I knew that there was something at the other end waiting for me that was good.*

The "darkness" of the dark tunnel is often described in a way that makes it sound palpable. It isn't just the absence of light it is a presence in itself. Comparisons have been made with concepts from Eastern religions such as Buddhism and Hinduism in which the ultimate reality of the universe is described as a "dazzling or shining darkness" or the "living void". It is also clear that the darkness is a channelling medium; it leads from one place or state of being to another.

Some people describe seeing a light at the end of the "tunnel", others of just being aware that they had a destination and that the darkness was something to be passed through. Commentators have compared the dark tunnel to the Greek myth of the river of the dead: a wide, dark body of water that separates the world of the living from the realm of the dead. In some myths souls are ferried across the River Acheron to the underworld, in others they are immersed in the River Lethe which washes away all memories of life.

At the end of the tunnel, the few experiencers who

get this far report visions of an almost clichéd paradise realm:

> *I saw the most beautiful lakes. Angels, they were floating around like you see seagulls. Everything was white. The most beautiful flowers. Nobody on this earth ever saw the beautiful flowers that I saw there . . . Of course I was so impressed with the beauty of everything there that I couldn't pinpoint any one thing . . . Everything was bright. The lakes were blue, light blue. Everything about the angels was pure white.*

Other accounts describe celestial cities or dramatic landscapes far more beautiful than anything on earth. It is here that experiencers often have encounters with long-dead relatives. Nobody who reports having seen this paradise wanted to return to life. For some, the initial wonderment turned to sadness when they realized that they would not yet be allowed to enter. Others commonly report speaking to relatives or hearing a disembodied voice that tells them they must return to earth. Often it takes the form of a reminder that the individual is still needed by living friends and family or of a command to return and finish a life's work.

Those who linger in the realm of light beyond the dark tunnel may experience the fifth and most profound stage of the NDE: encountering the light itself. Like the darkness the light is described as a physical presence. For many it is a god of compassion and forgiveness. In the presence of the light experiencers report reviewing their lives and answering questions about what they have done. This interrogation is never seen as threatening or judgmental but more as a form of guided self-understanding – the ultimate therapy session:

> *The next sensation is this wonderful, wonderful feeling of this light . . . It's almost like a person. It's not a person, but it is a being of some kind. It is a mass of energy. It doesn't have a character like you would describe another person, but it has a character in that it is more than just a thing. And also in size, it just covers the entire vista before you. And it totally engulfs whatever the horizon might be . . .*

The Experience of Death

1. Peace
Sudden sensation of bliss and calm
exit >>>   Relax into normal sleep
no >>>>   Out of Body

2. Out of Body
Looking down on the scene of one's own death with perfect clarity and detachment
exit >>>>   Snap back into unconscious body
no>>>>   The Dark Tunnel

3. The Dark Tunnel
Travelling at great speed to a different state of being
exit>>>>   Tunnel fades into normal sleep
no>>>>   The Realm of Light

4. The Realm of Light
A celestial paradise filled with light and warmth
exit>>>>   Told to return to earth
no>>>>   The Being of Light

5. The Being of Light
A presence of love and understanding helps the individual achieve perfect self-knowledge
exit>>>>   Individual decides or realizes they are not ready
no>>>>   Unknown

A great deal has been made of these reports from beyond. For those who have had NDEs the effect is often to completely change their lives. Most feel they have been given a second chance and are determined to make the most of their new opportunities. Many find it very hard to adjust to normal life again and find people's preoccupations petty and inconceivable. A few believe they have been given a specific mission or prophetic vision and set about campaigning to bring it about. In all cases the NDE is a spiritual experience that leaves them having to learn to live all over again.

For believers in established religions that have a specific afterlife as part of their theology, such as Christianity or Islam, the NDE phenomenon is taken as proof that there is life after death. They point out that many of those who experience NDEs were confirmed atheists who had no expectation of there being any kind of experience after death. It is also interesting that people from widely diverse ethnic and social backgrounds report very similar NDEs.

Scientists who try to explain the NDE in purely materialistic terms have a number of arguments that go some way to refuting the "religious" viewpoint. Sceptics claim that the similarity of NDEs indicates that they are a result of something that is similar in all humans: our brain chemistry.

Studies have shown that when the body undergoes

extreme stress or trauma a whole cocktail of chemicals are flooded into the brain – many of them known to produce euphoria or other altered states of consciousness. It is believed that this release of chemicals is a kind of self-anaesthetic administered by the brain once the body deteriorates to the point where death is inevitable. In fact such a huge dose is released that it begins a cascade of destruction in the brain that sees cells literally implode and die. It is this "death trip" that scientists identify with the euphoria stage of the NDE.

For doctors the notion of a tunnel of darkness immediately brings to mind the common effects of reduced blood flow to the brain. Fainting is almost always preceded by tunnel vision. A sudden drop in blood supply to the brain causes the optic nerves to shut down, among other things. First, the periphery of vision becomes blurred and then disappears. The area of functioning vision is quickly reduced to a contracting point of light and the effect is of looking at the world through a profoundly dark tunnel. The suggestion is that, as the brain dies, the "inner eye" or consciousness undergoes a similar process. Perceptions of light, sound and everything else die off peripherally leaving only a diminishing point of pure white light that represents the last random firings of dying brain cells.

The final stage of the NDE, entering the light and achieving a sense of perfect peace, is identified as the brain entering the final stages of shutdown. All but the basic animal functions have already ceased and the last, tiny glimmer of blind consciousness is engulfed in a vast ocean of tranquillizing chemicals. The sensation of profound peace and contentment is nothing more than the combination of a much-reduced capacity for thought of any kind and a huge dose of narcotics. All the other details of the phenomenon, such as visions of paradise, meetings with dead relatives or profound insights, are dismissed as embroidered experiences of dream states during the period of recovery or as the subconscious addition of preconceived ideas of what it is like to die.

Although it is often claimed that similar NDEs are reported by people of widely differing ethnic backgrounds it should be noted that those people who have recovered from extreme near death states are likely to be citizens of industrialized, Western nations where sophisticated resuscitation equipment is readily available. Clearly there are many differences between the cultural background of an Israeli, a German and a Japanese, but in today's global culture they probably share a lot of basic beliefs. Very few people in the developed nations have a rigid and specific set of religious beliefs. Their visions of paradise are as likely to be as similar as they were thousands of years ago before organized religion; beauty, plenty and freedom from worry – exactly the elements we find in NDE reports.

One element of the NDE that scientists have a great deal of trouble explaining is the out-of-body phase. According to current medical understanding, once the brain has shut down there can be no perception of the outside world and certainly no understanding and yet time and again NDEs include detailed accounts of events that the experiencer couldn't have heard or seen from inside their essentially dead bodies.

Aldous Huxley, author of the classic dystopian fantasy *Brave New World*, was convinced that universal drug addiction was an inevitable feature of humanity's future. This startling claim was not meant as a criticism of human nature but as an expression of Huxley's own experiences of mind-altering substances. Whilst experimenting with LSD, Huxley realized that the human sensory apparatus was designed mainly to shut out information rather than to let it in. In effect he was pointing out what others had noted before: our senses allow us to focus on the few things that are important to us and to shut out the rest as irrelevant background – that's how we are able to conduct a conversation with one person in a room full of other people talking.

Huxley believed that LSD and other substances allowed the mind to open the "doors of perception" fully and allow everything to flood in. In many ways the experience he was describing sounds similar to the heightened awareness of out-of-body NDEs. It's conceivable that once the person is freed of the body he or she no longer needs those filters and becomes aware of everything that is happening all at once. On the other hand, if this is an effect that artificial substances can create it is equally possible that a natural version is manufactured by the brain along with the rest of its death cocktail.

There are other things that don't ring true about the "religious proof" hypothesis. Naturally we only receive reports when the NDE ends in return to the world of the living; people describe "deciding" to return, or being "ordered" to return which begs the question of why this hasn't happened before.

There were cases of NDE in the era before modern medicine, but not many. It seems odd that the ultimate authority in these matters seems to have decided to send large numbers of people back only since the advent of sophisticated resuscitation techniques. It seems clear that people return to life because medicine brings them back not because they decide to. Reports of deciding to return sound a lot like a subconscious sleight of hand that allows the experiencer to believe that he or she had something to do with the process.

Despite these objections it can't be denied that NDE is a new and unique human experience. Like many such phenomena it's unlikely that we will be able to explain it completely with existing theories and concepts; new perceptions always lead to new and deeper understandings. NDE is undoubtedly a spiritual experience and as such has become linked with our views of religion and the afterlife. Even if NDE is not proof of such a thing it is a fascinating window onto a part of the human mind or soul that we rarely have access to.

The Ghost in the Machine

The most important distinguishing feature of a soul is that it isn't there. The soul is supposed to be immaterial, invisible and untouchable, and yet to exist, somehow, in a form beyond the physical. It is this very characteristic that supposedly gives the soul the ability to survive the death of the body. On the other hand the soul is seen as inextricably linked to the body – the soul never leaves before the body dies – it is death that sets it free.

It was the philosopher Gilbert Ryle who first used the phrase "Ghost in the Machine" to refer to a problem that had perplexed generations of his colleagues and continues to do so today. Simply stated the problem is this; if the soul is not physical and not bound by the physical laws of the universe how does it manage to control the body and why should it be trapped inside it? Rene Descartes, the founder of modern philosophy, made it his life's work to tackle this problem – although it was several years before he realized that this was the problem he had set himself.

Descartes set out to construct a new science that could explain every phenomenon in the universe. Before he could do this however, he decided that he must establish a few basic truths from which everything else could be built up. After years of contemplation he came to the conclusion that there was only one truth that could not be doubted; the fact that he existed. Famously expressed in the phrase "I think therefore I am" Descartes created philosophy's first catch-phrase.

For Descartes there were essentially two things in the universe, his mind or soul and his body – everything else was open to doubt. He believed that these two things were completely different in nature. The body is physical, occupies space and is subject to the laws of physics; the soul is not physical, occupies no space and is unaffected by physics. It wasn't long before Descartes' critics pointed out that he was going to have a hard time explaining how such completely different entities could interact.

That they do interact seems obvious. Every religion holds the individual responsible for his or her actions and identifies the individual as the soul. When the body dies it is the soul that faces retribution or reward in the next life – hardly fair if the soul didn't actually have control of the body. Equally punishments from

God on earth are usually described as taking the form of physical discomfort, presumably because this will in some way impact on the soul.

Descartes had stumbled across a problem that had stood at the heart of humanity's idea of itself for thousands of years. People instinctively believe that the essence of themselves is somehow distinct from their physical body and that this essence is essentially immaterial and immortal. Few people had stopped to think how this supernatural substance they called a soul could be anchored to the natural world. Descartes never did solve the problem to the satisfaction of his critics and nobody else has since.

Descartes' solution was to suggest that an area of the brain, specifically the pineal gland, acted as a kind of conduit through which the soul could act on the body. Really this was no solution at all. The pineal gland is no less physical than any other part of the brain or body so there is no particular reason to believe that it could act as some kind of communication centre.

With the advent of modern computers the question of what constitutes a soul has again become interesting. For the first time humanity has a technology that can hope to approach the storage capacity and molecular-level complexity of the brain. Some believe that this means we will be able to create a purely artificial life form with a mind or even a soul.

Fundamentalist artificial intelligence researchers speculate that if a replica could be built of the human brain that matched its physical functions and parameters exactly, then that brain, attached to an appropriate artificial body, would have as much right to say of itself that it had a mind or a soul as any natural-born human being. They point out that this is essentially what a human mother does, the only difference is in the materials and the method of manufacture: silicon and copper in place of carbon and water, laser etchers and soldering irons in place of cells and hormones.

For a lot of people there remains a deep resistance to this concept – they simply refuse to believe that a human is no more than the sum of its material parts and insist that some supernatural entity or spirit must be injected into the biology before it becomes any more than an intricate machine.

Unfortunately computer technology isn't anywhere near the point where such a machine could be built, it may never be, and even if it were it's unlikely that the argument would be settled. Even if the artificial human could be made to look and act like a real human in every way there would always be the sneaking suspicion that it was nothing more than a very sophisticated mimic with no real internal life of its own.

By winding the technology clock forward a few hundred years we can speculate about what such an experiment might be like. Imagine that a device exactly like the human brain could be built and that it was small enough to house in a perfect artificial body indistinguishable from a real human body without actually slicing it open to look inside.

The first problem arises when you consider where the model for the artificial brain comes from. There is of course no such thing as the human brain. The structure of each individual brain is subtly different. Suppose the scientists take the brain of a volunteer, copy it exactly, and then put the brain back in the volunteer's head before he even wakes up from the anaesthetic.

They now have two functionally-identical brains in

two different bodies. If the mind and the soul is no more than the structure of the brain then they also have two identical souls in two different bodies. Few people are willing to accept that this is possible but, on the other hand, it would be very difficult to explain to the artificial human that he wasn't real and that he didn't have a soul or a mind.

Even more literally mind-boggling experiments are not hard to envisage. Suppose that the artificial brain and the flesh-and-blood brain are stored separately from the volunteer's body. Both brains are then connected to the body by means of radio waves so that either one can control the body and will feel as if they are walking around in it, but only one brain can be in control at any one time. Now suppose that the control function is set up to switch automatically between the real and the artificial brain once every few hours. Now imagine you were to meet this person with two brains.

Of course, nobody can be sure what such a person would be like. According to some theories two separate personalities would emerge as the two brains developed along slightly separate paths, in which case the person would appear to suddenly switch personalities in mid-sentence. Others maintain that the two brains would remain exactly in synch and that it would be impossible to tell when the switch took place. Either way, it would certainly be impossible to tell when you were talking to the biological brain and when the silicon brain. Under such conditions would it be possible to say that the person sitting in front of you had a soul sometimes but at other times had none?

Recently it has been suggested that a kind of immortality could be achieved by "downloading" an individual's mind into some kind of memory chip or disk which could then be uploaded into an artificial brain in an artificial body as many times as the individual wanted over the course of thousands of years. The notion of immortality has always been closely associated with the soul. Life after death is generally assumed to be eternal, otherwise there seems to be little point in it, but it is only the soul, our essential selves, that experience it.

If physical immortality became a possibility it would raise interesting questions about the usefulness of the soul. In a sense the soul only really comes into its own when the body dies. As long as the body is alive the soul is pretty much trapped. Would we cease to need souls if our bodies never died? Or would we find after a few thousand years that death is a process we somehow have to go through, otherwise we become stagnant and inhuman?

These questions lead down endless corridors that have been explored for thousands of years under different names and with different motives. Medieval theologians believed that the answers were just as critical and pressing as the modern-day artificial intelligence programmer. No doubt they will continue to be long after both are a forgotten footnote in history. Whatever our minds or our souls might be, at least we can be certain that we will never cease wondering what they are.

Proving the Soul

Belief in an afterlife and the survival of the soul has been a part of human culture for as long as anyone can tell. Proof has always been rather harder to come by.

For much of history, religious beliefs have been held with absolute conviction by vast numbers of people. It's difficult to understand this conviction in the modern secular age but, for a medieval peasant, the idea that the soul went to heaven or hell after death was as certain as the fact that spring followed winter. Heresy was common but atheism had been virtually unknown since the days of the ancient Greeks. It wasn't until the late nineteenth century that the notion that there may be no God or heaven or hell began to gain a little ground in the West.

One of the consequences of the migration of thought away from the centuries-old teachings of the established churches was that the impulse to believe in a soul that survives death began to take on new and distinctly odd forms. Without a strict framework imposed by a church that described what people could expect in the next life the whole concept began to disintegrate into a plethora of amorphous beliefs about the fate of the soul. It was almost as if the lack of specific, concrete beliefs about the afterlife among the living doomed the souls of the dead to a kind of shadowy hinterland.

This is the afterlife of the séance and the spirit medium. Disembodied souls contacted through mediums often seem to be rather sad and pathetic figures with little to do other than gossip with the living and make complaints. The grand visions of an eternity spent in the presence of God or enduring the tortures of hell has been replaced by a kind of disembodied soap opera where souls spend most of their time seedily spying on the living.

A classic example of this rather absurd eternity comes from the late 1930s. Two Icelandic mediums,

Hafsteinn Bjornsson and Einar Kvaran, were holding a séance when the voice of a spirit began to speak through Bjornsson. The visitor proved to be an irritable and difficult man who refused to identify himself and kept demanding that the assembled group should find his leg and give it back. The baffling behaviour got worse when a new member, fish merchant Ludvik Gudmundsson, joined the regular séance group. The spirit now insisted that Gudmundsson had his leg and grew enraged when the bewildered merchant denied any knowledge of the offending limb.

Eventually the spirit identified itself as Runulfor Runolfsson, a fisherman who had drowned in 1879. He explained that when his body was washed ashore several days later it had been torn apart by wild dogs and partially consumed. When locals discovered the remains they gathered up as much as they could find and gave them a proper Christian burial. One thighbone, which was overlooked, eventually turned up several weeks later and nobody could be bothered to dig up the grave again to put it with the rest of the remains. The bone was kept as a curiosity and eventually a carpenter placed it in a wall cavity as he was renovating the house that Gudmundsson was to live in many years later.

Gudmundsson duly returned home, opened up the section of wall that the spirit had identified, and found a human thigh bone inside. Amazed, he arranged for the bone to be given a proper burial and the spirit that had invaded their séance was never heard from again. Like many such tales the case of the missing leg is compelling and faintly absurd. The notion that a soul would go to the trouble of spending fifty years in a bad-tempered attempt to get a piece of bone buried suggests that there is very little to do in the modern afterlife.

Another case with a slightly more serious theme but with the same disturbing echoes of post-mortem boredom is known as the Lethe case. Frederic W. H. Myers was a classical scholar at Cambridge University and a leading investigator of psychic phenomenon until his death in 1901. The idea that the soul survived death had long fascinated Myers and, after his demise, several mediums claimed to be in contact with him. One of Myers' former colleagues, George Dorr, determined to try and find out if these claims could be true.

In 1908 Dorr approached Boston medium Mrs Piper and asked her to try and contact Myers. Once the medium claimed to have established contact, Dorr told her to ask Myers the question "what does the word Lethe suggest to you?" Dorr figured that since Myers had been a classicist he should be able to give an informed answer to the question. Lethe was the Greek name for a mythical river that flowed through the underworld and bestowed utter forgetfulness on those who touched its waters.

The answer that Dorr received didn't fill him with confidence. It seemed to be a garbled account of some classical story, but Dorr didn't recognise it and wasn't even sure that it had anything to do with Lethe. Disappointed he nevertheless sent the result to another classical scholar for interpretation. When the answer came back that the message did indeed seem to refer to the Lethe and was from an obscure passage in the works of the Roman poet Ovid, Dorr's flagging interest was rekindled.

Cambridge physicist Sir Oliver Lodge suggested that a way to obtain further proof of Myers' survival beyond

death was by a method he described as cross-corre-
spondence. The idea was to ask several different
mediums to communicate with Myers and see if a
consistent picture emerged when all of their messages
were put together. In 1910 Lodge engaged a prominent
British medium, known as Mrs Willet, to carry out the
experiment. Mrs Willet did not know about the
message delivered by the Boston medium, nor did she
know Myers. Lodge gave her an envelope that
contained the question "what does the word Lethe
suggest to you?"

Mrs Willet produced a long message that convinced
Lodge and Dorr that Myers had indeed answered the
question and that he knew why he had been asked the
same question twice. Over the course of several years
Mrs Willet and Mrs Piper produced over two thousand
scripts allegedly dictated by the spirit of Myers, and
many of them were published in the journal of the
Society for Psychical Research. An intriguing case but
again it seems to beg the question why would the dead
waste their time indulging in trivial message sending?

These odd features of modern beliefs about the
afterlife can be traced to a connection with the very
cultural forces that largely destroyed belief in
organized religion in the West. A strong current in
modern thinking says that there can be no afterlife or
God because there is no scientific proof of these things.
At the same time people cannot really bring themselves to totally let go of the instinctive belief that the
personality survives death. The two have come
together in a bizarre fusion that is modern spiritualism.

The idea that the dead can be communicated with
through specially receptive people is found in cultures

throughout history. Even most primitive shamanistic faiths tend to include a belief that the shaman or witch doctor can communicate with the spirits of the ancestors. Modern spiritualism is unique in its somewhat contradictory appeal to proof. In the past, people had little trouble believing that messages could be received from the dead because they already "knew" that the dead inhabited a very real but separate world. Today we have lost this faith in a real, unequivocal afterlife and therefore insist that spirits must prove they are who they say they are before we will believe anything they say.

The missing leg case and the Lethe case are classic examples of this trend. We only find these stories compelling because they seem to offer proof that an individual personality can survive death. The entombed thigh bone and the erudite classical references persuade us that the medium is receiving a genuine message and not just making stuff up to sound impressive. The pattern is familiar. Once the identity of the spirit has been "proved" its messages are listened to with much greater attention. It's a pattern that can be traced back to the birth of the modern spiritualist movement: the case of the Fox sisters.

In 1847 a farmer named J. D. Fox moved into a new house in Hydesville, New York with his wife Leah and two young daughters Margaretta and Katy. Almost immediately the family was disturbed by inexplicable knocks, raps and bangs that kept them awake at night. By the spring of 1848 they were convinced that the house was haunted. One night Katy, then twelve years old, was sitting listening to the constant rapping when she suddenly said "Do as I do" and began clapping her hands in a simple rhythm. Everybody was astounded when the sounds began to imitate the pattern of Katy's clapping.

Soon Mrs Fox was attempting to interrogate the presence by means of a primitive Morse-like code. She reported that the noises were being made by the spirit of a man who had been murdered and buried in the cellar of the house. Soon, all three women in the Fox household were communicating freely with the spirit and friends and neighbours were invited to marvel at the strange goings on. News of the Fox's communicating spirit spread all across America and then the rest of the world. Within months a new craze had been born. People all over the United States were sitting in darkened rooms and listening in awe as mysterious knocking noises answered their questions.

Many people were more than a little sceptical. One commentator famously remarked "It seemed as if the spirit world, having at last hit upon a means of communicating with ours, could not get enough of it". The Fox family were visited by huge numbers of people and, in the summer of 1848, Mr Fox claimed to have unearthed human remains in the cellar of the house providing the vital "proof". Séances soon became a global phenomenon that reached its peak around the turn of the nineteenth century and continues to this day.

A striking feature of these communications with the dead is the way that they are used as a desperate attempt to fill the gap left by the demise of organized religion. Once the identity of the spirit had been established the first question that everybody wants answered is "what is it like to be dead?" Lacking a clear and commonly accepted cultural vision of an afterlife people are keen to hear the reports of "eye-witnesses". The effect of this backwards faith has been to create a loose system of belief that has no clear idea of what the afterlife might be like. All mediums agree that the personality can survive death but their ideas about what we can expect to find on the other side are wildly different and often barely coherent.

Just as believers in the kind of spirituality that began with the Fox family rely on a kind of faith-by-proof the sceptics are equally obsessed with the idea of proving that the whole thing is a sham. Psychic investigators like Harry Price were as common a sight at séances as the mediums themselves. Fraud was apparently very common and many mediums were exposed as using mechanical devices to create the phenomenon they attributed to the spirit world.

Many years after the events at the Fox household Margaretta confessed in an interview with the *New York World* that the whole thing was a childish prank that had got out of hand. She told the magazine that her sister Katy had first shown her how to produce the rapping sound with her knuckles and the joints of her big toe. Once they had the method perfected the sisters had concocted the entire ghost story and, once it gained public attention, had been unable to go back on it. In a damning indictment of the spiritualist movement that she and her sister had apparently inadvertently started she said: "I have seen so much miserable deception . . . That is why I am willing to state that spiritualism is a fraud of the worst description . . . After my sister Katy and I expose it I hope spiritualism will be given a death blow."

Margaretta's confession did little to stem the growth of spiritualism – it clearly tapped into a basic need in the human psyche at a time when the church was failing to do so. The great illusionist and escape artist Harry Houdini saw this clearly and hated it. Houdini became the leading spiritualist debunker of his day. A lifetime of creating startling illusions had given him the ideal training to expose the tricks used by fraudulent mediums. His motive was simple. Like many people he dearly wanted to believe that death was not the end of the person and that members of his family who had died could still be contacted. He regarded fraud that played on this desire to be the lowest form of crime and worked tirelessly to stamp it out. His favourite method was to conduct fake séances and then show his audience how he had done it.

A bizarre example of the way that the search for the soul has turned to the pseudo-scientific demands of proof resulted in one of the longest trials in American legal history. In November of 1949 a seventy-year-old copper miner named James Kidd went missing from his simple shack in Arizona. He had no family and few friends and was regarded as bit of an oddball by the local community. It was several weeks before anyone even realized he was missing. A police investigation failed to find Kidd's body but it also failed to find any sign of foul play either and, in time, Kidd was declared legally dead.

Several years later the case of James Kidd became the business of Geraldine Swift, an Arizona estate-tax commissioner. Kidd had apparently died without making a will and had no living relatives so it was Swift's job to liquidate what few assets he may have had and turn the proceeds over to the state. In fact it turned out that Kidd had somehow stashed away a great deal of money during his life and had invested it wisely so that the total sum of his estate came to almost two hundred thousand dollars – a very considerable sum at the time.

For some reason Swift was reluctant to let go of the Kidd case and held off making a final decision until 1964. Just as Kidd's assets were about to be turned over to the state Swift made a remarkable discovery among a box of papers that had belonged to Kidd – she had apparently found a will. Although hastily and badly written it was clearly the statement of James Kidd's intentions about what should happen to his money. It was no ordinary bequest:

> *Phoenix, Arizona, Jan 2nd, 1946*
> *This is my first and only will and is dated the second day in January 1946. I have no heirs have not been married in my life, after all my funeral expenses have been paid and one hundred dollars to some preacher of the hospital to say fare well at my grave sell all my property which is all in cash and stocks with E F Hutton Company Phoenix some in safety box, and have this balance money to go in a research or some scientific proof of a soul of the human body which leaves at death I think in time their can be a Photograph of soul leaving the human at death.*

Kidd was asking for nothing less than proof of the existence of the human soul, and he was willing to put his money where his mouth was to help achieve that goal. Geraldine Swift was tempted to just lose the will – she could foresee all too easily the legal nightmare that it would create. First it would have to be established that this highly irregular document could be recognized as a legal will, then there would be the hordes of

fortune seekers, crackpots and other assorted undesir-
ables who would try to lay claim to the fortune. But
Swift had done her job up to this point and she wasn't
about to give up now, besides she rather relished the
thought of the modern legal system having to deal with
such a fundamental and controversial issue.

Even before the trial began the presiding judge,
Robert Myers, was besieged with calls and letters
laying claim to the money. One persistent caller identified himself as St Mark; Myers told him to lodge a
formal claim like all the others. Three years after the
discovery of the will, and almost twenty years after the
death of James Kidd, hearings began to determine who
was entitled to the money.

One hundred and thirty three claimants lined up
hoping for a slice of the pie. Many were discharged
pretty quickly, such as the woman who wanted some
of the money to buy herself a new set of false teeth and
the man who claimed that extraterrestrials had
revealed the secret of the soul to him. Several peti-
tioners claimed to be acting on the authority of Kidd
himself, one even claimed that she had brought his
spirit along to the courtroom as a witness.

The trial had been scheduled to take eighteen days;
after three months of non-stop testimony Judge Myers
decided it was time to reach a conclusion. Keeping in
mind Kidd's request that he wanted a "scientific" proof
Myers awarded the money to the Barrow Neurological
Institute of Phoenix – a respected research institute
dedicated to the study of the nervous system and life
processes.

Needless to say groups that took a less materialistic
view of the soul were outraged that the money had
gone to an already well-funded organization that

hadn't even made any specific promises about how the money would be used. A number of spiritualist and psychical research bodies banded together and lodged an appeal. The legal wrangle continued for another five years. Eventually the original ruling was over-turned and the Arizona Supreme Court awarded two-thirds of the money to the American Society for Psychical Research and the rest to the Psychical Research Foundation. Much of the money was spent on a study of hospital patients near death. A great deal of interesting evidence was collected from interviews with patients who had been through near death experiences but the proof that Kidd had longed for never emerged.

The Kidd case reveals some fundamental truths about the modern incarnation of the oldest mystery of them all – what and where is the soul? The triumph of the scientific method over the past two centuries has taught us to replace faith with proof; it has not taught us how to overcome the need to believe, or even if we should try and overcome it. Like so many other features of our culture the modern vision of the soul is unprecedented in human history.

The instinctual belief in some kind of immortal soul or life-force remains as common as ever but we lack the context of organized religion to give it shape. In many ways the popular modern vision of the soul has reverted to a primitive, shamanistic model. Unlike our prehistoric ancestors, however, we know too much about the universe to believe in a simple and neat afterlife laid out by the gods specifically for humans. Unfortunately we are also too ignorant of the universe to be able to replace that vision with something else.

Visions and Prophecies

•••••••••••••••••••••••••••••••••••••••

The End of the World

Every major religion has a story about the end of the world – it is an integral and vital part of the religious model of the universe. Just as a faith describes the journey and fate of the soul it must also describe the birth and death of the world. The two stories often mirror each other closely. In the Western religious tradition that manifests itself in Christianity and Islam, the journey of the soul is a one-way trip and the fate of the world is equally linear; it has a definite beginning and a definite end. In the Eastern tradition the same mirroring can be seen. In Hinduism and Buddhism the soul is destined to be reborn many times in an endless cycle. The world too is seen as passing through a cyclical pattern of destruction and rebirth that stretches infinitely into the future.

Aside from this fundamental difference there are a number of remarkable similarities in the promised events of the end days. A very common feature is the overthrowing of the natural order of the universe; day becomes night, the sun and moon stand still in the sky and the stars cease to wheel around the sky. Death and destruction on a global scale is also an essential ingredient. Typically the vast majority of non-believers are wiped out in these cataclysms and even believers suffer terrible torments. The destruction is typically envisaged as a war between good and evil fought by terrible supernatural beings, and as vast natural catastrophes such as earthquakes, floods and falling stars. Another common element is the arrival of a saviour who will guide humanity out of the disaster and create a new and better world.

For most Europeans the defining vision of the end of the world is the version given in the Christian bible, particularly the words of the the final book of the New Testament, The Revelation of St John the Divine. Supposedly written in the last decade of the first century after Christ by the apostle John, the powerful images of Revelations lie at the heart of Western civilization's vision of the apocalypse.

At the beginning of Revelations John describes how the vision of what the end of the world would be like came to him. One Sunday, as John was deep in prayer, he heard a voice "as of a trumpet" behind him and heard these words:

> *I am Alpha and Omega, the first and the last: and, what thou seest, write in a book, and send it unto the seven churches which are in Asia; unto Ephesus, and unto Smyrna, and unto Pergamos, and unto Thyatira, and unto Sardis, and unto Philadelphia, and unto Laodicea.*

The strange and terrible messenger than proceeds to show John how the apocalypse will occur in vivid detail. "Come up hither and I will show you things which must be hereafter" invites the messenger. John sees a great book closed with seven seals and as each of

Revelation prophecies: the four riders of the apocalypse.

the seals is broken the events of the end of the world unfold before his eyes. The breaking of the first four seals releases four horsemen, the four horsemen of the apocalypse, who represent conquest, slaughter, famine and death. Each rides forth to bring destruction to humanity.

As the fifth seal is broken the martyred saints appear and are told to wait until others of their kind who are to come will join them. The sixth seal brings a great earthquake; the sun is blotted out and the moon becomes blood red. On Earth men run and hide in terror as nature is overturned and the stars rain down on them, from caves and cellars they cry out "the great day of his wrath is come, and who shall be able to stand." Before the seventh and final seal is opened and the destructive angels are released on the earth a hundred and forty four thousand chosen people are taken off the Earth and delivered to heaven.

A terrible silence follows the breaking of the seventh seal. Then seven angels with trumpets appear and surround the earth. As each angel blows its trumpet a new disaster descends on the Earth:

> The first angel sounded, and there followed hail and fire mingled with blood, and they were cast upon the earth: and the third part of the trees was burnt up, and all green grass was burnt up.
>
> And the second angel sounded, and as if it were a great mountain burning with fire was cast into the sea, and the third part of the sea became blood. And the third part of the creatures which were in the sea, and had life, died and the third part of the ships were destroyed.
>
> And the third angel sounded, and there fell a great

star from heaven, burning as if it were a lamp, and it fell upon the third part of the rivers, and upon the fountains of waters; and the name of the star is called Wormwood and the third part of the waters became wormwood; and many men died of the waters, because they were made bitter.

And the fourth angel sounded, and the third part of the sun was smitten, and the third part of the moon, and the third part of the stars; so as the third part of them was darkened, and the day shone not for a third part of it, and the night likewise.

With the sounding of the fifth trumpet a star falls to the earth and opens up the pit of hell. A flood of locusts emerges from the smoke and sting everyone on earth with a bite that is so painful that people wish for death but are denied it. This torment continues for five months before the sixth trumpet is sounded. Now four angels of death are released who lead an army of two hundred million to massacre a third of the population of the world. Despite these ravages John sees that humanity has not yet turned away from its evil ways.

The climax of Revelations comes with the sounding of the seventh trumpet. The kingdom of God is proclaimed on earth and a new saviour is born in heaven to lead all the nations of the earth. After vast battles and tribulations lasting thousands of years a series of beasts are defeated and the new Jerusalem is built on earth:

And there shall be no night there; and they shall need no candle, neither light of the sun; for the Lord God giveth them light: and they shall reign for ever and ever.

In the Islamic tradition the end of the world is described in very similar terms. In the Koran the apocalypse is known as *Qiyaamah*. Events begin with an earthquake or a collapse of the ground in the east, in the west and at Hejaz in modern-day Saudi Arabia. This is followed by a terrible fog or smoke that fills the air and blots out the sun for forty days. The fog will be so noxious that unbelievers will fall unconscious and even believers will become dizzy and ill. Next comes a night that lasts for three days and, when the sun does finally rise, it will rise in the west instead of the east. This is the final sign that the end has come. After the rising of the sun in the west it will be too late for unbelievers to save themselves by converting to the true faith.

For a long period after the final sign a beast that has emerged from the earth will torment the people of the world and will mark believers with shining faces and non-believers with darkened faces. War and fire will see the destruction of the Ka'aba – Islam's most holy monument – as Mecca and humanity will enter a dark period in which even the teachings of the Koran are forgotten. Diseases borne on the wind will be rife across the world. The final destruction, which will see the sweeping away of all evil, will begin with the sounding of a trumpet.

Similarities in the tone and some details of the Christian and Islamic apocalypse are evident. This is unsurprising since both derive from the same core ideas of the ancient civilizations of the Middle East. A highly influential branch of religious thought originated with the Persian prophet known as Zoroaster. Very little is known about the man who founded Zoroastrianism, but he is thought to have lived sometime between 1000 and 1200 BC in the region of what is now Iran and Iraq, making this faith one of the oldest still practised today. It is to Zoroastrianism that later religions such as Christianity owe their concepts of good and evil and the coming of a saviour to cleanse the world of evil.

The Zoroastrian vision of the apocalypse also contains the seeds of the features that we find in the Islamic and Christian version. According to the surviving scriptures of this ancient faith the end of the world will come about when a mighty comet or star known as *Gochihr* strikes the earth. Its terrible heat will melt all the minerals of the earth so that a river of molten metal sweeps across the surface of the world. Every person will have to pass through this molten sea, the evil will have their sins burned away by it and the good will pass through it as if it were no more than warm milk. This event is known as the *Freshegird*, meaning the "making wonderful".

In Zoroaster's hymns or psalms, the only script generally accepted as having actually been composed by the prophet himself, he promises that three saviours will be born to bring peace to the world. The saviours will be born from virgins after they bathe in a lake that holds the spirit of Zoroaster himself. At specific moments in the lives of these future saints the heavens will show signs that prove their divinity. On one occasion the sun will stand at mid-day for ten days; on another, for twenty days.

There is also a beast to match the beast of the Christian and Islamic traditions. During the reign of the saviours all of the wolves in the world will gather into one place and join to form a single mighty wolf bigger than a giant. It will take a mighty army of righteous soldiers to defeat the wolf and after the victory the world will be swamped with rain.

Unlike later traditions in the West Zoroaster gives specific dates for the end of the world. According to Zoroastrians there are two types of time: true infinity, which is the time of the gods, and sovereign time, which is the time carved out of infinity for the span of the existence of the world. Sovereign time is set to last twelve thousand years and is closely related to ancient astrological beliefs. Each millennium is ruled by a sign of the zodiac which determines its character. The final millennium was supposed to begin with the birth of Zoroaster himself and was said to be destined to pass through seven ages; an age of gold, of silver, of copper, of brass, of lead, of steel and finally of iron.

With the coming of the last age humanity will sink deeper and deeper into misery and poverty. Rains will fail, crops will refuse to grow and humans will themselves become stunted and incapable of skilled work. Greed, false religions and a hunger in the soul will all presage the final end of Zoroastrian creation.

The few surviving practitioners of Zoroastrianism are to be found in India today. Perhaps the faith has survived only there because it bears some resemblance to the other ancient faith of the region, Hinduism. The Hindu vision of the end of the world is in many ways less dramatic than the Christian or Hindu versions, perhaps because it is seen as an almost routine event. According to Hindu mythology we are currently living in the fourth age of the world, known as the age of Kali. As with the three previous ages the world will die after a time and then be reborn in a fifth age. The central figure in this drama is the god Vishnu, the preserver. At the end of each age Vishnu is incarnated on earth as a saviour and destroyer. The world is dissolved and absorbed into his body before it is reborn in a new and different form.

The main feature of the Kali age, which is destined to become worse over time, is a weakness in the moral standards of humanity. Texts speak of rulers who, lacking in tranquility, take pleasure in inflicting pain on their subjects, are short-lived, greedy and lack wisdom. Their subjects are unlikely to be much better. In the Kali age humans are weak in spirit, mind and body. They are easily misled by false religions and give in to the temptations of the physical world with relish.

The Kali age sees a people totally out of balance with the world. The earth is valued only for its mineral wealth, nobility is equated with wealth, power with virtue and lust with love. Eventually civilization will break down to such an extent and the decisions of the world's rulers will become so hard to bear that people will run away from the towns and cities and take to living in the woods. Here they will revert to primitivism, hunting and gathering their food and wearing clothes of tree bark or animal skins. In this condition no one will live beyond the age of twenty-three. At last, cold, hungry, spiritless and little better than animals the human race will be put out of its misery by Vishnu who will appear in the form of a white horse. Vishnu will then remake the earth and the human race in a new and higher form.

Nostradamus

Few names are as instantly recognizable as that of the sixteenth-century seer Nostradamus. Not only does almost everyone know his name today, almost four hundred and fifty years after his death, but he has been studied and revered during the whole of those four centuries.

Born in the town of St Remy de Provence on 14 December 1503, just a few years after the region became a part of the Kingdom of France, Michele de Nostradame was the eldest son of a family of good but not wealthy lineage. Nostradamus' family was Jewish – like many other periods in European history, the early fifteenth century was not a good time for Jews. The Inquisition was in full swing and many Jews took the path of least resistance and converted to Catholicism; by the time Nostradamus was nine his family had done the same. Although he never denied his Jewish roots it was something that he kept well hidden for the rest of his life.

Young Michel was obviously a highly intelligent child. His early education was at the hands of his grandfather, Jean, who taught him Latin, Greek, Hebrew, mathematics and the rudiments of astrology. This last subject was to become a fascination for Nostradamus. When he started attending school in Avignon his interest and knowledge of the subject quickly became a talking point among the students. Astrology and what we would call astronomy today were not distinguished in Nostradamus' time and one of his favourite methods of enraging his masters was by insisting on the Copernican theory that the Earth revolves around the Sun. Galileo would be arrested for

Michel de Nostradamus.

supporting the same theory more than a century later.

Worried about their son's capacity for causing controversy at a time when such activities could easily lead to an "interview" with the Inquisition, Nostradamus' parents packed him off to Montpellier to study medicine. Three years later he had achieved his first degree and, with a certificate to practice medicine tucked into his pocket, he set off to offer aid to rural victims of the plague. The Great Plague of two centuries before which wiped out somewhere between a third and a half of the population of Europe had never really gone away. New outbreaks of the Black Death appeared sporadically all over the continent for the next four hundred years. Southern France was particularly badly hit at the time the twenty-two-year-old Nostradamus completed the first part of his medical training.

After four years of working tirelessly to combat the plague Nostradamus returned to Montpellier to obtain his doctorate. Practical experience had introduced him to some very unorthodox remedies and practices and he had trouble persuading the university that he had not abandoned their teachings altogether. After a year of teaching at Montpellier Nostradamus' theories became too much for the college authorities and he was forced to leave. One of his "outrageous" teachings was that patients should not be bled because it only served to make them weaker – at the time bleeding was considered to be the cure for just about everything from a headache to a case of the plague.

The next stage of the future prophet's life is obscure and punctuated by tragedy. By 1534 he was living and practising medicine in Agen and had become a friend of the philosopher Julius-Cesar Scaliger. He had married a woman described as "of high estate, very beautiful and admirable" and had a son and daughter. Sometime in the period between 1534 and 1538 plague came to Agen and Nostradamus' wife and children were among its victims. His practice went into decline – nobody wanted a doctor who could not even save his own wife and children – and his wife's family sued him for the return of the dowry. In 1538 he was accused of heresy. It was common practice at the time to persecute Jews and other minority groups as the cause of the plague and, despite the years he had spent combating the disease and the fact that it had taken away his own family, Nostradamus came under superstitious suspicion.

Not relishing the prospect of a heresy trial and with no reason to stay in Agen Nostradamus took to wandering the countryside again. Very little is known about his movement between the time he left Agen and sixteen years later when he settled in Marseilles. He clearly travelled widely and there are reports of him in Sicily, Venice and even as far afield as North Africa. It seems to be during this period that his true vocation as a prophet and seer emerged. Devastated by the loss of his family and outraged by the way that former friends and family had turned against him, Nostradamus wandered from city to city amid a landscape ravaged by the almost apocalyptic plague. Perhaps he followed the plague in the hope that it would kill him too or perhaps it was simply his old desire to help that drew him to it.

At Marseilles in 1554 Nostradamus witnessed one of the worst floods the city had ever seen. Coupled with fresh plague outbreaks the city came to resemble a biblical horror. Starvation and plague decimated the population and bloated, plague-ridden bodies from all along the Rhone valley were washed into the city streets and the harbour. Nostradamus worked tirelessly giving what aid he could but, like every other doctor, there was simply nothing he could do to stem the flow of death. The experience seems to have affected him deeply. A year later we find him living in the pretty little town of Salon and working on his first book of serious predictions *The Prognostications.*

Nostradamus had in fact been producing a yearly Almanac of predictions since 1550, but these were largely small-scale tit-bits concerning weather and harvests and aimed at the rural population. The *Prognostications* were different in tone and Nostradamus increasingly began to take on more political issues. In 1555 the first volume of Nostradamus' *Centuries* was published and became an overnight sensation. *The Centuries* were to be the works on which his fame would rest. So named because each section contained a hundred four-line verses the first published volume contained the first three Centuries and part of the fourth – over three hundred predictions.

The four-line verses, or quatrains as they are known, were written in the attic of Nostradamus' house in Salon. Every night he would lock himself in and work into the small hours, exactly how he received his inspiration remains something of a mystery. He reputedly used a number of obscure occult books, including one called *De Mysteriis Egyptorum*, and he was said to see visions swirling in water contained in a copper or pewter bowl that he kept for the purpose. Whatever the source of his predictions they brought him immediate fame.

By August of 1555 Nostradamus had been summoned to the royal court in Paris by Queen Catherine, wife of King Henry II. His book was already all the rage at the court and the queen spent two hours in private discussion with Nostradamus. It is likely that they discussed the verse that was believed to predict the death of the king – quatrain thirty five of the first century:

> *The young lion will overcome the older one,*
> *On the field of combat in a single battle;*
> *He will pierce his eyes through a golden cage,*
> *Two wounds made one, then he dies a cruel death.*

Nostradamus reputedly warned the king that his death was imminent, but Henry was far less impressed by the prophet than his wife and refused to believe him. In June of 1559 Henry agreed to take part in a jousting tournament against the Comte de Montgomery. During the final pass, de Montgomery failed to lower his lance in time and it shattered against the king's helmet. Two large splinters of wood were driven through the king's visor, one destroyed his eye and the other entered his head just behind the eye, both lodged in his brain. Henry died after ten days of agony.

Those at the court were quick to point out the accuracy of Nostradamus' prophecy. Both men's shield devices had been lions; the Comte was six years younger than the king; the accident had happened during a single combat and there had been two mortal wounds.

Soon after the king's death Nostradamus returned to Salon. The accuracy of his prediction had impressed many but it also raised suspicions in the church that black magic might be involved. Eager to avoid another encounter with the church and perhaps a little shocked at the power of his own predictions Nostradamus decided to lie low for a while. Back in Salon he continued writing his *Centuries* and drawing up horoscopes for the increasing number of rich and powerful people who beat a path to his door. In 1564 the queen herself, now regent of France, came to visit her old favourite. Perceiving that he was exhausted, ill and near the end of his life she bestowed the title of Physician-in-Ordinary and a generous pension on him.

Two years later Nostradamus lay on his death bed. One night he called to be given the last rites and told the priest when he left that he would be dead by morning – he was. In his will, which he made two weeks before his death, he left a large sum in gold and instructions that he should be entombed standing up in the wall of the church. His instructions were carried out to the letter and much of France mourned the passing of a great and gifted man.

By the time of his death Nostradamus had completed several hundred quatrains and many people believed that a fair number of them had already come true. Like other prophets Nostradamus couched his predictions in a cryptic form. His odd use of language is a notorious difficulty for researchers who have attempted to translate and interpret his writings. He often used standard French words liberally mixed in with Provençal French, Greek, Latin and a number of other sources. Rather than making direct statements his quatrains often allude to places or persons with symbolic language. For example, in his prediction of the death of the king he talks about the young "lion" overcoming the older rather than mentioning the king or his killer by name.

Soon after his death a rumour emerged that Nostradamus had been buried with a document that contained the key to decoding all of the quatrains. The idea persisted and became part of local folklore. In 1700 it was decided to move the tomb to a more prominent part of the church. When the wall was taken down a number of priests couldn't resist the temptation of opening the coffin to see if they could find the legendary document. No paper was found but the priests were astonished to discover a medallion plainly inscribed with the date 1700 strung around the neck of the grinning skeleton.

Ninety years later Nostradamus' rest was disturbed again. In 1791, at the height of the French Revolution, a group of drunken soldiers broke into the church at Salon and decided to smash open the tomb of the famed prophet. The commotion alerted the mayor who arrived at the scene to find soldiers dancing around the church with various skeletal limbs as partners and one guardsman drinking wine from Nostradamus' skull. The mayor managed to calm the situation down and warned them sternly that they risked instant retribution for interfering with the grave of the powerful Nostradamus. It isn't clear whether Nostradamus ever pronounced any kind of curse against future grave robbers but it is reported that the soldiers who raided his tomb that night were all cut down in an ambush the next day.

The French Revolution is just one of dozens of major historical events that Nostradamus is said to have predicted. Of course he never made explicit predictions of the kind that could leave no doubt but one of his verses is believed to relate to the event:

> *From the enslaved people songs, chants and*
> *   demands,*
> *The Princes and Lords are held captive in prisons;*
> *In the future by such headless idiots*
> *These will be taken as divine utterances.*

Many quatrains have been identified as referring to the Second World War and the life of Adolf Hitler. Several seem to use a slightly garbled version of the Nazi leader's name:

> *Beasts ferocious with hunger will cross the rivers,*
> *The greater part of the battle will be against Hister;*
> *Into a cage of iron will the great one be drawn,*
> *When the child of Germany observes nothing.*

Another startling Hitler reference comes later:

> *In the mountains of Austria near the Rhine,*
> *There will be born of simple parents;*
> *A man who will claim to defend Poland and*
> *   Hungary,*
> *And whose fate shall never be certain.*

Hitler was of course born in Austria near the German border, his parents were ordinary folk and his promises as dictator of Germany to remain at peace with his neighbours were broken when he invaded Poland and Hungary's neighbour Czechoslovakia. There is certainly no shortage of doubt over his ultimate fate either. The charred body found in his

Berlin bunker could never conclusively be identified and rumours have persisted for decades that he may have escaped Europe after Germany fell.

Most terrifying of all are the numerous quatrains that seem to predict apocalyptic cataclysms and wars. Many of the scholars who have spent years interpreting Nostradamus' labyrinth of verses conclude that he correctly predicted the sequence of the reigns of the Catholic Popes. According to these interpretations the present pope, John Paul II, will be followed by only one more whose term will see the end of the world. Appalling global catastrophes are predicted:

> *After a great misery for mankind an even greater*
> *approaches.*
> *The great cycle of the centuries is renewed;*
> *It will rain blood, milk, famine, war and disease.*
> *In the sky will be seen a fire dragging a tail of*
> *sparks.*
>
> *The sky will burn at forty five degrees latitude.*
> *Fire approaches the great new city*
> *Immediately a huge, scattered flame leaps up*
> *When they want to have verification from the*
> *French.*
>
> *The speeches of Lake Geneva become angered.*
> *The days drag out into weeks;*
> *Then months, then years, then all will fail,*
> *The authorities will damn their useless powers.*

Perhaps we can take hope from the apparent failure of one of Nostradamus' most famous predictions which seems to have failed:

In the year 1999 and seven months
The Great King of Terror will come from the sky,
He will bring back to life the great king of the
   Mongols.
Before and after the god of war reigns happily.

The Hopi Vision

In 1948, four young men from the Hopi tribe of Arizona were selected by their elders to guard their people's prophetic visions and to teach them to the world. Fifty years later, only one remained. Now an old man, Thomas Banyacya led a group of nine other native Americans who gave a presentation before the United Nations General Assembly in New York. In calm and compelling tones Banyacya warned the representatives of the world's nations that the end times were fast approaching and that humanity would surely be destroyed unless a balance with nature could be restored; this was the message of the Hopi prophecies.

That evening, the state of New York was hit by some of the worst storms in decades. Major highways were closed and the sub-levels of the UN building were flooded causing power blackouts and the failure of other utilities. Banyacya led other native peoples and a large number of UN officials in forming a prayer circle until the storms subsided. For many it was clear that Banyacya was speaking the truth.

The native peoples of North America are perhaps better placed than most to prophecy the end of the world. In a very real sense they have already experienced an apocalypse. Over the course of two centuries they have been systematically dispossessed of their lands and witnessed millions of their people die from diseases imported from Europe and from violent persecution. In many ways these once sophisticated and free-living people already feel as if they are no more than a handful of survivors living in twilight world ruled by insane devils.

The Hopi tribe have a particularly strong tradition of prophecy and their vision indicates that the world is approaching the end of one of its periodic cycles of destruction and rebirth. According to the Hopi we are living in the final days of the fourth world cycle and signs that the fifth cycle is about to begin are all around us. The Hopi believe that nine signs of the end of the world have been fulfilled over the past two centuries. These signs are recorded in detail in the traditional Book of the Hopi.

This is the first sign; we were told of the coming of the white-skinned men . . . Men who took the land that was not theirs and who struck their enemies with thunder.

Prophecies of the arrival of a white-skinned people from the east are surprisingly common in native American culture – many people have seen this as proof that Europeans had visited the American continent long before Columbus. The Hopi vision is particularly specific in that it takes this as the first sign of the end of the world as they knew it and with its reference to guns; the ultimate source of the white race's power.

This is the second sign; our lands will see the coming of spinning wheels filled with voices.

This sign is often taken to refer to the covered wagons that Europeans settlers used in their relentless push west. Native peoples had never developed the wheel, which explains why they should feature so centrally in the second sign.

> *This is the third sign; a strange beast like a buffalo but with great, long horns will overrun the land in huge numbers.*

Before the arrival of the Europeans vast buffalo herds ranged across the North American plains and hunting them provided the native peoples with almost everything they needed. The few animals taken by the tribes had no effect on the million-strong herds. European hunters used machine guns to slaughter them by their thousands so that they could be stripped of their hides. For the native Americans this was inconceivable insanity. To destroy so many animals and to then leave their valuable flesh and bones to rot on the plains was an offence to nature that convinced many that the white races must be demons. The prime motive behind the Europeans' hunger for the native people's land was commercial cattle farming. The cow, although distantly related to the buffalo, was an entirely new introduction to the American continent. As the buffalo disappeared they were replaced by vast herds of long-horn cattle.

> *This is the fourth sign; the land will be criss-crossed with snakes of iron.*

> *This is the fifth sign; the land shall be criss-crossed by a giant spider's web.*

This is the sixth sign; the land shall be criss-crossed with rivers of stone that makes pictures in the sun.

These three signs are interpreted as predicting the coming of railways, the power line and telephone line networks and concrete roads respectively. These are all fundamental elements of modern American culture and are totally alien concepts to the native peoples who travelled on foot and had no need to communicate over long distances. The reference to "pictures in the sun" remains obscure; it has been suggested that it refers to mirage effects that occur over the long, straight roads that run through Arizona, or that it is an oblique reference to the use of fuels such as petroleum which are essentially fossilized sunlight.

This is the seventh sign; you will hear of the sea turning black and many living things dying because of it.

Again this has been taken as a reference to modern society's reliance of fossil fuels and, in particular, the disasters that result from massive oil spills at sea. Such spills can cover hundreds of square miles and are lethal to fish, birds and marine mammals that get caught up in them.

This is the eighth sign; you will see many youths, who wear their hair long like our people, come and join the tribal nations to learn our ways and wisdom.

The only positive and hopeful sign, the eighth, seems to predict a growing awareness of environmental issues among the young. Although such organizations haven't literally joined the Hopi tribe they often look to the way of life of ancient indigenous peoples for clues about how we can live in closer harmony with nature.

> *This is the ninth and last sign; you will hear of a dwelling-place in the heavens, above the Earth, that shall fall with a great crash. It will appear as a blue star. Very soon after this the ceremonies of the Hopi people will cease. These are the signs that great destruction is here. The world shall rock to and fro . . . There will be many columns of smoke and fire such as the white man has made in the desert not far from here [the Hopi's lands are not far from nuclear weapon test ranges in New Mexico]. Those who stay and live in the places of the Hopi shall be safe.*

This final prophecy is perhaps the most intriguing of all and contains many key elements of Hopi belief. The reference to the ending of the ceremonies of the Hopi people is of particular significance. For the Hopi and other tribal peoples the cycle of ritual ceremonies is seen as being intimately connected with the very existence of the world – they are as much a part of nature as the people and the animals. For the Hopi ceremonies to end must mean the end of the world. Another compelling prophecy clearly invokes this connection.

> *The end of all Hopi ceremonies will come when a Kachina removes his mask during a dance in the plaza before uninitiated children. For a while there will be no more ceremonies and no more faith.*

The unmasking of the shaman in front of children who have not yet been initiated into the faith and wisdom of the Hopi is a powerful symbol of the death of a religion. The Hopi believe that they are a chosen people intimately bound up with the fate of the Earth – for their faith to end is for the force that holds the world together to dissolve.

Hopi prophecy is said to reside in a set of stone and ivory tablets given to the Hopi people at the beginning of the current fourth age by Masawa, the caretaker of the Earth. The tablets contain instructions to the Hopi about how to preserve the Earth and what signs to look out for as it comes to an end. One of the tablets, in the possession of the Fire Clan, is a four-inch square of dark coloured stone engraved with strange symbols and pictures of headless men. One corner of the tablet has been broken off and, according to the legend, will be presented to the Fire Clan by a saviour named Pahana as proof of his identity.

Pahana is sometimes identified as the shaman who will unmask and end the ceremonies. In other places he is said to be a blue star or, surprisingly, a fair-skinned man from the east. Whatever his identity, his role is clear. He will arrive near the end time and show the Hopi how to survive the apocalypse and rebuild a new world afterwards. Before he disappeared from the Earth leaving behind the tablets, Masawa told the Fire Clan what they could expect in the centuries ahead. He told them that a strange people would come to steal their lands and subjugate them but that they must not resist. He also warned that the leader of the clan must not adopt any other religion or he would have to be beheaded when Pahana arrived to erase the evil influence on his people.

For the Hopi the whole Earth is a living goddess but one particular area, the tribal homelands, are of particular significance. This, they believe, is the only part of the Earth that will not be cleansed of human life in the wars of the end times. It will become the centre from which a new civilization is built at the beginning of the fifth age.

The Hopi see their land as a symbolic microcosm of the whole world, a kind of seed from which the whole planet can be reborn. This is why it is particularly important to the Hopi that their land should not be developed or exploited in any way; any damage to the template for the new world could have dire consequences for the future of the human race. Of particular concern is the proposed exploitation of coal and uranium deposits. The Hopi believe that the Earth's minerals are akin to the vital internal organs of the human body. By removing these minerals they say we are literally disembowelling the goddess. Her pain is manifested in earthquakes, tidal waves and wild fluctuations of global temperatures.

One particularly strange Hopi prediction warns against the deadly consequences of bringing material back from the Moon or other planets. In the early 1960s Hopi traditionalists predicted potential disaster if samples of Moon rock were returned to the Earth with the Apollo astronauts. In the Hopi vision the entire universe is in delicate balance. The removal of even a tiny piece of matter from one heavenly body and its relocation to another could throw the whole system out of kilter. Many Hopi are convinced that recent changes in global weather patterns are a direct result of their warnings being ignored.

Unlike many apocalyptic visionaries the Hopi traditionalists remain hopeful that something can be done to avert disaster. The Hopi have actively been campaigning against the rape of the Earth and the lunacy of keeping the peoples of the world divided for decades, long before the current awareness of ecological issues in the industrialized West. In a book entitled the *Hopi Survival Kit* Dan Evehema, a modern Hopi elder, describes the coming shake-up with characteristic down-to-earth humour and hope:

> *The liberators will come in from the west with great force. They will drop down from the sky like rain. They will have no mercy. We must not get on the house tops to watch. They will shake us by our ears, like children who have been bad. This will be the final decisive battle between good and evil.*
>
> *When the end is near we will see a halo of mist around the heavenly bodies. Four times it will appear around the sun as a warning that we must reform, telling us that people of all colour must unite and arise for survival . . . Unless man-made weapons are used to strike first, peace will then come.*

The Fatima Prophecies

Somewhere deep inside the Vatican City, among the thousands of historical documents in the possession of the Catholic Church stretching back over two thousand years, there is a letter written by a Portuguese nun. For more than ninety years the full contents of this letter have remained a secret and successive Popes have refused permission for the letter to be published. Very few within the church itself have been permitted access to this document, only the Popes and a few senior cardinals. Known as the third prophecy of Fatima the document remains one of the most speculated about and tantalizing mysteries of our age.

On 13 October 1917, an estimated 70,000 people gathered in the fields outside the town of Fatima in Portugal. Expectations ran high and there was an element of religious hysteria among the mass of pilgrims. They had come to witness a miracle and they were far from disappointed.

It had all begun exactly five months earlier, on 13 May when three children from the town had received a vision of the Virgin Mary. Three cousins, Lucia, Jacinta and Francisco, were keeping watch over their flock of sheep at a natural hollow known as Cova da Iria when they were surprised by tremendous flash of light in the sky. Thinking that a storm was on its way the children began gathering their flock when a second flash caused them to fall to the ground and huddle together in fear.

Looking up the children saw the shimmering, luminous figure of a woman standing nearby smiling at them. Nervously they got to their feet and plucked up the courage to ask who she was. "I am from heaven" she replied and the children later recalled that the air was filled with the scent of roses as she spoke. She told the children to return to the same spot on the same day of the following month and then floated into the sky on a radiant cloud.

Lucia warned her cousins to tell no one about what had happened but the other children were far too excited to keep it to themselves and both Jacinta and Francisco told their parents. The unfortunate pair were punished for their pains and mercilessly ridiculed by the other children, but they returned to the hollow at the appointed time the following month. The mysterious lady appeared to them again and announced that the three of them were to be messengers for the world of God. Over the following months the children returned to the same spot on the same day of each month and were shown visions of heaven, hell and the future of the Earth.

The children's persistence eventually began to arouse the curiosity of the townsfolk and soon many people came to believe that they were indeed receiving messages from a visitation of the Virgin Mary. The children told them about their vision of hell and that the Virgin had told them that God intended Fatima to become a place of pilgrimage that would save many people from damnation.

The second prophecy reported by the children was that the war in Europe would soon be over. By the summer of 1917 the First World War had been raging for more than three years and had claimed millions of lives. The Virgin promised that the war would end but that if people did not turn away from their wicked ways it would be followed by an even greater war that would be heralded by a "night illuminated by an unknown light". If this happened she warned, the people of Russia would be doomed to follow a godless path for many decades before their land could be consecrated by a future Pope. The Virgin also made a third prophecy which did not come to light until many years later when Lucia, then a nun, wrote it down and sent it to the Pope.

In the month before her final visitation the Virgin promised the children that she would perform a "miracle of the sun" to demonstrate her divine origins. It was this promise that brought thousands to Fatima in the autumn of 1917. People over many square miles both in and outside of the town witnessed the strange events that manifested themselves that afternoon.

One man who was there that day, Dr Jose Marie de Almedia, later recorded what he saw in a document that survives along with a large number of other eye-witness accounts. According to de Almedia the day was cloudy and grey and all attention was focused on the three children who were standing in their customary spot in the hollow. At about half past one in the afternoon the sky began to clear very rapidly and the crowd were delighted find themselves bathed in warm sunshine. The mood became good humoured and people's attention remained focused on the children. Suddenly de Almedia heard an uproar of voices that spread through the vast crowd and everybody turned their backs on the children to look at the sun.

There was something very odd and beautiful about the appearance of the sun at that moment that witnesses have struggled to describe:

> . . . I could see the sun, like a very clear disc, with its sharp edge, which gleamed without hurting the sight . . . It kept its light and heat and light and stood out clearly in the sky, with a sharp edge, like a large gaming table. The most astonishing thing was to be able to stare at the solar disc for a long time, brilliant with light and heat, without hurting the eyes or damaging the retina . . . the sun's disc did not remain immobile, it had a giddy motion, not like the twinkling of a star in its brilliance for it spun around itself in a mad whirl.

Another witness interviewed in 1960 remembered a similar experience:

> *The sun started to roll from one place to another and changed to blue, yellow – all colours. Then we see the sun coming towards the children. Everyone was crying out. Some started to confess their sins . . . My mother grabbed me to her and started to cry saying "It is the end of the world!" And then we see the sun come right into the trees.*

De Almedia and many others also noted the strange kaleidoscope effect and a final plunge of the sun earthwards before the phenomenon ceased. A priest remembered that the strange light of the sun caused the faces of the crowd and the whole landscape to be bathed in weird blue, yellow and red light. He also said that the sun seemed to be huge and very near him and that he thought he was going to die. The climactic moment left a deep impression on de Almedia:

> *Then, suddenly, one heard a clamour, a cry of anguish breaking from the people. The sun, whirling wildly, seemed all at once to loosen itself from the firmament and, blood red, to advance threateningly on the earth as if to crush us with its huge and fiery weight. The sensation during those moments was truly terrible.*

The three children were found to be in a state of near-fainting ecstasy. Lucia was decked with garlands of roses and carried through the crowd on the shoulders of a great, tall man. As she passed she shouted out reminders of the Virgin's prophecies: the ending of the war, the danger of a second war and the peril for Russia. Gradually and quietly the crowds dispersed and returned to their towns and villages to spread the word about what they had seen. The first prophecy came true within a short time. Fatima quickly became a centre of pilgrimage and has remained one to this day.

The following year the first part of the second prophecy also came true when the First World War finally ground to a halt. In the few years after the war an influenza epidemic swept across Europe claiming more victims than the war itself had; among them were Jacinta and Francisco, only Lucia survived. People continued to make the journey to Fatima but few remembered the second part of the prophecy, that another war would break out and would be preceded by an "unknown light".

On the night of 25 January 1938 Lucia went to the window of her cell in the nunnery where she lived and looked up at a strange sky. All over Europe people were doing the same thing. That night saw one of the most spectacular and eerie displays of the northern lights, or aurora borealis, in recorded history. Later, the same phenomena was seen over the United States. Contemporary newspaper reports reveal the impact of this display:

> Thousands of frightened Portuguese rushed from their homes one night recently and pointed to huge shafts of blood red, greenish, blue and purple light shimmering on the northern horizon. "It's the end of the world", they cried.
>
> In London the luminous heavens also caused alarm. Half the city appeared to be ablaze. Frantic

NOSSA SENHORA DO ROSARIO DE FÁTIMA

Vision of Our Lady of Fatima.

citizens telephoned newspaper offices. "Where's the fire?" they asked. Out in Windsor fire engines clanged through the streets. "Windsor Castle is afire!" they said.

In south-western France, in the Alpine villages of Switzerland and along the Danube in Austria, the heavenly blaze brought thousands onto city streets and country roads. "Fire?" they asked one another "War? Doomsday?"

Few people knew or remembered the Fatima prophecy, but Lucia knew exactly what that strange night meant – the second great war was coming. In March 1938 Germany and Austria were united and the first step was taken down the short road that would lead to global war within a year. As the apparition at Fatima had promised the second war was to be far greater in scope and horror than the first. By this time it had also become clear to believers in the Fatima prophecies that the fate of Russia was sealed.

The Bolshevik Revolution of 1915, two years before the Fatima visitations, had swept all before it. By 1938 the Communist regime was firmly in control of the vast Russian hinterland and looked set to stay that way for a long time to come. A central tenet of communist philosophy was the suppression of religion. Churches were torn down and cathedrals were boarded up; the people of Russia had to practice their religion in secret. It wasn't until eighty years later that restrictions were lifted fully. In 1984 Pope John Paul II carried out a ceremony consecrating the Russian nation. For believers in the Fatima prophecy this was the promised liberation that the Virgin had spoken of.

In the early 1960s it became known that Lucia had

divulged the third prophecy of the Virgin to the then Pope. She had entrusted the envelope containing the prophecy to the Bishop of Leiria with strict instructions that it should not be opened until 1960. When the time came Pope John XXIII opened the envelope and read the prediction. To this day few people know what Lucia had written. John refused to divulge the full contents saying only "This prophecy does not relate to my time".

Evidence has emerged that Pope Paul VI thought the prophecy important enough to send extracts of it to President Kennedy of the United States, Prime Minister Macmillan of Britain and Premier Kruschev of the Soviet Union just before a series of meetings in Moscow which resulted in a 1963 agreement to limit the testing of atomic weapons. This was a tense time in world history; the year before had brought the super-powers closer to war than ever before over the Cuban missile crisis.

Reputed extracts of the text of the third prophecy have since emerged, although their authenticity remains open to doubt. Essentially these extracts predict a time of extreme hardship for the world between 1960 and the year 2000. They also hint that a failure to reform will eventually lead to a terrible war that will result in the death of a large proportion of the human race and the near-total destruction of the earth.

Many Catholics continue to believe that the true message of the third Fatima prophecy has never been revealed. It is certainly odd that the Church would want to keep the document secret if it merely predicted the end of the world; many such prophecies have been made before and have never been suppressed. Speculations about the true content of the prophecies are numerous and varied.

Some have suggested that it predicts the downfall of the Catholic Church itself, a fact that senior Catholics would be keen to keep secret, or that it reveals a deep level of corruption in the hierarchy of the Church. Others suspect that the prophecy gives the precise date of the promised second coming of Christ, which may explain Pope John XXIII's statement that the prophecy was not of his time. Many non-Christian scholars think that the prophecy may simply be banal or has already been proven wrong and that it is being kept secret to prevent disappointment and a loss of faith. Whatever the truth there are no signs that the Vatican is about to publish the prophecy any time soon.

The Scientific Apocalypse

Science has often been described as the modern religion. It would be more accurate to say that science has taken the place of religion, but it's easy to see how the cliché came into being. In the past organized religion provided us with our world-view. Priests and sacred texts such as the Christian Bible answered all the fundamental questions: where did the world come from? where did we come from? what happens after death and what is the ultimate fate of the world? This has been the pattern since the very earliest days of religious thought, in fact the need to have answers to these questions can be seen as the very reason for the existence of religion.

Today, things are different. Science has provided us with new answers to the age-old questions and introduced the world to the idea that proof is superior to faith. Religion claims the authority of God, via prophets and sacred texts, for the validity of its world-view. Science claims the authority of observation and verifiable experiment but it also holds doubt and uncertainty as fundamental.

The mythology of science, the stories that have shaped its place in our culture, are overwhelmingly concerned with the idea that theories are constantly being overthrown. Indeed this is the founding myth of science – the story of how a centuries-old world-view based on religion was overthrown in favour of a radically new theory, the world-view of science. The myth is represented by classic stories such as Copernicus' formulation of the theory of the sun-centered universe or Darwin's epic voyage that led him to formulate his theory of evolution by natural selection. In the traditional religious world-view there is no room for change, since it is based on the word of God it cannot admit change or compromise.

These fundamental differences in the approaches of science and religion to the great questions clearly show that science is not just a new religion – it is an entirely new way of thinking about the world. However, it is fair to say that science has taken over some of the functions of religion, the most obvious being providing answers to the great questions, but other similarities can also be traced. Just like priests and shamans, scientists are held in awe by our culture. This is partly because scientific disciplines are difficult to understand for the layman, which makes them seem mysterious, and partly because scientists seem to hold the fate of the world in their hands. Science has created terrible weapons of destruction and wonderful cures for disease; these are powers that have always been associated with the gods.

In some respects science has also taken over the moral and taboo functions of religion in the sense that it warns of terrible consequences of certain actions. Medical science advises us not to smoke or eat too much fatty food and demonstrates the punishments for breaking these taboos. In recent years science has also moved into the apocalypse-predicting game. Growing awareness of environmental issues in the second half of the twentieth century led people to turn to science for predictions and cures of the world's ills.

On 18 November 1992, a large group of the world's leading scientists issued a statement voicing their concerns about humanity's mismanagement of the planet. Seventeen hundred scientists, including most of the living Nobel Prize winners in science, put their name to the document. Expressed as an open letter to the world and aimed specifically at political and industrial leaders this remarkable statement can be seen as a modern counterpart to biblical predictions of apocalypse. Today the document is little known but historians of the future will probably regard it as one of the most significant of our age. It is reproduced here in full:

Human beings and the natural world are on a collision course. Human activities inflict harsh and often irreversible damage on the environment and on critical resources. If not checked, many of our current practices put at serious risk the future that we wish for human society and the plant and animal kingdoms, and may so alter the living world that it will be unable to sustain life in the manner that we know. Fundamental changes are urgent if we are to avoid the collision our present course will bring about. The environment is suffering critical stress.

The statement opens with a clear, apocalyptic warning; if we don't change our ways life will be unsustainable. Compare this to prophecies such as the Fatima prophecies in which the Virgin Mary supposedly revealed to three children that humanity would face a terrible war unless it changed its ways. The scientists' statement goes on to list the specifics of the threat.

The Atmosphere
Stratospheric ozone depletion threatens us with enhanced ultraviolet radiation at the earth's surface, which can be damaging or lethal to many life forms. Air pollution near ground level, and acid precipitation, are already causing widespread injury to humans, forests and crops.

Water Resources
Heedless exploitation of depletable ground water supplies endangers food production and other essential human systems. Heavy demands on the world's surface waters have resulted in serious shortages in some 80 countries, containing 40% of the world's population. Pollution of rivers, lakes and ground water further limits the supply.

Oceans
Destructive pressure on the oceans is severe, particularly in the coastal regions which produce most of

the world's food fish. The total marine catch is now at or above the estimated maximum sustainable yield. Some fisheries have already shown signs of collapse. Rivers carrying heavy burdens of eroded soil into the seas also carry industrial, municipal, agricultural, and livestock waste – some of it toxic.

Soil
Loss of soil productivity, which is causing extensive land abandonment, is a widespread byproduct of current practices in agriculture and animal husbandry. Since 1945, 11% of the earth's vegetated surface has been degraded – an area larger than India and China combined – and per capita food production in many parts of the world is decreasing.

Forests
Tropical rain forests, as well as tropical and temperate dry forests, are being destroyed rapidly. At present rates, some critical forest types will be gone in a few years and most of the tropical rain forest will be gone before the end of the next century. With them will go large numbers of plant and animal species.

These are of course the key elements that support life on earth. In apocalyptic vision down the ages the final end of the world is preceded by cataclysms that lay waste to these vital resources. In the Book of Revelation in the Christian Bible for example a third of the grass and a third of the trees are destroyed by hail and fire mixed with blood. A third of the life in the seas is killed by a "great mountain burning with fire" and a

third of the world's springs and rivers are poisoned and
made bitter by a falling star.

Living Species

*The irreversible loss of species, which by 2100 may
reach one third of all species now living, is especially serious. We are losing the potential they hold
for providing medicinal and other benefits, and the
contribution that genetic diversity of life forms
gives to the robustness of the world's biological
systems and to the astonishing beauty of the earth
itself. Much of this damage is irreversible on a scale
of centuries or permanent. Other processes appear
to pose additional threats. Increasing levels of gases
in the atmosphere from human activities,
including carbon dioxide released from fossil fuel
burning and from deforestation, may alter climate
on a global scale. Predictions of global warming
are still uncertain – with projected effects ranging
from tolerable to very severe – but the potential
risks are very great. Our massive tampering with
the world's interdependent web of life – coupled
with the environmental damage inflicted by deforestation, species loss, and climate change – could
trigger widespread adverse effects, including
unpredictable collapses of critical biological
systems whose interactions and dynamics we only
imperfectly understand. Uncertainty over the
extent of these effects cannot excuse complacency
or delay in facing the threat.*

Destruction of all other forms of life on earth apart
from humanity is also a common feature of ancient
prophecy. The most familiar example is the flood of

Noah when the animal population of the world was only saved by a hair's breadth. Today there are an alarming number of species that only exist in small numbers in captivity. Unlike Noah modern attempts to rebuild their populations have met with only limited success.

Population

The earth is finite. Its ability to absorb wastes and destructive effluent is finite. Its ability to provide food and energy is finite. Its ability to provide for growing numbers of people is finite. And we are fast approaching many of the earth's limits. Current economic practices which damage the environment, in both developed and underdeveloped nations, cannot be continued without the risk that vital global systems will be damaged beyond repair.

Pressures resulting from unrestrained population growth put demands on the natural world that can overwhelm any efforts to achieve a sustainable future. If we are to halt the destruction of our environment, we must accept limits to that growth. A World Bank estimate indicates that world population will not stabilize at less than 12.4 billion, while the United Nations concludes that the eventual total could reach 14 billion, a near tripling of today's 5.4 billion. But, even at this moment, one person in five lives in absolute poverty without enough to eat, and one in ten suffers serious malnutrition. No more than one or a few decades remain before the chance to avert the threats we now confront will be lost and the prospects for humanity immeasurably diminished.

In 1999, only seven years after this statement was issued, the world population reached the six billion mark. Worry about the sheer number of people on earth is not a new thing. In the seventeenth century a man named Malthus voiced similar fears when he pointed out that the human race would inevitably grow at a faster rate than its ability to produce food. Fortunately he turned out to be wrong; new methods of farming have so far kept us ahead of the game in theory at least. In reality of course the world's food is far from evenly shared out.

Warning

We the undersigned, senior members of the world's scientific community, hereby warn all humanity of what lies ahead. A great change in our stewardship of the earth and the life on it, is required, if vast human misery is to be avoided and our global home on this planet is not to be irretrievably mutilated.

What We Must Do – Five inextricably linked areas must be addressed simultaneously:

1. We must bring environmentally damaging activities under control to restore and protect the integrity of the earth's systems we depend on. We must, for example, move away from fossil fuels to more benign, inexhaustible energy sources to cut greenhouse gas emissions and the pollution of our air and water. Priority must be given to the development of energy sources matched to third world needs – small scale and relatively easy to implement. We must halt deforestation, injury to and loss of agricultural land, and the loss of terrestrial and marine plant and animal species.

2. We must manage resources crucial to human welfare more effectively. We must give high priority to efficient use of energy, water, and other materials, including expansion of conservation and recycling.

3. We must stabilize population. This will be possible only if all nations recognize that it requires improved social and economic conditions, and the adoption of effective, voluntary family planning.

4. We must reduce and eventually eliminate poverty.

5. We must ensure sexual equality, and guarantee women control over their own reproductive decisions.

The developed nations are the largest polluters in the world today. They must greatly reduce their over-consumption, if we are to reduce pressures on resources and the global environment. The developed nations have the obligation to provide aid and support to developing nations, because only the developed nations have the financial resources and the technical skills for these tasks.

Acting on this recognition is not altruism, but enlightened self-interest: whether industrialized or not, we all have but one lifeboat. No nation can escape from injury when global biological systems are damaged. No nation can escape from conflicts over increasingly scarce resources. In addition, environ-mental and economic instabilities will cause mass migrations with incalculable consequences for developed and undeveloped nations alike. Developing nations must realize that environmental damage is one of the gravest threats they face, and that attempts to blunt it will be overwhelmed if their populations go unchecked. The greatest peril is to become trapped in spirals of environmental decline, poverty, and unrest, leading to social, economic and environmental collapse.

Success in this global endeavour will require a great reduction in violence and war. Resources now devoted to the preparation and conduct of war – amounting to over $1 trillion annually – will be badly needed in the new tasks and should be diverted to the new challenges.

A new ethic is required – a new attitude towards discharging our responsibility for caring for ourselves and for the earth. We must recognize the earth's limited capacity to provide for us. We must recognize its fragility. We must no longer allow it to be ravaged. This ethic must motivate a great movement, convince reluctant leaders and reluctant governments and reluctant peoples themselves to effect the needed changes.

The scientists issuing this warning hope that our message will reach and affect people everywhere. We need the help of many.

We require the help of the world community of scientists – natural, social, economic, political;

We require the help of the world's business and industrial leaders;

We require the help of the world's religious leaders; and

We require the help of the world's peoples.

We call on all to join us in this task.

Unlike traditional apocalyptic visions the scientists' vision ends on a note of hope. The future is not fixed and, in the end, we choose at least this part of our fate.

It's conceivable that the scientists' canon of "five things we must do" could become an adjunct to our general morality. At least we can hope that the new century will see an improvement on the last.

The Problem with Prophets

Contrary to the popular expression, prophecy is probably the oldest profession. Ever since the earliest emergence of religious feeling there has been a shaman or priest figure to mediate between the earthly world and the realm of the spirits or gods. Primitive religions of this kind are essentially concerned with bringing about favourable conditions by appealing to gods that control such things as weather or the migration of prey animals. A vital part of the shaman's job is to interpret signs of the mood of the gods and thereby deduce when disaster or good fortune can be predicted.

Prophets can be found in abundance in the history of the world's major religions. The founders of these religions have all been prophets of some form or other and credited with knowledge of what lies in store for the human race or the individual after death. In more recent times the profession of prophecy has taken on a life of its own independent of organized religion. Prophets such as the legendary Nostradamus used religious language and operated within the bounds of prevailing theology but were not representatives of any church. Britain's Mother Shipton is another historical example. Today the world is full of people who claim to be able to see into the future.

In modern times prophets and seers claim a wide

variety of sources for their miraculous foreknowledge. These can range from psychic powers to visitations by extraterrestrials. In ancient times the gods were usually claimed as the whistle-blowers on the future – an obvious choice since they were believed to make the future. Since the failure of universal faith and the general collapse of organized religion in the developed nations, science has become the new arbiter of truth. In this new climate many people have suspected that the whole business of prophecy may be nothing more than a massive fraud.

One of the most famous pure prophecy makers of the ancient world was the Oracle of Delphi. Generations of ancient Greeks relied on the mystical priestesses at Delphi to advise and warn them about the future. Part of the attraction of tales of the Oracle is their twist-in-the-tail endings which seems to exaggerate their mystical character. A classic example is the story of King Croesus of Lydia, said to be the wealthiest man in the ancient world.

Contemplating an invasion on the neighbouring Persian empire Croesus sent envoys to the Delphic Oracle to find out if this would be a good idea. The envoys took the necessary offering, a large sum of money, and observed the priestess drink the holy potions and lapse into a trance. They returned some time later with the following message from the Oracle:

> When Croesus shall o'er Halys River go
> He will a mighty kingdom overthrow.

Croesus was overjoyed. The great god Apollo, who was said to be the source of the prophecies, was clearly smiling on his enterprise. The king gathered his army and crossed the Halys river to meet the Persian forces. In the battle that followed Croesus' forces were annihilated and Croesus himself was beheaded. The king had misunderstood; the mighty kingdom that was to be overthrown was his own. Awe at the power of the Delphic Oracle was substantially enhanced.

Modern debunkers have pointed out that this story reveals one of the basic flaws in the business of prophecy. If Croesus had been victorious and gone on to conquer the Persians the prophecy would still have been true; it works whatever the actual course of events turn out to be. With such cleverly constructed prophecies the Oracle could keep its reputation going indefinitely, and reap the rich rewards. Sceptics claim that, by following a few simple rules, anyone can be a successful prophet.

The Canadian magician James Randi has spent much of his career debunking paranormal phenomena of all kinds. He has drawn up a set of seven rules for aspiring prophets which reveal some compelling truths about prognostication.

Randi's first rule is the necessity of the scatter-gun effect. In other words the more predictions you make the more often you will get lucky and predict something that really happens. Nostradamus wrote almost a thousand four-line verses over the course of his prophetic career. It's hardly surprising says Randi that some of them turned out to fit future events. As with every other element of prophecy human psychology plays right into the prophet's hands; even if only one in a hundred of your predictions come true they will be hailed as miraculous, all the others will be forgotten.

The second rule is vagueness. Seers commonly use language related to feeling and awareness. Successful prophecies should include terms like "I feel . . ." or "I sense . . ." or "I think I see . . .". This gives people the opportunity to fit events to the prophecy, which is what most people desperately want to do. A prophecy such as "I sense some kind of upheaval in the East" could refer to an economic problem, a war or even an unexpected political turn. The East could mean almost anywhere, the obvious interpretation is the Oriental sphere, but it could just as easily mean London's East End. All the prophet has to do is sit back and wait for someone to find a good fit, then he or she can nod sagely and say "Yes, that must be what I saw."

The third rule is the use of metaphor and symbolism. This forces people to search for meaning and almost always leads to some kind of triumphant interpretation. There is a great store of words in the English language that can be twisted into a whole variety of symbolic associations. Words such as "king" or "crown" or "throne" can be taken as referring to any position of power, authority or respected reputation. Predictions of kings losing their crowns or their thrones can be applied to the ups and downs of almost any career in politics or business. Animals, gemstones, elements and words like "vessel" or "wings" are also highly interpretable.

The fourth rule is contradiction. When asked to predict the outcome of an event such as an election or the outcome of vital peace talks the prophet should essentially predict both possible outcomes on separate occasions. Best of all is the kind of prophecy issued about Croesus: one that can be interpreted both ways. Failing this it's perfectly okay to make two contradictory predictions; only the accurate one will be reported and remembered.

The fifth rule is divine backing; the prophet should attribute his or her visions of the future to a god or some other mysterious agency. This magnifies the effects of vagueness and symbolism; people expect mysterious forces to manifest themselves in ways that are difficult to understand. Even if a prediction stubbornly refuses to come true the prophet can claim that he must have misunderstood the advanced intelligence that revealed it, or that everyone else simply does not have the understanding to see that the prediction has in fact come true.

The sixth rule, persistence, is related to the first, quantity. The mere fact of someone insisting that they are a prophet over a long period of time will convince some people that they must be even if there is no obvious proof of their claims. It also puts errors further in the past where they are even more likely to be forgotten; proof is rarely an essential element in persuasion.

The seventh and last rule, doom, is again related to patterns of human thought. For one thing people generally find it easier to believe that bad things are going to happen rather than wonderful things; for another, most events, even if they turn out to be good, are seen as bad at the time. Another advantage is that disaster is a common feature of the world. There are several major natural disasters every year and, as long as the prophet is careful to obscure actual dates and places with symbolism, these can be confidently predicted.

The best place to see these rules in action is in the works of Nostradamus, the most famous prophet of the modern era. Nostradamus, born in 1503, spent the latter part of his life engaged in writing his *Centuries* – collections of four-line verses or quatrains that were believed to reveal all kinds of future events. Nostradamus was a legend in his own lifetime and has remained a favourite for more than four hundred years.

Running through the rules it's clear that they offer an explanation of Nostradamus' success. He certainly cannot be faulted on the first: quantity. Over the course of his career he published ten of his *Centuries*, not all of them are complete but they still amounted to over nine hundred predictions. Even the most ambitious of Nostradamus' numerous interpreters haven't attempted to offer fits for all of his predictions, since few of them give dates they are no doubt expected to come true at some future time. Given the long-term appeal of Nostradamus and the huge number of events that occur in an ever-accelerating culture like ours this will no doubt happen in time.

Vagueness is almost a defining feature of Nostradamus' predictions. His verses are notoriously difficult to interpret because of their bizarre mix of languages. He used French, the dialect of his native Provence, and a generous smattering of Latin and Greek. Not only that but they were written in such an obscure and elliptical style that they are virtually incomprehensible on first reading:

> *The ancient work will be accomplished*
> *And from the roof evil ruin will fall on the great*
>   *man*
> *They will accuse an innocent, being dead, of the*
>   *deed*
> *The guilty one is hidden in the misty copse.*

Taken out of context of the expectations that surround Nostradamus this is clearly a piece of random nonsense. Once the magic of expectation, and judicious translation, is applied however, many interpreters have seen these lines as a clear prediction of the assassination of President Kennedy in 1963 complete with reference to the conspiracy of the hidden assassin on the grassy knoll. Notice that there is no mention of a date, a place or a name in the quatrain, neither is there any mention of death or the consequences of the "evil ruin". These are surely key elements that one would expect from a prediction of the assassination of a key figure in world politics.

Another obvious feature of the quatrains is their heavy use of symbolic language. This is perhaps the key to their success. A verse that is supposed to foretell the Second World War is a good example:

> *Beasts ferocious with hunger will cross the rivers*
> *The greater part of the battlefield will be against*
> * Hister*
> *Into a cage of iron the great one will be drawn*
> *When the child of Germany observes nothing.*

The presence of the name "Hister" in this quatrain is what gives it its power. Endless interpreters have pointed out the similarity to the name "Hitler" as if this is absolute proof of the prediction's authority. In fact it's more likely that Nostradamus was referring to the name of a river in Germany that he thought would be near the battlefield. Symbolic elements are rife, there are "beasts", there is "hunger", a "cage of iron", a "great one" and "the child of Germany". Possible interpretations of these elements allow the verses to fit just about any European war or battle in the past thousand years.

Next up on the prophecy wish-list is contradiction. Notice in the "Hister" quatrain that there is actually no mention of "the great one's" final fate, there is no prediction of either victory or defeat, or rather there is a hint of both. The "cage of iron" into which the great one is drawn could be seen as a kind of defeat, although it doesn't really fit the actual defeat of Hitler. Of course the great one could equally refer to Hitler's enemies. If the war had ended with a German victory it's easy to see that this quatrain would still have that quality of eerie accuracy.

Nostradamus certainly made full use of the rule of divine backing. He did not claim that his visions came from God, that would have been a dangerous game for a man born a Jew in the sixteenth century, but he did claim mystical precedent. The Jewish tribe from which his family was said to be descended had a reputation as a tribe of seers; we only know this because Nostradamus dropped heavy hints about it in his lifetime. The actual source of his predictions is something of a mystery, which is the best kind of source to have. He described them as visions and later accounts of uncertain origin have described him using a magical bowl or "seeing glass". In the fifteenth century such props were the standard equipment of alchemists and seers alike; the general public would have instantly recognized these as the necessary tools of a man in touch with unseen powers.

The sixth rule is persistence, something Nostradamus clearly had in bundles. There is only one clear case of his predictions coming true within his lifetime, the quatrain that was taken as predicting the

death of King Henry II of France in 1559. This apparent
lack of success did nothing to harm Nostradamus'
career; one spectacular success was enough to
persuade Queen Catherine for one that he had supernatural powers.

The final rule is fulfilled by Nostradamus like no
other. His predictions are unremittingly disaster filled
and gloomy and people love every second of it. Two
classic examples represent the general tone of the
Centuries:

> *After a great misery for mankind an even greater*
>   *approaches*
> *The great cycle of the centuries is renewed*
> *It will rain blood, milk, famine, war, disease*
> *In the sky will be seen a fire, dragging a tail of*
>   *sparks.*

> *Leave, leave Geneva everyone!*
> *The grim reaper will change gold to iron*
> *Those against Rapoz will be exterminated*
> *Before the invasion the heavens will show signs.*

Loaded with the symbolic language of death and
destruction quatrains such as these crop up with
monotonous regularity. The addition of a reference to
"the great cycle of the centuries" adds an air of millen-
nial fever that made this example particularly popular
as the twentieth century neared its conclusion.

Seen from the point of view of a sceptic Nostodamus'
predictions seem less than impressive. Probably much
of his reputation rests on the fact that few people who
know the name and have heard of his miraculous
predictions of the Second World War and the assassi-

nation of Kennedy have actually seen the verses on which these claims rest. Even his rare "successes" are far from persuasive; they lack dates or names and rely almost exclusively on tortuous interpretations of vague, symbolic language. Randi is right in one sense at least, when you follow the rules of prophecy as closely as Nostradamus did, success is inevitable.

Of course, just because features such as Randi's seven rules can be found in the works of numerous prophets doesn't prove that all prophets are frauds. For one thing it's highly unlikely that the founders of the world's great religions made prophecies for financial gain; they genuinely believed that they were conveying messages from a higher power. It's equally certain that a lot of modern prophets are not deliberately misleading people.

It's very easy for the rules of prophecy to become internalized so that the prophet doesn't even realize that he or she is following a rule. It becomes a way of looking at the world. Vague thoughts or feelings already amplified by a fantasy-prone personality become prophetic visions, people and things become symbolic of deeper, hidden powers and occasional successes become proof that the prophet is in tune with some supernatural force that they long to believe in.

Prophecy as Politics

George Washington is regarded almost a god by the people of the United States of America. As the first president of the union and the man who commanded the rag-tag army that defeated the British in the War of

Independence he is regarded as the father of the nation. Numerous legends and folk tales have grown up about the man that illustrate his moral and modest character. Some of them are no doubt true, others are pure invention; the same things have happened to admired leaders down the centuries.

Washington was born in 1732 into a Virginia planter family. He first became involved in politics through his involvement as a serving officer during the Seven Years War, or the French and Indian War as it is known in the United States. Although never a brilliant strategist he was a fine speaker and his solid command abilities and prudence impressed many in the growing movement for independence. In 1775, at the Second Continental Congress, Washington was elected Commander in Chief of the Continental Army, the force that was to end British rule. For six years he struggled against insufficient supplies, poorly disciplined troops and the military superiority of the British before finally forcing the defeat of the British commander Cornwallis at Yorktown.

The economy of the former colony had suffered terribly during the war and many of Washington's troops had not been paid for months. Angry at this treatment his officers asked Washington to lead them against the Capital where they would take over the government. In what was probably one of his most significant acts Washington refused and persuaded his army to respect the elected council. It was decisions like this that earned Washington his special place in American history. He became the standard by which all future presidents were judged and, more often than not, found wanting.

Washington was elected president of the new nation

in 1787. He served two terms and retired in 1796. During his farewell address he warned the nation to never disband the union and to beware of regional splits. After only three years of retirement he died in December of 1799. Just sixty-one years after his death the United States was facing the greatest crisis in its history: the Civil War.

By this time the area of the United States had expanded hugely and it was becoming one of the world's leading economies. All that was put at risk when the southern states decided to reject the authority of the Federal Government in the city which had been named after Washington. In 1859 the *National Tribune* newspaper published a remarkable document that was said to recount a vision that Washington had received of his country's future. In that year tensions between North and South reached new heights and there was widespread talk of dissolving the union. The ghost of George Washington was raised as a political act to try and avert the coming conflict. In his vision Washington sees vast conflicts and three perils that will face the United States. Several times an angel emblazoned with the word "Union" saves the day – the message is clear; without Union the peoples of America are lost.

George Washington's Vision of the Perils of the United States.

I do not know whether it is owing to the anxiety of my mind, or what, but this afternoon, as I was sitting at this table engaged in preparing a dispatch, something seemed to disturb me. Looking up, I beheld standing opposite me a singularly beautiful female. So astonished was I, for I had given strict orders not to be disturbed, that it was some moments before I found language to inquire into the cause of her presence.

A second, a third, and even a fourth time did I repeat my question, but received no answer from my mysterious visitor except a slight raising of her eyes. I would have risen, but the rivetted gaze of the being before me rendered volition impossible. I assayed once more to address her, but my tongue had become useless, even thought itself had become paralysed. A new influence, mysterious, potent, irresistible, took possession of me. All I could do was to gaze steadily, vacantly at my unknown visitor.

Gradually, the surrounding atmosphere seemed as though becoming filled with sensations and luminous. Everything about me seemed to rarefy, the mysterious visitor herself becoming more airy, and yet more distinct to my sight than before. I now began to feel as one dying, or rather to experience the sensations which I have sometimes imagined accompany dissolution. I did not think, I did not reason, I did not move; all were alike impossible. I was only conscious of gazing fixedly, vacantly at my companion.

Presently I heard a voice saying, "Son of the Republic, look and learn," while at the same time my visitor extended her arm eastwardly. I now beheld a heavy white vapour at some distance rising fold upon fold. This gradually dissipated, and I looked upon a strange scene. Before me lay spread out in one vast plain all the countries of the world. I saw rolling and tossing between Europe and America the billows of the Atlantic, and between Asia and America lay the Pacific. "Son of the Republic," said the same mysterious voice as before, "Look and learn."

At that moment I beheld a dark, shadowy being floating in mid-air between Europe and America, dipping water out of the ocean in the hollow of each hand. He sprinkled some upon America with his right hand, while with his left hand he cast some on Europe. Immediately a dark cloud raised from these countries and joined in mid-ocean. For a while it remained stationary, and then moved slowly westward, until it enveloped America in its murky folds. Sharp flashes of lightning passed through it at intervals, and I heard the smothered groans and cries of the American people.

A second time the angel dipped water from the ocean, and sprinkled it out as before. The dark cloud was then drawn back to the ocean, in whose heaving billows it sank from view. A third time I heard the mysterious voice saying, "Son of the Republic, look and learn." I cast my eyes upon America and beheld villages and towns and cities springing up one after another until the whole land from the Atlantic to the Pacific was dotted with them. Again I heard the mysterious voice say, "Son of the Republic, the end of the century cometh, look and learn."

At this the dark, shadowy angel turned his face southward, and from Africa I saw an ill-omened spectre approach our land. It flitted slowly over every town and city. The inhabitants presently set themselves in battle array against each other. As I continued looking, I saw a bright angel, on whose brow rested a crown of light, on which was traced the word "Union," bearing the American flag, which he placed between the divided nation, and said, "Remember ye are brethren." Instantly the inhabitants, casting from them their weapons, became friends once more and united around the National Standard.

And again I heard the mysterious voice saying, "Son of the Republic, look and learn." At this the dark, shadowy angel placed a trumpet to his mouth and blew three distinct blasts; and taking water from the ocean, he sprinkled it upon Europe, Asia, and Africa. Then my eyes beheld a fearful scene: from each of these countries arose thick, black clouds that were joined into one, and throughout this mass there gleamed a dark red light by which I saw hordes of armed men, who, moving with the cloud, marched by land and sailed by sea to America, which country was enveloped in the volume of the cloud.

And I dimly saw these vast armies devastate the whole country and burn the villages, towns, and cities that I beheld were springing up. As my ears listened to the thundering of the cannon, clashing of swords, and the shouts and cries of millions in mortal combat, I heard again the mysterious voice saying, "Son of the Republic, look and learn." When the voice had ceased, the dark, shadowy angel placed his trumpet once more to his mouth and blew a long and fearful blast.

Instantly a light as of a thousand suns shone down from above me, and pierced and broke into fragments the dark cloud which enveloped America. At the same moment the angel, upon whose head still shone the word UNION, and who bore our national flag in one hand and a sword in the other, descended from the heavens, attended by legions of white spirits. These immediately joined the inhabitants of America, who I perceived were well nigh overcome, but who immediately taking courage again, closed up their broken ranks and renewed the battle.

Again, amid the fearful noise of the conflict, I heard the mysterious voice saying, "Son of the Republic, look and learn." As the voice ceased, the shadowy angel for the last time dipped water from the ocean and sprinkled it upon America. Instantly the dark cloud rolled back, together with the armies it had brought, leaving the inhabitants of the land victorious. Then once more I beheld the villages, towns, and cities springing up where I had seen them before, while the bright angel, planting the azure standard he had brought in the midst of them, cried with a loud voice, "While the stars remain, and the heavens send down dew upon the earth, so long shall the Union last." And taking from his brow the crown on which was blazoned the word "Union," he placed it upon the Standard, while the people, kneeling down, said, "Amen."

The scene instantly began to fade and dissolve, and I at last saw nothing but the rising, curling vapour I at first beheld. This also disappearing, I found myself once more gazing upon the mysterious visitor, who, in the same voice I had heard before, said, "Son of the Republic, what you have seen is thus interpreted: Three great perils will come upon the Republic. The most fearful is the third, passing which the whole world united shall not prevail against her. Let every child of the Republic learn to live for his God, his land, and the Union." With these words the vision vanished, and I started from my seat, and felt that I had seen a vision wherein had been shown me the birth, progress, and destiny of the United States.

Mystical Places

•••••••••••••••••••••••••••••••••••••••

The Nazca Plain

Two hundred miles south of the Peruvian capital Lima, in the heart of the Peruvian desert, lies the Nazca Plain. A barren upland separating the valleys that were once home to the Inca people to the east and the Nazca people to the west, it is one of the driest places on earth. Receiving the equivalent of just twenty minutes of rain a year the plain is devoid of vegetation and human habitation. In many years, there is no rain at all; droughts can last for decades. Not surprisingly water has always been a problem for the peoples that live on the fringes of this region.

In the 1930s government pilots overflying the area during a survey for water were astonished to observe huge shapes and figures etched into the desert. They were so big that nobody had noticed them from the ground. In the decades since their discovery the lines of the Nazca Plain have been studied by dozens of archaeologists, anthropologists and assorted others in an attempt to figure out how, and why, they were made. The sheer scale of the figures has ensured that theories have not been in short supply.

The figures on the plain cover an area about 37 miles in length by about a mile and a half in width. Within

Nazca Plain geoglyphs on the Nazca desert, Peru.

this flat pan there are three basic types of figure; animal forms, abstract geometric shapes and straight lines. There are dozens of lines criss-crossing all over the plain. Some run in parallel over many miles, others cross at apparently random points. The longest extend for about five miles. The geometric shapes tend to be three- or four-sided and can have edges up to two and a half thousand feet long. Interspersed among the other forms are shapes that are recognizable as stylized line drawings of various animal forms. They include a bird-like form, a whale, a spider and a lizard.

Although the animal figures are the most famous feature of the Nazca Plain they are in fact dwarfed in scale by the lines and geometric shapes. Even so, they are so large that they are only recognisable as drawings from at least a thousand feet in the air – the so-called "hummingbird" pictogram is over three hundred feet long. On the ground the Nazca Plain features are far less impressive. They consist of lines or areas where the hard, stony crust of the desert has been scraped away to reveal the darker soil beneath. Leaving aside the question of how they were created there is no real way to even prove when they were created.

If the Nazca Plain features were indeed created by the Nazca people then they are at least 1800 years old – the Nazca civilization flourished between 200 BC and 200 AD. Unfortunately the features themselves cannot be carbon dated since they contain no organic material. The best archaeologists have been able to do is to date fragments of wood and other materials thought to have been left at the site by its creators, and these tend to fit the Nazca period. In fact this proves only that the Nazca visited the site, not that they built it. As any archaeologist knows it is somewhat akin to dating the Egyptian pyramids according to the age of an egg sandwich that some passing tourist has left nearby.

An added problem is the almost total absence of natural erosion processes on the plain. There is very little sand or dust and the ground is so flat that wind erosion is cut to a minimum. Water erosion is, of course, almost non-existent. The practical upshot is that the features could have been there for thousands of years or a couple of weeks before they were discovered. The connection with the Nazcas is mainly established by the plain's proximity to their centres of civilization and the fact that the ruins of their cities and temples indicate a strong taste for the geometric. In the end the question of who created the Nazca Plain features is far less interesting than the questions how and why?

Ever since the features were first spotted from the air there has been a great temptation to suggest that they were only meant to be seen from the air. This raises the intriguing question of why a people would go to the enormous trouble of creating vast pictograms that they themselves could never hope to see.

With characteristic boldness the Swiss author Erich von Daniken suggested in 1969 that the corridors and lanes were meant to guide extraterrestrial spaceships in to land – a kind of cosmic aerodrome. The patterns do bear a startling resemblance to a modern airport with its crossing runways and taxi ways but few have been convinced by von Daniken's argument. Apart from the rather grand assumption that alien visitors may have wanted to visit the Nazca Plain in the distant past there is a singular lack of other physical signs that the area might have been used to land intergalactic craft. Firstly, the soil of the desert is actually very soft and cannot even support a safe landing by a modern light aircraft. Secondly it's hard to believe that an advanced space-faring civilization would have to rely on crude lines scratched in the dirt to achieve a landing.

Part of the appeal of von Daniken's idea is that it seems to offer an explanation of how the features were laid out. The sheer technical difficulties involved in drawing a straight line five miles long across undulating terrain are mind-boggling. Modern road builders use laser sights, Global Positioning Satellite systems and powerful optical aids to build straight roads. However, as appealing as the idea of airborne surveyors sounds, it's difficult to see how it would really help. Just having someone in the air looking down at the people inscribing the line doesn't actually make their job any easier. It is hard to see what an airborne observer could do to affect the accuracy of the course the line is taking – at best the observer could simply report errors. There is no evidence that lines have been "erased" and corrected.

Several studies have been carried out which suggest that the process of creating terrain-covering markings with very primitive equipment is not actually that difficult. Field archaeologists have shown that remarkably accurate straight lines can be created using string and wooden posts. Any two posts stuck in the ground are, of course, in line with each other. All it takes is for one person to direct the placing of another post directly in line of sight of the first two for all three to be in a perfect line. String stretched between the posts indicates the route for the line cutters to take. This process can be repeated indefinitely. With practice and the use of posts with "sights" – for example a sighting hole drilled through the middle – long, straight lines can be achieved.

More complex, geometric patterns can be created just as easily. The designers probably drew their patterns at a small scale to start with and then used simple mathematics to scale them up to a size more suitable for the plain. Similar methods could be used to draw the animal shapes. As long as you can draw straight lines and know when to turn corners almost any shape can be drawn at any scale – there is no need to be able to see what you are doing and no real advantage in it.

It seems entirely possible that the Nazcas could have created the plain features without being able to see them from above but the vexing question remains; if the Nazcas weren't going to see the pictograms in their full glory, who were they meant for? The most likely theory is that they were meant to be seen by the gods of the Nazcas. Almost all primitive religions regard the sun and the sky as gods, these concepts generally evolve into personified figures like the Greeks' Zeus or the Scandinavians' Odin. It is highly likely that the Nazcas had similar sky and sun deities. Most mythologies also involve gods and goddesses that fly, and often, fight in the heavens. In fact it was partly the prevalence of such myths that led von Daniken to propose his rather literal prehistoric flying aliens.

The Nazca Plain is ringed by uplands and mountains dominate the western and eastern skyline. The little that is known of Nazca mythology suggests that their gods were believed to reside in those mountains. It's not difficult to see why – not only are mountains naturally awe-inspiring they are also the source of rivers and therefore quite literally the source of life for a people living in an arid environment.

The Nazcas believed that their gods soared over the landscape in the form of eagles or condors, a belief they shared with the later Inca peoples who lived to the west. The logic is clear. If your gods live at the tops of mountains and soar through the air as eagles the best way to communicate with them is by writing messages in very large letters on the ground. Something about the vast flatness of the plain and the hugeness of the desert sky seems to make this the obvious thing to do.

Among the many theories about the purpose of the Nazca Plain markings one current of thought comes up time and again. Lines, visible or otherwise, across the landscape are strongly reminiscent of the concept of ley lines. These are variously associated with lines of magnetism, channels of mysterious earth energies or subterranean water courses. It has been suggested that the lines and geometric markings on the Nazca Plain may mark subterranean water courses.

David Johnson, an American amateur dowser, is the most recent proponent of this theory. Using simple rods that he claims were found at a Nazca burial site, he has established to his own satisfaction that water does indeed run beneath the major surface features. He also claims the intersections of lines mark the ideal places to dig wells – a theory he intends to test in the near future with a well-drilling machine.

Even if Johnson finds no water beneath his line intersections it is likely that the features have a lot to do with water, if only in a symbolic sense. For peoples in arid environments the major problem with rain is not its scarcity but its unpredictability. The Nile Valley is essentially an arid location but the annual flood of the

Nile River is predictable, once the local inhabitants had figured out how much water they would get and when agriculture became easy. The problem with desert fringe regions like the Nazca Valley is that the rains may completely fail to come for years. It is almost inevitable that, under such conditions, a people will develop a religion centred around encouraging the rains to be regular. In all probability this is what the markings on the desert are all about.

Seen from the ground the long parallel lines and oblong shapes recede with perspective, and many of them recede directly in line with prominent mountain peaks on the horizon. We will never know exactly how these features were meant to work but they seem to be like a kind of invitation to the rain, a sort of royal road drawing the divine, life-giving force into the heart of the Nazca realm. It is likely that the plain features were created over a long period and probably with a number of different underlying beliefs about the best way to draw the rain from the mountains. Of course the rain came in the form of the Nazca River not as actual downpours, no Nazca would have expected that. And when it did come, the Nazca were more than ready for it.

The irrigation methods used by the Nazca, and many of their original artificial water courses, are still very much in use by the people of the area today. The aqueduct and irrigation technology of the Nazca was astounding. At one spot archaeologists have uncovered vast stone-lined spirals cut into the ground that swirled water into channels and fed it to the cities. Each spiral is sixty feet across and is designed to channel rushing water deeper and deeper into the ground with each loop. Remarkably, similar spirals are also found among the other features out on the plain.

The English explorer Tony Morrison has suggested that the tracks and alleys of the Nazca Plain may have been directly involved in Nazca worship. Researching existing folklore among the peoples of the Andes region he uncovered a widespread network of roadside shrines connected by straight pathways. Many of these shrines are extremely ancient and may consist of no more than a small pile of rocks suggesting that the custom could stretch back into the era of the Nazca. The suggestion is that the longer lines on the plain may have been procession routes along which Nazca priests may have made ritual pilgrimages to enhance or charge the magic of the lines themselves.

The notion of flying Nazcas refuses to lie down and die however. Even if the Nazca had no need of an eye in the sky to create their geoglyphs it's hard to believe that sheer human curiosity wouldn't have driven them to want to see what their creations looked like. According to the International Explorers' Society of Miami they may have done just that in a hot air balloon. The story began when researchers found loose fragments of cloth in a Nazca tomb. The Nazca are famous for the quality of their fabrics – many of which have survived in almost pristine condition to this day – and these samples seemed to be particularly fine. Members of the Explorers' Society had long been fascinated by the Nazca Plain lines and got to thinking that cloth of such high quality could conceivably be used to make the envelope for a hot air balloon.

It turned out that the weave of the cloth was so tight that it even exceeded the standards used by modern balloon-making companies. Fascinated, the Society decided to try and make a replica of what a Nazca balloon could have been like. Using only materials that would have been available to the Nazca they constructed a balloon large enough to carry two men. On 23 November 1973, Condor I carried two brave volunteers to a height of three hundred and eighty feet above the Nazca Plain. The heat was provided by a wood fire on the ground which allowed the envelope to be fully inflated and gave several minutes of flight time.

Of course the successful flight of Condor I does not prove that the Nazca made hot air balloons, it just proves that they could have done if they had thought of it. No direct evidence has been found of ancient balloons although there are features on the plain dubbed "burn pits" which cover an area 30–50 feet in diameter and show evidence of intense fires.

Interestingly, the Nazca Plain is not the only site in the area which has such geoglyphs. Eight hundred and fifty miles to the south is the world's largest known representation of a human figure, the Atacama Giant. Almost 400 feet from head to foot it is etched into the side of Solitary Mountain overlooking the scorching Atacama desert. Thought to date from around the tenth century AD the Atacama Giant is also surrounded by long, straight lines. Like the Nazca Plain features the Atacama Giant has been the subject of much fevered speculation. Surely the most compelling evidence that these vast geoglyphs are religious symbols is the wonder and awe they still provoke today.

The Lost City of a Lost People

The turn of the sixteenth century marked the moment when the indigenous peoples of the South American continent crested the peak of their civilization's achievements. More than a thousand years of civilization was about to come crashing down around their ears, vast empires, sophisticated cities and social systems that had endured for centuries were on the verge of oblivion. The year 1500 saw the empire of the Inca peoples reach its greatest extent – in fact, so total was the devastation that was about to descend on them that we do not even know the true name of these proud empire builders; they are referred to as the Incas only because they called their emperor Inca.

The seed of what was to become their Armageddon had only taken root eight years before, when Christopher Columbus set foot on a tiny Caribbean island and named it San Salvador. As yet the notion that the glory and power of the Incas would be brought to its knees within thirty years was unimagined and unimaginable.

The scale of the tragedy that was about to overtake the continent is almost inconceivable from a European viewpoint. Imagine if an unknown people from the Far East had landed in Europe in the Middle Ages and overthrown every empire in the region within a generation – culture, tradition, history and religion all wiped out and forgotten within a century. This is essentially what happened all across South America. Almost nothing is known today about the history of the continent before the arrival of the Europeans, a whole swathe of human history was virtually wiped out leaving only mysterious ruins and wild myths.

125

Archaeologists and scholars who have studied later Spanish records have been able to put together only a sketchy picture of the development and way of life of the people of the Inca empire. They seem to have first emerged as a distinct group in the Andean mountain region of what is now southern Peru sometime in the twelfth century.

Over the next two to three centuries they gradually subjugated other peoples and created an efficient administration to control their expanding empire. An ancient Inca myth states that the Inca people were born from an island in Lake Titicaca and spread out from there to bring civilization to the world. In fact far older civilizations had risen and fallen in the area long before the Incas emerged; the people of the Nazca valley for example were building vast, irrigated cities in Peru's western desert more than a thousand years earlier.

By the end of their third century of expansion the Incas had created the largest empire that the region had ever seen. It stretched from the Pacific coast inland to the high peaks of the Andes and covered more than two and a half thousand miles of territory from north to south. Incan civilization was strikingly different to the kind of civilization that had developed in Europe. The entire empire operated like a smoothly regulated machine. Every citizen had a clearly defined and limited role to play and the ultimate component was the Inca himself who ruled with an absolute authority only dreamed of by European monarchs.

From his splendid palace at the city of Cuzco the Inca could oversee his empire via a vast network of roadways. Messengers, couriers and officials travelled these roads constantly bringing reports to the centre and taking detailed instructions to the furthest reaches of the realm. Few ordinary people travelled along these roads since special permission was required to leave the place of one's birth. Money was an unknown concept; everybody simply did the job that was expected of them and received the basics of life in return. Failure to work or neglecting a duty were the worst imaginable crimes.

The region was rich in gold deposits, a factor that was to ensure the empire's destruction at the hands of the Spanish, but all gold was automatically the property of the Inca. Gold was said to be the "sweat of the sun" and since the Inca was believed to be an incarnation of the sun god nobody questioned his divine right to it. The gold was taken to Cuzco and other centres where it was formed into stunning adornments and decorations to further the glory of the Inca. A whole wall of the palace was said to be plated in gold and engraved with a representation of the sun and moon gods and a history of the Inca people. Almost all of these treasures were lost – melted down by Spanish adventurers so that the gold was easier to transport.

In 1527 a wave of excitement spread through the empire: some very strange travellers had arrived at the northern port of Tumbes. The fourteen "bearded ones" were of course Spanish explorers under the command of fifty-year-old Francisco Pizarro. The small group caused considerable wonder, no Incan had ever seen a European before and the Inca was kept fully informed of their brief visit. Pizarro for his part acted friendly but had far from friendly motives for the visit.

Only six years before, another Spaniard, Hernando Cortés, had conquered the wealthy Aztec empire in what is now Mexico and Pizarro was looking for an opportunity to do a bit of giant killing of his own. Two things impressed Pizarro. Firstly the stories he heard of the Incas' wealth convinced him the region was rich in gold; secondly he learned that the usually rock-solid regime of Inca rule was in crisis for the first time in living memory.

When the eleventh Inca, Huayna Capac, died at the northern city of Quito a crisis occurred. Huayna had spent much of his life on the battlefield extending the territory of the empire to the north into modern-day Equador. Normally the succession would have been simple – the Inca chose a successor from his sons by his chief wife, who was also traditionally his sister. Unfortunately Huayna wanted to leave part of his empire, the new territories that he had added, to a son he had by another wife in the north. Civil war became inevitable. After several years of bloody fighting Huayna's northern son Atahualpa, who had gained a lot of experience fighting beside his father, overcame the rightful successor and had his entire family butchered. The year was 1532.

Soon after the victory and as the empire was still reeling from this unprecedented upset in the smooth running of their society, Francisco Pizarro returned. In the intervening years he had returned to Spain and obtained permission from the king to attempt a take-over of the Inca empire.

Pizarro landed at Tumbes on 13 May 1532, with 106 foot soldiers and 62 men on horseback. Immediately he proceeded inland, hoping to find the capital Cuzco and buoyed up with news that the empire was in chaos. Atahualpa was informed of their arrival at a mountain spa where he was recovering from a wound he had received in the battle to defeat his half-brother.

He ordered that the "bearded ones" should be watched but there seemed little reason to be concerned and there were far more pressing issues to attend to.

As the Spaniards travelled deeper into the empire they were astounded by what they saw. All across the vast, fertile plains of the empire's eastern region villages had been depopulated by the war and by a strange plague that had ravaged the area. The sheer scale of the Incas' realm began to impress itself on Pizarro's men and many feared that they had taken on an impossible task – what could 169 men hope to do against so vast an empire?

Pizarro, however, remained undaunted. He was on a mission from his king and, therefore, from God. The Spanish themselves were a source of amazement for the locals they met during their journey, especially the mounted soldiers. Horses had never been seen before and people were convinced that the men they saw riding them were some kind of god-like creatures. Despite their fears the Spanish were not challenged and made good progress towards the capital.

In fact the Inca was much closer than Pizarro had imagined. He had taken a number of local people to be trained as interpreters during his first visit five years before and from these he learned that the Inca was at the city of Cajamarca high in the mountains, only about 350 miles south of Tumbes. The Spaniards followed the Inca roads deep into the hills, crossing ravines and chasms on rope bridges and drawing ever closer to the supreme power of the new Inca.

On 15 November 1532, Pizarro and his men arrived in Cajamarca. Pizarro sent an emissary to the Inca inviting him to dine with him. The Inca declined to attend on the first day, but agreed on the second. He walked straight into a carefully arranged trap. As the Inca and his retinue of warriors approached the Spaniards a friar stepped forward and demanded that the Inca declare allegiance to the Catholic Church. Enraged at this slight the emperor tossed the Bible he was offered to the ground and, pointing to the sun, declared "My god still lives." It was all the justification Pizarro needed. At his signal his soldiers opened up with a volley of musket fire and the cavalry descended on the Inca's retinue.

It was all over in half an hour. Battle-hardened and experienced as the Inca's soldiers were, they had never experienced musket fire or mounted soldiers and they were thrown into total disarray. With his proud guard lying at his feet the Inca was taken captive by Pizarro and locked in a storeroom. Already blessed with incredible luck Pizarro made the most fortunate move of his life. By keeping the Inca prisoner he effectively paralyzed the entire empire and prevented any kind of counter-attack. Warriors in the south had yet to even see their new emperor and those in the north who were loyal to Atahualpa were impotent without direct orders from the Inca himself. Officials were totally unused to making decisions for themselves and so did nothing.

Atahualpa was stunned by the audacity of these strange invaders but could do nothing. Noticing the Spaniards' strange hunger for gold he offered to buy his freedom by filling the room he was held in with gold. Initially Pizarro agreed and runners were sent out all across the empire to collect the precious metal. Amazingly the Inca fulfilled his promise – eye-witnesses record that the room the Inca was kept in was

22 feet long by 17 feet wide by 7 feet high. The ease with which the Inca had collected such a vast quantity of gold to pay his ransom simply whetted the Spaniards' appetites. Pizarro decided that the Inca had to die.

In a bizarre travesty of justice a trial was held in Cajamarca in which the Inca was charged with raising a force to resist the rightful rule of the Spanish, blasphemy and incest for marrying his own sister. Unsurprisingly he was found guilty on all counts and executed. The ruler of one of the world's largest and wealthiest empires was strangled to death by two brutal soldiers. Pizarro had the fabulous gold statues and jewellery melted down into ingots and shipped back to Spain.

The Inca empire was essentially finished – Pizarro marched on the capital and Cuzco was systematically looted. Its inhabitants were tortured and butchered. Centuries of total obedience had left the Incas completely unable to deal with the Spanish threat now that the Inca was dead and the Christians met virtually no resistance. By now reinforcements were beginning to flood into the country and Pizarro took control of the empire in the name of the Spanish king.

At Cuzco a puppet Inca was installed, Manco Capac, a young son of Huayna Capac. Now that they had an emperor again the Incas were prepared to fight the invaders, despite the fact that they were fighting for a man who had been installed by those very invaders. The conditioned belief that the Inca was a god was so strong that it simply didn't matter where he had come from. In the spring of 1536 the great uprising began. The Inca's forces laid siege to Cuzco and attacked Spanish columns at will.

The Incan soldiers were highly experienced at

mountain warfare and still held bases deep in the Andes that they could retreat to whenever the Spanish tried to pursue. For months Pizarro was virtually cut off at his new capital city, Lima. Eventually the Incas became too confident and Pizarro lured them into an open battle on the plains near Lima. Out in the open Spanish military superiority came into play and the Incan army was annihilated. By this time Pizarro had acquired allies among peoples whom had been subjugated by the empire.

Despite defeating the Incan army Pizarro was unable to totally break their power. It proved impossible to pursue the retreating army into the mountains and Manco Inca, the puppet who had turned against the Spanish, led his forces to secret fortresses and cities that the Spanish didn't even know existed. Exactly where the Manco Inca established his new court remained a mystery for almost 400 years until the American explorer Hiram Bingham stumbled across the city we know as Machu Picchu.

Bingham found the lost city in 1911 after hearing that some interesting ruins could be found along the steep Urabamba valley north of Cuzco. Traces of a roadway and a number of small sites convinced Bingham that he was on the verge of a major discovery. For a month he toiled up the heavily overgrown valley until, one day, he came across a beautifully preserved set of stone steps leading up the mountain side. At the top he was astonished to discover an impressive fortress-city perched on the very shoulder of the mountain. A quick look at the forms of the buildings and the characteristic masonry confirmed that it was the product of the height of Incan civilization.

The city in the mountains was dubbed Machu

Machu Picchu in Peru.

Picchu after the peak that towers over it, nobody knows what its original name was or how it came to be there. As centuries of undergrowth were cleared away it became clear that the city had been built long before the fall of the empire and that it had been hastily enlarged by Manco Inca after he retreated there from Cuzco. The isolation of the city, its awe-inspiring setting and the grandeur of its buildings all suggest that it was probably a religious centre of some kind before it became Manco Inca's new capital.

Exploration of burial caves near the city revealed that most of the bodies were female which suggests that the city may have been the centre of a group known as the *aclla cuna*, or Virgins of the Sun. Little is known about this mysterious branch of Incan society which seems to have played a central role in the religious life of the empire. The Virgins of the Sun seem to have been recruited from the general population. Young girls who showed particular beauty, grace or skill at weaving were identified by travelling officials and sent for initiation into the order. There may have been as many as 15,000 Virgins of the Sun at any one time living in compounds similar to nunneries all over the empire.

The Virgins were the servants of the supreme sun god and, as such, were also the servants of the Inca. The emperor and other nobles chose their wives from among the Virgins and they were absolutely forbidden to have any contact with other men. According to legend the punishments for such a liaison were harsh in the extreme. The lapsed Virgin would be buried alive, the man strangled to death and his entire household razed to the ground. Such a transgression would have been considered an act of blasphemy against the sun god and a direct infringement of the supreme authority of the Inca.

The women of the order seem to have fulfilled three roles in society. A few were accorded the supreme honour of becoming sacrifices to the sun god, others were married to top officials and the rest spent their time weaving garments for the Inca and his representatives. The Inca was provided with robes of the finest vicuna wool and wore each one only once before it was discarded and burned. Among the older generation of Virgins certain individuals were selected to teach the new initiates. Known as *Mama Cuna* these women controlled their young charges and introduced them to a way of life that must have been stark and unforgiving.

The evidence of the burial caves strongly suggests that Machu Picchu was a centre for the Virgins of the Sun and its grandeur suggests that it may even have been the administrative capital of the order. It is almost impossible to say how long the remnants of the Incan empire hung on at Machu Picchu. The period immediately after the defeat of Manco Inca at Lima was a sad one for the people of the region. Manco was assassinated, possibly by Spanish agents, in 1545 and his successor Titu Cusi remained hidden in his mountain stronghold.

The vast majority of the Inca's former subjects were left to fend for themselves. Systems of communication and irrigation that had fed and organized the empire for hundreds of years collapsed and the people reverted to a primitive stage of development. The Spanish were mainly concerned with looking for gold and an eleven-year-long war broke out among the conquerors over the division of the spoils. Both

Pizarro and his chief rival, Diego de Almagro, wound up dead.

The last certain contact with the Incas came in 1571 when a Spanish expeditionary force hunted down the Inca known as Tupac Amaru. The Inca had ordered the execution of a Spanish emissary and paid for it with his own life. It was clear from the ease with which he was captured that the remnants of the Incan army had lost much of their skill and strength. It's impossible to say how long after the death of Tupac the Incan people survived as a distinct group. Neither the Spanish nor any other Europeans saw Machu Picchu until 300 years later.

The death of this last great city must have been a slow and painful process. Tupac probably ordered the abandonment of the city during his final fight with the Spanish. It isn't known if he had a successor but it's almost certain that the survivors of his band would have returned to the city after their defeat. The Virgins of the Sun probably provided a degree of stability and kept the Incan way of life going for longer than it would have survived otherwise. Gradually however the population would have slipped away into the surrounding countryside to find a sustainable way of life.

We can only speculate but it's appealing to imagine a hard core of true Incas remaining in the city and preserving the ancient rites for decades after the fall of the last Inca. Perhaps the last Mama Cuna, herself the great-granddaughter of one of the young girls that witnessed the arrival of the defeated Manco Inca, still lit the flames and carried out the rituals in the abandoned and forgotten city a century after the arrival of the Spanish. As the sun rose every morning she may have repeated the words of the doomed Inca Atahualpa when he first met Pizarro generations before: "My god still lives".

Rapa Nui

A tiny speck in the vastness of the Pacific Ocean, Rapa Nui, or Easter Island, is one of the remotest inhabited parts of the Earth. The nearest inhabited island is equally tiny Pitcairn Island 1400 miles to the north west. Apart from that the closest population centre is the coast of Chile more than 2000 miles due east. Not only is the island unbelievably isolated, it holds the clues to a great human tragedy and mystery that has fascinated people ever since its re-discovery in 1722 by the Dutch mariner Jacob Roggeveen.

Dotted around the 64 square miles of the island are almost 900 huge and enigmatic statues known as *moai*. Ranging in height from 72 feet to only 4 feet and weighing as much as 160 tons the moai are among the most extraordinary cultural achievements of any civilization, especially considering the size of the place. The appeal of Rapa Nui has always been the haunting appearance of these statues. Their vastly enlarged heads, angular features and blind eyes have a mysterious quality quite unlike anything else on earth. In the barren and silent setting of an island so isolated from the rest of the world they have the ineffable aura of giants who have witnessed great and terrible things.

In 1989 the archaeologist Jo Anne van Tilburg completed the first comprehensive survey of the moai of Rapa Nui – her results were startling. Van Tilburg counted 887 moai on the island. Of these almost 400 were still lying in the quarries that they had been carved from. A further 47 were thought to have been left in various stages of transport from the quarries to their intended sites and only 288 had been taken to their intended sites. In fact, when Roggeveen arrived on the island, none of the moai were standing upright, all had apparently been torn down by the island's inhabitants at some time in the distant past.

The questions raised by these results are numerous and intriguing. Why were so many moai constructed? Why were so many of them left in the quarries and why was the effort to move them into their final positions abandoned so suddenly? In order to answer these questions archaeologists and anthropologists have tried to reconstruct the history of the island. The first and most obvious question to be answered was how people came to be on this remote and tiny rock in the first place.

In the early days it was believed that the original inhabitants had come from the South American mainland. The adventurer Thor Heyerdahl believed that he could see similarities between the architecture of the island and that of ancient Peru. To prove his point he made an incredible voyage in a reed boat named the *Kon-Tiki* to show that it could have been done.

While Heyerdahl certainly showed that such a voyage was possible recent theories suggest that it didn't happen. DNA tests carried out on twelve ancient skeletons from the island in 1994 showed conclusively that they were of Polynesian descent. A study of the Rapa Nui language also reveals links with Polynesian culture. It is clear then that the original inhabitants of the island came from the west, not the east, but how and why would these people have made such a hazardous journey to an island that has little to offer?

Recent studies have shown that between about 400 and 750 AD the Polynesian peoples, originally from the South-east Asian mainland, made a series of incredible migrations eastward across the Pacific. Their journeys took them as far as Hawaii and Tahiti and they also discovered and settled New Zealand. A number of theories have been advanced to explain these migrations but the most widely accepted has to do with overcrowding and cultural pressures.

The Polynesians were a highly successful people. On their journeys they found rich new lands and settled a vast area. Unfortunately many of the lands they settled just weren't big enough to support their expanding population so there was always pressure to find new land. Sometimes this paid off, such as the discovery of New Zealand, but usually they just found yet another small island chain. In Polynesian culture power is passed from the chief to his eldest son, other sons and daughters have no special status. Its possible that the younger sons of chiefs led these expeditions; if they found new lands they would automatically become chiefs in their own right.

Probably towards the end of this period of expansion, around 750 AD, one group of intrepid Polynesians wound up on Rapa Nui and decided to make it their home. Today the island has no tree cover and is mostly made up of grassy slopes; when the Polynesians first arrived it must have been covered in lush forests. Apparently the culture on Rapa Nui thrived. Archaeologists have found evidence of villages and farmland all over the island. They estimate that the population probably peaked at about 10,000.

Unfortunately this turned out to be rather more than the island could support using primitive agricultural methods.

This ecological imbalance probably coincided with a change in climate patterns which made the island's weather much more inhospitable. A rapid and tragic crash of the Rapa Nui civilization apparently followed.

The Rapa Nui had probably been carving moai since they first arrived on the island. The earliest sculptures are modest in size and are thought to represent chiefs who had died. Between about 1400 and 1600, however, the Rapa Nui apparently massively accelerated the rate at which they were producing moai; the sculptures also became much larger in this period. This sudden spurt of essentially religious activity seems to suggest that this is the period when the island hit an ecological brick wall. The weather had changed and the land was exhausted. All the beleaguered inhabitants could do was make bigger and better offerings to the ancestor gods who were supposed to ensure the fertility of the land – hence bigger and better moai.

Almost all the moai that were erected originally faced inland, looking across the fields that they were supposed to protect. Recent research into the scant folklore of the island has also revealed that the moai were not originally blind. In fact they were fitted with huge staring eyes made from white coral. Reconstructions of these eyes placed on re-erected moai completely transform the character of the statues. Instead of gentle giants they become wildly staring and terrifying colossuses that seem to sear the landscape with their gaze.

Eventually the situation worsened to the point

where the civilization collapsed. The moai simply were not working and, by association, the ruling class – seen as living gods – were not doing their job. As the culture wound down there seemed no point in finishing and transporting the moai that were still being carved in the quarries; statues already in transit were simply abandoned where they lay. At some point the ruling class was overthrown and the symbols of their rule were toppled. As a final gesture the staring eyes of the discredited gods were torn out and smashed.

The Rapa Nui civilization probably collapsed pretty rapidly from that point. It must have been a terrifying time. The crops were getting worse each year, there was no wood left to make boats for a mass exodus and the people had probably forgotten where they had come from anyway. They were left completely stranded and alone. The few thousand people of the island surely came to believe that they were the only people in the world, indeed that their island was the world, a speck of land in an infinite sea. The arrival of a Dutch merchant ship 200 years later must have been something of a shock.

When Roggeveen arrived the people were living very simply and had invented a new religion to replace the old. A "birdman" cult emerged which survived until the end of the nineteenth century. Representatives from each of the island's tribes would meet on a clifftop overlooking tiny islands offshore. A race was then held and the first warrior to return with an egg from the nests of the seabirds that colonized the islands would become ruler of Rapa Nui for a year.

As with many cultures the arrival of the Europeans proved to be a seriously unfortunate event. Many islanders were wiped out by disease and those that survived were shipped off as slaves. By 1877 only 111 islanders remained, and a once proud and sophisticated culture had been utterly destroyed. Today there are about 2000 islanders. Many have mixed Latin and Polynesian blood but a good number are thought to be more or less direct descendants of the original Rapa Nui.

One of the most interesting aspects of the archaeological investigation of Rapa Nui has been the study of how the moai were transported and erected. Inevitably there have been the usual crackpot theories about the use of mystical powers or extraterrestrial intervention but, as usual, it has been demonstrated that moving large lumps of rock around is well within the limits of human ingenuity.

According to Rapa Nui folklore moving the moai was very simple: they were just told where to go and they walked there. The Rapa Nui believed that certain ancient chiefs had control over force they called *mana* and that by using this force they could command the moai to move. As folklore goes it's an attractive idea but it should be remembered that the Rapa Nui who told Europeans these stories were separated from the culture that had erected the moai by at least two centuries. Probably this mana is no more than a garbled reference to the right of the ancient chiefs to command that the statues be carved and moved. With such a small population even at its height the right to command a large proportion of the work force to work on a moai must have been no small thing.

One modern theorist has taken the idea rather more literally. Earlier attempts to reconstruct the transport methods of the ancient Rapa Nui had focused on the obvious method of dragging the statues across the ground on sleds or rollers. The disadvantage of these methods is that they require a lot of manpower and wood, both of which would have been in short supply. The Czech engineer Pawel Pawel decided that there might be an element of truth in the walking myth. Noticing that the moai have a very low centre of gravity he suggested that they could have been moved while upright with a kind of rocking motion on the base.

In 1986 Pawel put his theory to the test using two original moai. They proved to be so stable in an upright position that they could tilt 70 degrees without falling. Progress was good until the swivelling motion began to cause damage to the base of the statue and the experiment had to be halted. Pawel concluded that this method may well have been used in the final positioning of the statue, but that the roughness of the terrain made it unlikely that it could have been used to transport the sculptures over long distances.

In 1998 another team led by Jo van Tilburg, the archaeologist who had surveyed all the moai on the island, tried a more direct method. Tying a prone replica statue to a wooden sled the team pulled it along a prepared roadway using logs as rollers under the sled. Seventy volunteers managed to pull the statue along the short roadway and up a slope before the statue was lowered into an upright position. The prosaic approach worked remarkably well.

Today a considerable number of moai have been re-erected and restored and most of the island is a United Nations-protected World Heritage Site. The culture of the Rapa Nui themselves, their language and customs, are almost lost but once again the great, staring images of their remarkable ancestors stare out across the tragic landscape of the island.

Shambhala

In 1900 a British Army major was part of a military expedition into the Himalayan mountains on the north-eastern border of India. It was a zone of critical importance for the British at the time and one of the prime arenas of the "Great Game" described by Kipling and other writers, the hidden struggle for power in the region between the British and the Russians.

By 1900 the British had been in India for more than 200 years and a lot of people had seen some very odd things across that vast and mysterious continent. The major, who wasn't named in the newspaper article which reported his story, was startled one day to see a very tall, lightly-clad man with long hair wandering through the snowy wastes. The major called out to the intruder who turned to observe him with a nonchalant gaze and then, quite deliberately, leapt down a near vertical slope. The major rushed to the spot fully expecting to see his broken body on the crags below, but instead there was no sign of the man and neither were there any footprints to show that he had been there.

When the major returned to his camp and told his native guides about what he had seen, none of them were remotely surprised. They assured him that he had seen one of the "snowmen"; magical guardians of the legendary land of Shambhala. These figures were well known to the locals who occasionally caught sight

The Himalayan mountains.

of them flying across the snows of the remotest regions with steps so light that they left no trace. Able to appear and disappear at will the locals knew that it was folly to try and follow them since they would inevitably lead the unwary into deadly crevasses or bury them in avalanches.

The explorer Alexandra David Neel spent fourteen years in the Tibet region and also reported an encounter with a mysterious "snowman" who she saw moving with incredible speed across the snowfields:

> *I could clearly see his perfectly calm impassive face and wide-open eyes with their gaze fixed on some invisible distant object situated somewhere high up in space. The man did not run. He seemed to lift himself from the ground, proceeding by leaps. It looked as if he had been endowed with the elasticity of a ball, and rebounded each time his feet touched the ground. His steps had the regularity of a pendulum.*

So who were these strange figures and what were they guarding? According to Tibetan Buddhism there is a secret land named Shambhala hidden somewhere in the empty region between the Gobi deserts and the Himalayas. In the West this secret kingdom is better known as Shangri-La.

The Tibetans believe that a race of secret masters who control the fate of the world live in Shambhala and that they have incredible psychic powers. They are the masters of Kalacakra, the most secret and advanced form of Buddhism which teaches the acolyte how to use godlike powers. Unfortunately the Shambhalans rarely allow outsiders into their kingdom and those that do gain access never want to leave.

Some claim that Shambhala is hidden beneath the ground but, in fact, Tibetan scriptures give a detailed picture of a kingdom that is above ground. The land is described as being made up of eight concentric ring valleys separated by walls of mountains. In the centre of the innermost ring is Kalapa, the capital city, and the palace of the king of the Shambhalans.

The capital is surrounded by mountains of shining ice and the king is a great scientist as well as a religious head. The windows of his palace point skywards and act as powerful telescopes that allow his astronomers to study life on distant planets. The Shambhalans are also said to possess magical means of transport that allow them to travel underground and to have a network of tunnels that enables them to emerge anywhere in the world.

Although many have tried to find the secret kingdom, mostly Tibetan lamas or holy men, few have ever returned from the attempt. There is said to be no road to the kingdom and it is protected by a psychic field that makes it invisible. Animals and people who approach its borders are said to become confused and to tremble. If they persist they lapse into unconsciousness and, if they ever awake, find themselves many miles away from the spot where they felt the disturbance. Lamas who attempt the journey must first spend much of their lives in mental and spiritual preparation. Only if they have achieved sufficient purity of mind will the mysterious guards admit them.

Tibetan texts go into great detail about the history of Shambhala and contain a prophecy that the last king of the region will one day reveal himself and his kingdom to the world. The prophecy states that thirty-two kings will reign in Shambhala and that each one will rule for exactly a hundred years. During this period the world beyond the borders of the kingdom will slowly deteriorate until the whole world is ruled by materialism and greed and the teachings of Buddhism are forgotten. Only then will Shambhala be revealed. A mighty army will be raised to plunder its riches but the last king, Rudra Cakrin, will defeat the invaders and bring a new, enlightened peace to the world.

In the 1880s the Theosophical Society, founded in New York by Russian mystic Helena Blavatsky, incorporated the myth of Shambhala into its strange and diverse world-view. Blavatsky claimed that the kings of Shambhala are already actively engaged in the world and that they essentially guide the fate of humanity from their hidden temples beneath the earth. The Theosophists attracted many converts in their time, even after Blavatsky herself was exposed as a fraud who had used conjuring tricks during her séances.

Even today the legend of Shambhala or Shangri-La encapsulates a sense of wonder about the strange physical and spiritual borderlands of Tibet. For Westerners the very real kingdom of Tibet was itself a mysterious and forbidden country for centuries. It wasn't until 1904 that Europeans first reached the Tibetan capital Lhasa. They found a land almost cut off from the rest of the world and home to strange and wonderful beliefs.

It was the novelist and Hollywood scriptwriter James Hilton who created the enduring image of Shangri-La in Western culture. His novel *Lost Horizons*, published in 1933, tells the tale of four Westerners who are kidnapped and taken to the hidden kingdom. In a secret valley deep in the mountains they find a rural paradise watched over by a group of holy men who have lived for centuries. Their leader, the head lama, is more than two hundred years old and first came to the valley as a Christian monk in 1719. He found it such a wonderful place that he adopted Buddhism and decided to stay on.

Hilton's novel was a fantastically successful piece of fantasy in a time when the world was gloomily expecting a second world war that many felt could spell the end of civilization. Like the Tibetan vision of Shambhala, Shangri-La became the promise of civilization renewed from the shattered ruins of a greedy and warlike culture. As long as humanity has wishes and hopes for the future and as long as those hopes are dashed by foolishness and short-sightedness Shambhala will always be out there, just beyond our grasp.

Atlantis

The legend of Atlantis is surely the greatest and most complex mystery of the modern era. In many ways it is a no more than a formless and insubstantial concept that has been incorporated into virtually every mystical and occult theory of recent times. Unlike the mysteries of lost and abandoned cities such as Machu Picchu there is no undeniable physical evidence that such a place ever existed; practically all the "evidence" that has been advanced has been cultural or derived by occult means such as spirit communication. The very formlessness of the myth is what has made it so attractive to our culture. Atlantis is a rare and powerful

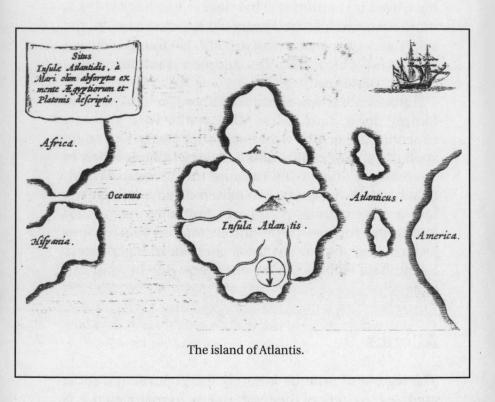

The island of Atlantis.

myth of faith; for some reason the notion that a powerful civilization existed before recorded history is extremely attractive to modern sensibilities.

It's undeniable that Atlantis is a modern myth. Although the seed of the idea is contained in texts written by the ancient Greek philosopher Plato, the torrent of books speculating about the reality of such a place did not begin until the late nineteenth century. Any attempt to trace the details of such a formless concept is doomed to failure, it has been connected to so many phenomena from UFOs to spiritualism, and has been interpreted in so many blatantly contradictory ways that there can be no single account of what the myth of Atlantis actually is. At its most basic the Atlantis story is the story of a powerful civilization that was destroyed at some point in history before the rise of classical Greece in the fifth century BC.

The mysterious quality of this tale can be traced to elements of the original Atlantis story – that told by Plato in his dialogues *Timaeus* and *Critias*. Plato expressed his philosophical ideas in the form of dialogues or conversations between a number of characters. In *Timaeus* one of Plato's characters, Critias the historian, recounts a tale that was told to the semi-mythical Athenian law-giver Solon.

Like many Greek leaders before and after him Solon was said to have travelled to Egypt where he heard about a war that had taken place thousands of years before his time. The protagonists of this war were the Atlantians and the early founders of the city of Athens. According to the Egyptian story Atlantis was already a mighty and powerful civilization when Athens was first founded. The Atlantians were warlike and had conquered most of Europe and North Africa. Athens alone remained unconquered and it was the Athenians who eventually defeated the Atlantians.

In the later dialogue, *Critias*, Plato provides more details of the story. The continent of Atlantis is said to have lain beyond the Pillars of Hercules and to have been larger than North Africa and Europe put together. The Pillars of Hercules are thought by modern scholars to refer to the Straits of Gibraltar, which would place Atlantis in the Atlantic Ocean.

The Atlantians were incredible engineers who had remodelled the very geography of their land. They lived on a mighty mountain surrounded by alternate circular bands of land and water. These bands of water were connected by huge tunnels, large enough for a ship to sail through, and the outer band was connected to the sea via a canal 300 feet wide and 100 feet deep. Behind the central mountain on which the Atlantians had built their splendid capital was a vast fertile plain 230 by 340 miles across. This plain provided the Atlantians with all their food and was defended by a mighty ditch that enclosed the entire area.

For centuries the Atlantians lived good and rich lives, they built incredible temples, harbours and palaces and literally lined their streets with gold and precious gems. Eventually, however, they lost their wisdom and became corrupt and greedy. It was in this period that they became conquerors and made the mistake of tangling with the tiny city state of Athens. The gods became angry at their arrogance and decided to teach them a lesson. At this point the account breaks off. Plato never completed *Critias* or the third dialogue in the series so the tale was never finished. For more than 2000 years Plato's account was regarded as little more than an historical curiosity and was interpreted as a political allegory.

This fantastic but rather basic story contains within it the essential elements that make the myth so appealing to the modern mind. Firstly the accomplishments of the Atlantians seem superhuman; the building of tunnels large enough to convey ships is far beyond anything achieved by ancient engineers. The scale is also incredible; the ditch that was said to surround the fertile plain would have been more than 1000 miles long; and a sea canal 300 feet wide and 100 feet deep dwarfs modern engineering achievements like the Suez and Panama canals.

Such tall tales are common in ancient literature and archaeology has dispelled many of them but, of course, there is no archaeology of Atlantis which leaves open the possibility that they could be true. Super-human achievements suggest superhuman powers and this is the root of one of our fascinations with the Atlantis myth. It has led to the suggestion that the Atlantians were a superior form of humans, or even that they were not human at all.

The second compelling element of Plato's tale is the apocalyptic fate of the Atlantians. Plato hints that it was their very grandness that led to their downfall because it offended the gods. This is a classic story-telling device; fate inevitably decrees that the mighty should fall. If you go as far as to believe that the Atlantians had supernatural powers it's an easy step to conclude that these powers got out of hand and led to the destruction of their civilization.

This is an idea that has strong resonances today; as much as we desire scientific progress there is always the fear at the back of our collective mind that these are powers that we shouldn't be toying with and that they could all too easily lead to our own destruction. This particular strand of the Atlantis myth has surfaced many times in suggestions that the Atlantians were technologically advanced extraterrestrials or that they were alchemists and magicians who meddled with dark powers.

In 1882 an American congressman, Ignatius Donnelly, opened the floodgates of the Atlantis myth when he published *Atlantis, the Antediluvian World.* Donnelly had become convinced that Plato was describing a real place when he wrote about Atlantis, a real civilization that had risen and fallen thousands of years before the classical period and which had been remembered in the myths and folk tales of the Egyptians and other ancient peoples.

Drawing on his own substantial scholarship and borrowing liberally from the ever-growing flood of new discoveries about the world that marked his time Donnelly constructed an elaborate argument for the existence of Atlantis. The basis of his theory was that a large continent had existed in the Atlantic, that it had been home to an advanced civilization and that it had eventually been destroyed by a natural cataclysm such as an earthquake or an explosive volcanic eruption. Donnelly was the first to provide evidence for his theory. If such a vast landmass had existed he reasoned it couldn't have disappeared without leaving any trace.

Donnelly believed that civilizations on both sides of the Atlantic show the imprint of contact with the same ancient people who must have been the Atlantians. He noted the similarity of flood legends in places as far apart as Egypt and Mexico, found similarities in the design of artefacts on both sides of the Atlantic and in writing systems. As physical evidence he pointed to the mid-Atlantic ridge, an underwater chain of mountains of then mysterious origin, and suggested that the Azores were the peaks of mountains on a large, submerged island.

Unfortunately, for all his scholarly efforts, much of Donnelly's evidence turned out to be false. The mid-Atlantic ridge is understood today as a fault where two of the Earth's tectonic plates separate and the geology of the Azores does not support Donnelly's conjectures. Despite its shortcomings Donnelly's book became the basis for a major strand in Atlantian folklore: the notion that an ancient advanced civilization was destroyed by a natural catastrophe and has left its marks in the mythology and technology of other ancient cultures. Later versions of this story have claimed that surviving Atlantians were the founders of every major civilization from China, to Peru, to Egypt or that they were the builders of Stonehenge, the Pyramids or the lost Mayan cities in the jungle.

The second strand of Atlantian myth, the supernatural and spiritual side, stems largely from the work of the Russian spiritualist Helena Blavatsky. As the leading light of the Theosophical Society, Blavatsky had achieved international renown with her strange blend of Eastern and Western occult traditions.

The Theosophical Society, founded in New York in 1875, can be seen as a reaction to the triumph of science and industrialization at the end of the nineteenth century. After the general acceptance of Darwin's theory of evolution by natural selection many educated people could no longer bring themselves to believe in the traditional Christian view of the world but still longed for some spiritual message to take its place. The domination of industry and the machine also created a thirst for a legendary past of magic and mystery. In *The Secret Doctrine*, completed just before her death, Blavatsky incorporated the Atlantis myth into her already complex world-view.

One of the doctrines of the Theosophical Society is the idea that all events are recorded in a permanent but ethereal medium known as the Akashic record. Those who knew how could witness any event in history first hand by accessing this medium and Blavatsky claimed that her writings were based on this first-hand record. According to the Akashic record modern people are the fifth race of humans to have lived on the Earth. The first race were beings of fire and mist, the second lived in Asia, the third were giants who lived on the vanished continent of Mu in the Indian Ocean and the fourth were the Atlantians. Although similar to us the Atlantians were all natural mediums and possessed occult powers undreamed of today. Their civilization died when war broke out between powerful magicians.

Not all Atlantians were destroyed when their continent sank – according to Blavatsky, the survivors migrated to Europe, Africa and South America where they built Stonehenge and the Pyramids of Egypt and Mexico. All this happened more than 100,000 years ago, making the Pyramids at least 25 times older than conventional archaeology would have us believe. After Blavatsky's death a number of warring factions within the Theosophical Society took over her ideas and elaborated on them. Rudolph Steiner developed a theory, based of course on the Akashic record, that saw the survivors of Atlantis as the Aryan master race. It was disturbing development that has lingered on to this day.

Elements of early twentieth-century scientific speculation were frequently appropriated by people wishing to make political points and the proponents of the Aryan master race were no exception. They believed that a single people had introduced civilization to the world during a long period of wandering in prehistoric times. When the idea of Atlantis became popular it was quickly incorporated into these racist theories. The Aryans became Atlantian survivors who were vastly superior in intellect and achievement to the rest of the peoples of the world. Much of this dangerous rubbish was later enshrined in the weird undercurrents of thought that underpinned the Nazi world-view. Numerous high-ranking Nazis were said to believe in the Atlantis–Aryan link among other bizarre theories.

Like the mystery of the Pyramids, which isn't really a mystery at all, the story of Atlantis has fascinated occult theorists and fiction writers. Those two elements implicit in Plato's tale – the superhuman achievements of the Atlantians and their cataclysmic end – have become the hooks on which a thousand theories have been hung. Despite the sea of dross and vague speculation that surrounds the Atlantis myth serious scholars continue to worry at the question of whether there could be a seed of truth in the tale. After all, many other supposedly mythical places have turned out to have been based on truth, the classic example being the city of Troy which everybody took to be a myth until a German archaeologist went and dug it up.

Perhaps the most convincing theory about the origin of the Atlantis myth was advanced by Greek archaeologist Professor Angelos Galanopoulos in the late 1960s. Around 2000 BC there was an advanced civilization in the Mediterranean, the Minoan culture, centred on the island of Crete. The Minoans built palaces and sophisticated cities and are known to have been the major sea power of the era. Minoan settlers are thought to have been the ancestors of the Greeks of the classical era. Archaeological evidence suggests that Minoan culture came to a rather abrupt halt around 1500 BC. Galanopoulos believes that the Minoans were originally Atlantians and that they were in fact destroyed by a natural catastrophe.

In about 1500 BC an explosive volcanic eruption devastated the eastern Mediterranean. Centred on the island of Santorini the explosion would certainly have killed tens of thousands of people and could easily have been the final blow that put an end to an already declining empire like the Minoans'. Galanopoulos speculates that the Egyptians may well have had a record of this event and of the destruction of an empire that must have been a great rival to their own in the area. Galanopoulos also makes the pleasingly simple suggestion that the account of the story that we have today, via Plato, may owe its apparently massive exaggeration to a simple copying error made by some Greek scribe translating from the Egyptian.

If the figures given in Plato's account are reduced by a factor of ten they begin to look a bit more realistic – it's entirely conceivable that the Egyptian symbol for a hundred was simply misread as the symbol for a thousand. A defensive ditch surrounding a plain 23 by 34 miles sounds feasible, as does a canal 30 feet wide by 10 deep. Other aspects of the story also fit Galanopoulos' model.

The Minoans were clearly the most advanced people of their age in that region and their achievements must have looked spectacular to their neighbours. They also grew extremely wealthy through trade, and great wealth is always exaggerated by time to sound like cities of solid gold and streets paved with gems. Finally it's likely that the Minoans were at war with the mainland inhabitants of Greece at least some of the time. These peoples, the ancestors of the Athenians, probably took full advantage of the cataclysm that devastated Crete to seize parts of the Minoan empire.

We are left with a story that fits strictly within the accepted time frame of Mediterranean civilization, explains a possible source of exaggeration and fits with most of the details of Plato's story. It seems reasonable to conclude that Crete was Atlantis and the Minoans were the Atlantians. They were not supermen, just more advanced than their neighbours, and they were not destroyed by the gods or by spacemen, just by a devastating but verifiable natural phenomenon.

In effect all this theory really does is explain the origin of Plato's story – it has little to do with the modern myth of Atlantis and has done nothing to stem the tide of speculation about it. Atlantis is a country of the mind, constructed from the most basic fears and needs of the modern mind and no amount of solid archaeological fact will make it go away, and nor should it.

The Great Pyramid

Just outside modern Cairo stands surely the most impressive ancient site in the world, the pyramids of Giza. Three massive structures placed side by side in descending order of size make up the most instantly recognizable landscape on Earth. The largest of the structures, known as the Great Pyramid or the Cheops Pyramid, has been a source of wonder and speculation for thousands of years.

The Great Pyramid is an undeniably incredible structure. Built around four and a half thousand years ago it was, until the turn of the twentieth century, by far the largest single structure on the planet. Its base covers thirteen acres (52,900 sq m) and its summit towers 450 feet (140 m) above the desert floor. More than two million blocks of stone were used in its construction, each one weighing between two and fifteen tons – that's more stone than was used to build every single church and cathedral in Britain.

Analogies used to try and convey the sheer scale of the building are numerous. Napoleon calculated that he could build a wall ten feet high and three feet thick around the whole of France with the material used in its construction. In terms of volume it is thirty times larger than the Empire State Building in New York. It is undoubtedly one of the greatest architectural achievements in human history. Apart from the scale of the monument there is the incredible accuracy of its design and construction. Surveys of the site have revealed that the length of the sides of the base differ by less than twenty centimetres, a deviation of just 0.0009 per cent!

The pyramid we see today is a highly degraded

version of the original. Today the sides of the Great Pyramid are made up of tiny steps and the stones are rough and chipped. This surface is in fact the inner shell of the structure. Originally all four sides were encased in polished, white limestone and were perfectly smooth; legend also says that the top was capped with gold. It must have been an incredible sight, the whole structure would have blazed with light under the fierce Egyptian sun. The name "Pyramid" is actually of Greek construction and brings together the words for fire or light "pyra" with the word for measurement "midos" to mean something like "measured light".

The earliest European reference to the Great Pyramid is found in the writings of the ancient Greek historian Herodotus who visited Egypt on his travels around the Mediterranean. Herodotus lived sometime in the sixth century BC so he must have seen the Great Pyramid in its full glory. The structure certainly impressed him mightily and he asked numerous questions about its construction. Priests told him that it had taken a hundred thousand men, working in three shifts, twenty years to build. Herodotus attributed its awesome dimensions to the work of the legendary Golden Age when everything on Earth was bigger, better and stronger, including the people.

For much of the Christian era, Egypt was inaccessible to Europeans since it was occupied by a hostile Islamic empire. It wasn't until 1798, when the future French Emperor Napoleon led an expeditionary force to the region, that the Great Pyramid entered the popular imagination of Western culture. Napoleon's campaign, which was aimed at threatening Britain's links with India, ended in disaster but he had taken a core of scientists and engineers with him who conducted the first comprehensive studies of the site. Their findings led to a rush of interest in the archaeology of the region that culminated in the great digs of the nineteenth and early twentieth centuries, not to mention the systematic looting of artefacts and monuments by European governments.

When Napoleon arrived in Egypt the Great Pyramid had already been stripped of its limestone casing and emptied of whatever treasures it had once held. According to legend the Great Pyramid was first breached by a caliph of Baghdad, Al Mamun, in about 800 AD. He was lured by reports of great wealth and secret knowledge sealed inside and spent a great deal of effort in forcing a way inside. All he had to go on was a legend that said that an entrance could be found on the north side of the building. Using fire and water to crack the outer casing Al Mamun eventually found his entrance and began exploring.

The interior of the Great Pyramid is every bit as awe-inspiring as its exterior. Al Mamun's entrance leads on to a downward sloping passageway that eventually leads to a chamber carved into the solid rock beneath the Pyramid. At a point just before the downward passage hits the bedrock a second, upward sloping passage leads off from its roof. This was originally concealed by a massive granite block suggesting that the down passage was a blind alley designed to mislead intruders.

Fortunately for Al Mamun this block had been dislodged and he was able to proceed up into the heart of the structure. The up passage leads to a high gallery which ascends to a large roofed chamber known as the king's chamber. This chamber and another, called the queen's chamber which is reached through a separate passage at the bottom of the gallery, were both concealed behind massive blocks. When Al Mamun eventually reached the king's chamber he found only an empty stone coffin; either somebody had got there before him or the chamber had never been used. The absence of any apparent purpose for such a vast monument has fuelled much of the mystery that has grown up around the Great Pyramid.

Perhaps because the original investigators of the Great Pyramid were surveyors, a great deal of speculation about the structure has involved studying its precise measurement. This numbers game has produced some fascinating observations and led to the formulation of some wild theories.

The most consistent claim is that the geometry of the Great Pyramid demonstrates and embodies a knowledge of the value of pi. The sum of the length of the Pyramid's base sides equal the circumference of a circle that could be drawn using the height of the Pyramid as a radius. The suggestion is that the Egyptians must have known the formula for calculating the circumference of a circle ($2\pi r$) in order to have incorporated this relationship into the design. Of course this takes for granted that the relationship between the length of the sides and the height is not pure coincidence. Theorists argue that the dimensions are too precise for the designers not to have known about this relationship, so it remains a possibility.

Another startling feature of the Great Pyramid is its compass alignment. It was noted early on that the four sides face exactly north, south, east and west. Modern surveying methods have confirmed that this alignment is incredibly accurate, the deviation is comparable to the best that could be achieved by modern methods – only 0.058 degrees. Even more incredible, the north orientation is towards true north not magnetic north which implies that it wasn't achieved by using a compass but is based on a startlingly comprehensive knowledge of the planet's form.

Both of these claims are hard to dispute. The truth of the measurements and relationships cannot be denied although it's unclear to what extent they represent happy accident and to what extent genuine knowledge on the part of the Pyramid builders. Once you start playing the numbers game the possibilities are endless.

Evidence that the Pyramid builders knew not only that the Earth was a sphere but also exactly how large it was has also been derived from measurements of the Great Pyramid. The sum of the lengths of the four sides of the Pyramid yields a figure that is exactly equal to half a minute of arc at the equator, within thirteen millimetres. If these figures are not coincidental they imply that the Egyptians knew the true radius of the Earth to within 280 metres!

In the 1940s aerial surveys of the Great Pyramid revealed that each of its four sides are very slightly concave. The arc of this bow is said to exactly match the arc of the surface of the Earth. Another compelling observation is that the height of the Pyramid is the same as the average height above sea level of all the land on Earth.

One theory of the origin of the Great Pyramid states that it was built under the direction of a Jewish prophet and that it embodies all kinds of prophecies about the coming of Christianity. As usual the theory relies heavily on numbers and measurements. It is based on a quote from the Biblical book of Isaiah:

At that time there will be an altar for the Lord in the middle of Egypt and a monument to the Lord at the border of Egypt.

Proponents point out that Giza lies at the centre of the ancient kingdom of Egypt and at the border that separated the old Upper Kingdom from the Lower Kingdom. The key to this theory is a measurement known as the Jewish Inch, which is slightly longer than the Imperial Inch. If the date for the completion of the Great Pyramid is taken as 2623 BC, an apparently arbitrary date, then every inch of the descending passage becomes a year of time. Features of the passage are taken as marking momentous events in what was the distant future to the descendants of the builders of the Pyramid. The point at which the ascending passage branches off is said to represent the exodus of the Jewish people from Egypt more than a thousand years after the structure was completed.

Slightly more convincing aspects of this "prophecy" theory include the observation that if the angle of the descending and the ascending passages are applied to a map from the centre of the Great Pyramid the line passes directly through Bethlehem, the reputed birthplace of Jesus. The theory also makes much of the fact that the descending passage was aligned so that, when it was built, the then Pole Star shone directly down its length. The procession of the stars across the night sky means that this is no longer the case. The next time that a star will shine directly down the passageway is said to be 2004 when the current star we refer to as the Pole Star moves into position. This date is taken as the moment of Christ's second coming.

There are far too many arbitrary dates and assumptions in the prophecy theory to make it anything more than of passing interest. Another theory that plays on the builders' apparent knowledge of the shape and size of the earth is the extraterrestrial theory. This theory also attempts to explain how the Pyramid could have been put together so accurately and how the huge blocks used in its construction could have been carved and moved. Speculations along these lines suggest that the design of the Pyramid was the work of non-human visitors who had precise knowledge of the planet, and that their technology may have been used to transport and place the stones.

Many Egyptologists feel that such theories are not only baseless but are vastly insulting to the ingenuity and imagination of our ancestors. It turns out that the Great Pyramid could have been built using nothing more than simple tools, human muscle power and the skills of highly accomplished stone masons. Archaeologists who have worked on the site and attempted to reconstruct some of the methods used by the pyramid builders are convinced that the structures are entirely within human capabilities.

The most thorough reconstruction experiment was carried out under the leadership of American archaeologist Mark Lehner. Over a three-week period they quarried stones, experimented with transporting them and built a small pyramid at Giza. The findings surprised even Lehner who had always been convinced that the pyramids were the result of strictly human labour. In 21 days his team of twelve masons quarried 186 blocks using only hand tools. Lehner estimates that for the Great Pyramid to have been completed within twenty years the builders would have needed 340 stones a day. Lehner's team were using steel tools, which the ancient Egyptians wouldn't have had, but even if the number of man-hours is triple to compensate for this, the job could have been done with about twelve hundred men, a surprisingly small figure.

Of course the actual stonecutters were just a part of the overall operation – a great deal of the labour must have gone into transporting and placing the stones. It is known that the bulk of the stone used in the Great Pyramid came from quarries very near to the site, so there was not a great distance to be covered. Using prepared roadways and oiled sleds each of the two-ton blocks could have been moved with as few as twenty men. To deliver the necessary 340 stones in a ten-hour working day the site would have needed about 2000 stone haulers. Adding the labour needed to place the stones brings the total up to a figure of about 5000, rather less than Herodotus' 100,000.

This figure of five thousand represents the raw labour that the task would have required. There must have been many more who were specialists. The cutting and placing of the stones that make up the interior bulk of the Great Pyramid is vastly inferior to the casing stones that once covered the outside. These precisely worked stones must have been produced and placed by an expert elite of the work force. Equally the construction of the inner chambers must have been the work of highly skilled and experienced engineers.

Five thousand men working ten-hour days over a twenty-year period represents an awful lot of hours of

Pyramids of Mykerinos, Khefren and Cheops at Giza, near Cairo.

labour. How could a kingdom, even one as wealthy as ancient Egypt, have afforded to lose so much labour from the general economy? In the traditional Hollywood version of the building of the pyramids the labour is usually provided by slaves but there is no evidence that Egypt ever had a slave culture. It is far more likely that the bulk of the labour that went into building the Great Pyramid was given willingly by the general population. Lehner suggests that it probably worked on a rota basis.

Lehner's suggestion is that a full-time crew, including the experienced engineers and the best stone cutters, probably lived on site all year round and spent much of their lives on the project. The main labour force probably arrived during the Nile flood season when there was little to be done in the fields. Lehner and his Egyptian colleague Zahi Hawass have excavated the bakeries that fed this army of workers and the cemetery where they were buried. Both suggest that the workers were well-cared-for average citizens of the kingdom. The bakeries are substantial enough to have provided ample rations for that many men and the skeletons in the cemetery show signs that primitive bone-setting methods were used to help heal the inevitable injuries.

The most compelling evidence turned up by Lehner and Hawass relates to the way that the work crews were organized. Graffiti found on hidden parts of the Great Pyramid and at other sites around Giza suggest that workers were organized into tight-knit groups with their own nicknames. Some groups were represented by names like "endurance" or "strong" perhaps denoting their specialities. Others have names like "friends of Khufu gang" or the "drunkards of

Menkuara" which give a rare insight into the human aspect of these enigmatic monuments and the people who made them. In some places it's clear that these work gangs competed to complete their part of the monument first.

A picture emerges of a very believable voluntary work force. Over the course of a construction project like the Great Pyramid a large part of the work force of the kingdom was probably involved in rotating shifts of a few months or perhaps only weeks. Time was given freely for the glory of the god-king, the pharaoh, and the kingdom. Other great construction projects throughout history have been carried out in the same way; the cathedrals of Europe were built largely with a voluntary work force directed by a full-time elite of stone masons and architects.

As attractive as the theories of supernatural intervention and lost knowledge are, they pale into insignificance beside the true story of the construction of the pyramids. A culture that was able to organize such massive projects as the building of the Great Pyramid must have been one of the greatest in the world's history, and the Great Pyramid is only a tiny part of what they achieved. There are more than sixty full-scale pyramids in Egypt built over a period of several thousand years. Then there are the temples and tombs of Luxor and the Valley of the Kings. Together they represent an unprecedented triumph over time and the elements, accomplished by people just like us.

Standing Stones

The countryside of northern Europe has some of the most enigmatic and atmospheric ancient sites in the world. The splendour of the Pyramids or the abandoned cities of the Incas inspire wonderment and awe but nothing compares to the sense of mystery that surrounds a circle of standing stones on a windswept moor.

Long after their original purpose was forgotten stone circles and monuments were regarded as sacred and magical places by the people who lived near them. In Britain they are called witch's or Devil's stones and are variously associated with good look, bad luck or fertility. Local legends speak of ancient magicians who placed the stones, or even of stones that move at night or that cannot be counted.

Certainly the most famous standing stone monument of them all is Stonehenge on Salisbury Plain. It is one of the most complex and intriguing mystery sites in the world and clearly represents the highest achievement of a civilization that is now forgotten. The name Stonehenge means "hanging stones" and refers to the fact that its most striking feature are the huge stones that make up the horseshoe of pillars and lintels, also known as trilithons. This is a unique feature in European stone circles and actually became a feature of the site fairly late in its long active life.

Stonehenge is one of the most extensively studied sites in the world and archaeologists have managed to piece together a fairly detailed history of the construction of the site. Carbon dating of burials at the site suggest that it had significance to the local people from as early as 8000 BC. In about 5000 BC the very first discernible built features on the site appeared. They consisted of a circular ditch and six-foot-high embankment about 380 feet in diameter. This space was accessed through a gap in the ditch marked with two stones. Around the enclosure there were fifty-six pits which probably held massive wooden pillars. Inside the enclosure were four small mounds topped by stones that formed a rectangle. About fifty feet beyond the entrance a massive stone, known today as the Heel Stone, was erected.

About a thousand years later a banked avenue leading up to the enclosure was constructed and two rings of massive bluestones were erected. Eighty of these stones, each weighing up to four tons, were brought to the site from the Preseli Mountains in south Wales over a hundred miles away. An even larger bluestone, known as the Altar Stone, was set in the centre of the rings.

Before about 2000 BC the most striking feature of the site, the Sarcen pillars and lintels, or trilithons, had been erected. Sixty vast Sarcen blocks were transported twenty miles over the plain from quarries in the Marlborough Downs to the north. The thirty uprights and thirty lintels were shaped and smoothed with stone hammers and then slotted together with cup-and-ball joints. An even more massive horseshoe of trilithons was erected within the circle and an oval of bluestones was also added.

By this time the site had been in continuous use for as much as six thousand years and there is evidence that it remained in use for another thousand years after it was completed. The sheer timescale is staggering; Europe's oldest churches are barely one thousand years old and many of them have already fallen into disuse. The Stonehenge site was important to people for a period at least three times as long as the entire Christian era.

No one can say for certain when Stonehenge ceased to be an active site. It probably fell into disuse sometime during the two thousand years prior to the Roman occupation at around about the beginning of the Christian era. By the time the Romans arrived, many of the stones had probably already been dragged away and put to other uses, a process that was to continue right up until the last few centuries of the second millennium AD. Some of the stones at Stonehenge have now been standing for more than 7000 years and today the site continues to attract pilgrims of a different kind from all over the world.

To anyone who visits Stonehenge it is clear that it was of enormous importance to someone. The question is who and why? Speculation about these questions really took off in the eighteenth century. Before then the site was little known to anyone but local people and they ascribed it to the work of ancient gods or heathen devils. In 1740 a clergyman named Dr William Stukeley published his theory that Stonehenge was essentially a solar observatory and this has remained a favourite idea ever since. Stukeley had made the key observation that the axis of the structure was aligned precisely with the point at which the sun rises on 21 June, the summer solstice.

Stukeley's observation has been confirmed many times and extended by other scholars to show that a large number of the features at Stonehenge align with other significant moments in the solar, lunar and astronomical cycles. In the 1930s Scottish engineer Alexander Thom decided to see if the same concept could be applied to other stone circles. Over the course of 40 years he surveyed more than 600 sites and found that almost all of them aligned with some significant astronomical moment or other. It seems clear that there is some essential link between structures like Stonehenge and astronomical cycles, but why would this have been so important to ancient peoples?

The answer to that question has a lot to do with a key moment in the development of civilization in Europe – the ending of the last ice age. The only known cultural expressions in Europe to pre-date the stone circles are the cave paintings found in southern France and a few other scattered sites. These are thought to have been created about 30–35,000 years ago. The climate of Europe was very different at that time from what it is today. Much of northern Europe was under ice sheets and even the Mediterranean regions were barely warm enough to support human life. At this time humans were hunter-gatherers.

Like their earliest simian ancestors these early people took everything they needed from nature. Life was nomadic and harsh. There was little point in building permanent shelters under such conditions and many bands of humans lived in caves or other natural shelters. After many thousands of years, and for reasons that we still don't understand, the ice began to retreat. At first people simply exploited the newly accessible landscapes in the same ways they always had but gradually a new way of living was developed – agriculture.

As the climate stabilized people in the southern regions began to learn how to get far more from the land by sowing and tending plants with food value. No

Cave painting at Lascaux in France.

one can say where or when this practice began, probably it evolved independently in several places. Within a few thousand years it had largely displaced the hunter-gatherer lifestyle all across Europe apart from the extreme north.

It is impossible to overstate the importance of agriculture in the history of civilization – it is the single most important step that humans have taken since coming down from the trees. Agriculture required people to stay in one place from one year to the next which meant that they had to develop ways of building artificial shelters. It also meant that not everybody had to be engaged in the vital business of getting food all the time. In this free time people developed technology to help them reap more food and also invented everything else from weaving to cities. Archaeologists believe that northern Europeans probably reached this stage between eight and ten thousand years ago. Interestingly this corresponds closely with the earliest signs of activity at the site that was to become Stonehenge.

The truth is that agriculture hadn't only changed the way people lived, it had radically altered their view of the universe. Judging from their cave paintings the religion of the hunter-gatherers was centred around animal spirits and "luck" magic. This is exactly what you would expect from a people whose survival depended on successful hunts and finding wild fruits and berries. The heavens were important to them only in so far as they were the source of harsh or good weather which made life a little easier or harder. For agrarian cultures the sky suddenly took on a new meaning. People must have realized very early on that rain and sunshine in the correct amounts were vital for crops to grow properly and no doubt the very earliest agrarian religions had a lot to do with making sure this happened.

Later it would have also become clear that the annual round of the seasons could be read in the cycles of the sun, moon and stars. In northern Europe, unlike equatorial regions, the seasonal differences are marked. Almost everything dies or stops growing in winter. It became extremely important to agrarian cultures living under these conditions that they could be sure that spring would come again and that they could tell when was a good time to plant crops; the weather in this region isn't predictable enough to be able to tell that spring is coming just because it's getting warmer.

This is the key to understanding the importance of sites such as Stonehenge. Understanding the seasons is vital for success in agriculture and to do that people need some kind of calendar. The builders of Stonehenge must have observed the way that the point at which the sun rose processed across the horizon in one direction for half of the year and then back again in the second half of the year. The turning points of this procession are known as the winter and summer solstices and have long played an important part in pagan religions.

Of course Stonehenge and other stone circles were not just observatories. You do not need several hundred tons of carefully worked stone just to tell when the solstice has arrived – two aligned sticks in the ground could do the same job. The procession of the seasons was so important to early agrarian cultures that it became the core of their religious beliefs. The alignment of Stonehenge doesn't so much

indicate when the summer solstice is reached, it celebrates the fact. It can be seen as a model of the
universe that fits into the cycles of sun, moon and
stars like a cog in a vast machine, lining up perfectly
with the important moments that it enshrines.

A less widely accepted idea as to what lies behind
monuments like Stonehenge is the concept of ley
lines. This theory was first popularized by Alfred
Watkins in his 1925 book *The Old Straight Track*.
Watkins noted that many ancient sites could be
connected by long, straight lines that seemed to
stretch for many miles across the landscape. These
sites include not just ancient monuments like stone
circles but the locations of more modern churches and
important buildings which Watkins speculated had
probably been built on top of the ruins of far more
ancient structures. Watkins speculated that these
straight lines may represent the courses of ancient
trackways that were used for trade or ceremonial
purposes.

Even in its initial incarnation the idea of ley lines
was widely ridiculed. The strongest and most persistent objection being that by selecting sites carefully,
straight lines can be found going in any direction you
desire. In the 1960s the ley line idea had taken on a
new form that largely discredited it in conventional
archaeological circles.

Watkins' original idea of trade routes had been
developed into a network of mysterious channels that
carried "earth energies". The suggestion was that
prehistoric peoples knew about these energies and
built monuments to mark their route and perhaps
even to tap into them. Ley line theorists don't deny
that stone circles are aligned astronomically but they

claim that this was just part of their function.

It is easy to dismiss ley line theories; there is no proof that the alignments are anything more than figments of that part of the human mind that loves to find patterns and there is no scientific evidence that these mysterious earth energies even exist. On the other hand the idea shouldn't be dismissed too lightly. If it occurred to modern humans then it may well have occurred to our prehistoric ancestors. There is evidence in European myth and folklore for long, straight tracks known as "corpse roads" or "ghost ways" and it's certainly not inconceivable that ancient monuments may have been lined up along these spirit tracks to guide the dead or even to ensure that they didn't stray into the world of the living.

The earth was certainly as important to early pagan religions as the sky and the seasons; the fertility of the Mother Earth is as essential to the growing of crops as the turning of the seasons. At Stonehenge there is evidence that a long, straight track extended far out from the centre of the monument, perhaps as far as the River Avon. Other stone circles also have avenues; the massive circle at Avebury has a particularly fine and clear avenue of stones leading up to it. It's possible that these man-made linear constructions were seen as symbolic of natural features of the spiritual earth in the same way that the monuments themselves stood for the turning of the seasons.

The notion of spiritual energies flowing in paths is certainly found in other parts of the world. It may lie behind the extraordinary straight lines inscribed over miles of the Nazca Plain in Peru and in Eastern mythology such channels exist in the earth just as they exist in the human body.

We will never know how Stonehenge was used by the people who built it. Over such a long period its use and the beliefs associated with it must have evolved into many forms. All that can be said for certain is that its construction was closely linked to ancient observations of the yearly cycles of nature and these must have played an important part in whatever ceremonies or rites were performed here. Above all it is clear that Stonehenge was meant to inspire awe in exactly the same way that the Pyramids or the cathedrals of medieval Europe were meant to inspire awe. They are a statement of the powers that surround us, that nurture us and sometimes terrify us, but always fascinate.

The Mystic Year

. . . .

Astrology

People have been watching the skies for an awfully long time. In the modern industrialized world we tend to forget what a fundamental part of humanity's experience of the world the sky was to our ancestors. Today we live and work largely indoors – when we do venture out at night it is onto streets illuminated by artificial lights; the night sky has all but disappeared from our consciousness. For most of human history this has not been the case. The division between the earthly sphere and the heavenly sphere has been fundamental to the world-view of every ancient culture since the human story began.

The source of this distinction is simple and practical. Everything on the earthly sphere is within our grasp, it can be touched, tasted or in some other way directly interacted with; the other half of the universe, the sky, isn't like that. It is always there and is clearly imbued with as much energy and life as the earthly sphere but we cannot reach it. It is at night the distinction becomes most obvious. The stars and the moon wheel about the heavens in vast patterns and with discernible rhythms but they remain forever beyond our grasp. This division in the universe, which must

Arabic astrologers.

have been one of the first realizations of human consciousness, can be seen as the root of almost every mystical and spiritual instinct. The earth is the realm of the humans, the sky is the realm of the gods or the spirits.

The very earliest evidence that humans took note of the movement of the heavenly bodies and realized that they had a pattern comes from between twenty five and thirty thousand years ago. Notches carved on reindeer bones and mammoth tusks seem to indicate that our cave-dwelling ancestors took note of the phases of the moon. Interestingly this is also the period of cave painting in Europe, the earliest known indisputable evidence that a distinct human culture had evolved. By the time the great civilizations of antiquity – the Mayan, the Egyptian, the Babylonian – had emerged, the science of watching the sky was already highly evolved. Neolithic monuments such as Stonehenge clearly indicate that even cultures that did not reach the heights of the Egyptians had a sophisticated view of the heavens.

The sky systems of the civilizations of the Near and Middle East are the root of the modern discipline of astrology. Few systems of belief are as widely known and grossly misunderstood as the system of Western astrology. Today the discipline is largely represented by sun sign horoscopes found in newspapers and popular magazines and is regarded as something of a joke even by those who read them regularly. No occult discipline, with the possible exception of crystal-ball gazing, is subject to as much ridicule in the modern world as astrology, yet this ridicule is often based on wildly mistaken views of the subject.

In the popular imagination astrology is the art of

telling what a person will be like by studying the position of the sun, moon and planets at the moment of his or her birth. In a world dominated by notions of scientific cause and effect there are two very obvious objections to this idea. The first objection can be called the "generalization objection" and it goes like this. There are only twelve sun signs on the zodiac, and everybody falls into one of these signs; therefore astrology says that there are only twelve types of people.

The second objection can be called the "midwife objection" and goes like this. Bodies such as stars and planets exert influence through gravity, even if every planet in the solar system were lined up their combined pull in one direction would be less than the gravitational pull of the midwife present at the person's birth; therefore the planets cannot be exerting any significant influence on our lives. Both objections are hard to fault, but they are arguments based on a complete misconception of what astrology is all about.

A better definition of astrology would be "the study of relationships between the heavenly and earthly spheres". "Influence" is a dangerous word to use in defining astrology because, to the modern mind, it implies direct, physical interactions of cause and effect. This is not what astrologers mean at all. The key to understanding what astrology is really about is in the ancient division between the heavenly and the earthly spheres. Almost all cultures that made the distinction came to regard one as the mirror of the other, in other words both were connected as if part of a whole that acts according to hidden, designed motives. Put simply, the passing of a comet in the sky does not cause the birth of a prophet, they are both aspects of the same event. By observing one aspect of the event, i.e. the comet, astrologers believed they could be certain that the other had occurred.

This notion of the interconnectedness of all things is extremely ancient and remains a powerful current in modern thought. Astrology was born as an attempt to decode and read this interconnectedness. At the heart of this attempt is the assumption that the universe works according to immutable laws that may or may not have been pre-ordained by a creator. Again this is an idea that has remained at the core of modern thinking; the latest search for these immutable laws of interconnectedness is the story of modern science just as it was the story of astrology.

The development of astrology is rooted in ancient theories about the symbolism of numbers, the business of star signs and planets is largely coincidental. Today we regard numbers as tools or meaningless abstractions but to the ancients numbers had deep meaning. The Greek philosopher Pythagoras, father of modern mathematics, was far more interested in the meaning of numbers than he was in mere arithmetic or geometry – his famous geometrical axioms are as much statements of cosmic and spiritual harmonies as they are tools for measuring triangles or building geometric shapes. It is a tradition that can plainly be seen in the careful geometry of the pyramids – they weren't built that way just to look good, they had meaning.

Numbers in their simplest form have always been used to represent or embody fundamental aspects of existence. The number one has always stood for unity or the absolute, the basic oneness of the universe.

Similarly the number two has stood for basic dichotomies or polarities such as light and dark, male and female, good and evil. Ancient philosophical systems realized that these are not enough on their own to explain the processes of the universe. The number three is taken to represent relationship. The model looks like this; the universe as a whole is "one", within that whole there are opposites, "two", and these opposites interact, "three". So with polarities like "man" and "woman" we find interactive forces like "attraction". Man-woman-attraction is a relationship, man-woman is just a static state of affairs.

Three distinctions is still not enough, the fourth step is actuality or realization; man-woman-attraction becomes man-woman-attraction-love. The number four stands for substance or matter. This is the notion that lies behind the ancient idea of the four elements of the universe; earth, air, fire and water. Philosophers found that they needed a total of twelve such steps to define everything in the universe at every level. These twelve principles are what lies behind the twelve houses of the modern Western zodiac.

The basic twelve steps, or sun signs as we call them today, were further distinguished by four more steps. Each sun sign is assigned a negative or positive polarity. Then they have a "mode of action" cardinal, meaning an instigator of action; fixed, meaning that which is acted upon; or mutable, meaning the facilitator of action. Thirdly the signs have an elemental quality – earth, air, fire or water. For example Aries, the first sign of the zodiac, has a positive polarity, is a cardinal and a fire sign.

The four cardinal points of the modern zodiac – Aries, Libra, Cancer and Capricorn – were said to have

been established by Egyptian astronomers during the
reign of Rameses II in about 1300 BC. Between that
date and the time of the next great astronomers, the
Babylonians, the sky had been divided into twelve
sections. The symbolism of the number twelve
continued to develop under the Babylonians between
about 700 and 400 BC and was woven into the very
fabric of their view of the world. The year was divided
into twelve months, the day and the night into twelve
hours and the geometry of the circle into 360 degrees –
the twelve months multiplied by the thirty days in
each month. The Babylonian calendar was slightly
inaccurate since it left out five days of the true solar
year, but its basic elements have survived to this day.

It was also the Babylonians who first identified the
constellations that we know today. An animal or
person symbolic of the character of each of the twelve
zodiac houses was assigned to each segment of the
sky. The earliest known horoscopes date from 409 BC
and were drawn up by Babylonian astrologers. The
Greeks gave us two of the key terms used in "zodiac"
and "horoscope", which means "to watch what is
rising". It was a Greek living in the second century AD,
Claudius Ptolemaius or Ptolemy, who first wrote down
a comprehensive overview of the origins and methods
of astrology in a set of four books known simply as the
Tetrabiblos. This work contains the accumulated
wisdom of the Egyptians and the Babylonians with the
numerology of Pythagoras. Ptolemy's *Tetrabiblos* was
to become the bible of astrologers for the next 1500
years.

The code or key to unlocking the patterns that had
been detected by the earliest astrologers is known as
the horoscope. Today the word has a very limited

general meaning as the snippets of garbled double-speak that appear in daily newspaper columns. For astronomers a horoscope is the tool by which the secret patterns of the universe can be understood and interpreted.

There are in fact three main branches of astrology, all using their own form of horoscope. Natal astrology is the most familiar. It is concerned with reading the character and predicting the course of an individual's life. The second type is known as mundane astrology and is concerned with general trends in the fate of the world as a whole. In mundane astronomy, nations, corporations or cultural movements are treated in similar ways to individuals in natal astrology. The third type is hororary astrology which is concerned with determining the answers to questions, specific prophecies or the outcome of specific events.

In each type of astrology the basic concept is that the position of the heavenly bodies against the background of the twelve houses and in relation to one another at a specific moment provide the pattern that will be reflected in the event or person that it relates to. A natal horoscope describes a person's character by finding the exact position of the heavenly bodies at the moment of his or her birth. A mundane horoscope describes the character of an institution or a nation in the same way and a hororary horoscope finds the answer to the specified question in the pattern that exists at the moment the question is asked.

The supposed meanings of the position of the heavenly bodies within the zodiac and, equally importantly, their position in relation to each other, or their "aspects", are extremely complex and open to interpretation. The complexity of the system and its sensitivity to the movement of every body and an exact moment means that no two natal horoscopes will be the same, even two people born on the same day will have widely different elements in their horoscopes. The earth's slight orbital wobble ensures that a moment in the zodiac is only repeated once every 25,000 years or so – this is known as the Great or Platonic Year and is itself divided into twelve. This mundane astrological consideration is the basis of talk of the Age of Aquarius, which the world is now entering and the Age of Pisces which it is just leaving.

Given this understanding of the principles of astrology it becomes clear that the "generalization" and "midwife" objections do not touch the actual beliefs of astrologers. The complexity of an individual horoscope is such that it could only be replicated once every 25,000 years – true astrologers certainly do not suggest that there are only twelve types of people. The midwife objection is based on the assumption that when astrologers talk about the influence of the planets they mean direct, physical cause and effect; astrologers do not believe that the planets affect the character, they simply reveal the character.

The importance of this thought cannot be over-stated. For the astrologer everything in the heavenly sphere is an aspect of an earthly event just as the redness of an apple and its taste are both aspects of the same apple – one does not cause the other. The universe is seen as a vast, vibrating whole. A specific event at a specific moment, such as a birth, will share the unique vibration of the universe at that moment. All the astrologer has to do is find out exactly what that vibration was.

For hundreds of years since the Renaissance

astrology has been under attack in the West. The demands for empirical evidence on one hand and the objections of the Christian churches on the other largely drove the study underground and robbed it of its respectability. In the twentieth century there were a number of attempts to put astrological theories on a firm scientific footing.

In 1950, Michel Gaurquelin, a French statistician and confirmed sceptic, set out to prove that astrology had no basis. In an experiment that was based largely on the "generalization" objection Gaurquelin surveyed large numbers of people to show that their lives could not have been predicted according to the time of their birth. Surprisingly he uncovered large discrepancies in his results which indicated that the time of a person's birth did have a correlation with his future career. He found that eminent scientists did tend to be born with Saturn in the ascendant aspect. A large number of soldiers and athletes were born with Mars in that position.

Apart from this statistical evidence, which has mounted up in subsequent surveys, other researchers have found evidence that the cycles of the sun and the moon do have some kind of correspondence with earthly phenomenon independent of their direct physical effects. In one experiment oysters were taken from the Atlantic and transported in dark containers to a lab in Ohio. According to accepted views oysters open and close with the rise and fall of the tides because they respond to the direction of water flow. The tides of the oceans are caused by the interaction of the gravitational fields of the earth and the moon. In water tanks in Ohio the oysters responded to the tides that would have existed had that area been under water; in other words their cycles of opening and closing were related directly to the cycles of the moon and not water flow.

Other experiments carried out in the same lab showed that rats in darkened cages are twice as active when the moon is above the horizon, even when they cannot see the moon. The growth rate of various plants was also found to vary in line with lunar and solar cycles even when the plants were not exposed to sun or moon light. Sunspots, huge magnetic disturbances on the surface of the sun, have been shown to relate to aspects of human behaviour. In major European cities studies have noted that incidents of road accidents, suicides and violent crimes all take a sharp upturn during periods of high sunspot activity. Cyclical patterns apparently related to the rhythms of the sun and the moon have been found in such diverse and unexpected areas as the price of pig iron and salmon catches in Canada.

Serious practitioners of modern astrology recognize the limitations of traditional methods that reach back thousands of years. They claim that the fundamental insight of astrology, that every aspect of the universe is interrelated in ways that we do not yet understand, has more evidence to back it today than ever before. The problem is that the key to understanding these interrelations has been shown to be wanting. One of the most embarrassing blows suffered by astrology came in 1781 when the planet Uranus was discovered. Until that date the whole system of horoscope prediction had been based on just seven heavenly bodies – Sun, Moon, Mercury, Venus, Mars, Saturn and Jupiter – which had been known since prehistoric times.

The situation worsened when Neptune was discovered in 1846 and then Pluto in 1930. Astrologers struggled to fit these new bodies into their charts but they were fighting a losing battle. The old system of interpretation floundered; how could astrologers have accurately predicted the character of a person from the position of the planets if they didn't even know that three of them existed? Clearly the answer is that they couldn't.

One aspect of astrology was discredited by these discoveries but the principles remain valid. Today, astrologers are attempting to find a new set of keys to unlock the patterns of the universe. One day somebody of the stature of Ptolemy will come up with this new interpretation and astrology will have a renaissance. This can only be a good thing: not only will it sweep away the populist nonsense of newspaper columns and teen magazines, it will provide us with an insight into aspects of the universe that pure, physical science cannot address, an insight that is sorely lacking in modern culture.

Vedic Astrology

Just as the Western system of astrology can be linked to general spiritual ideas that have dominated the history of religion in the West, the astrological system of the Indian subcontinent is linked to different spiritual insights. In the West fate and the journey of the soul is a linear process; the Western soul springs from nothingness, proceeds through life and then passes into an eternal afterlife of damnation or salvation. In Eastern thought the journey of the soul is cyclical and passes through aeons of reincarnation before achieving peace in oblivion.

Western astrology is characteristically linear and individualistic. The moment of birth is taken as the critical moment in the character of a soul. The position of the heavenly bodies at that moment is said to reflect the character and destiny of the individual. In Indian astrology notions of reincarnation and karma are naturally taken into consideration.

The Vedic tradition is very ancient and derives from the earliest era of Indian civilization. The word "Vedic" is derived from the Sanskrit word "Veda" which means knowledge in the broadest sense. The Vedas are also the most ancient scriptures of the Hindu faith. Vedic knowledge is said to encompass every area of human experience and understanding from spiritual to medical to political. Its origins can be traced to about 5000 years ago and clearly formed part of a world-wide development of astrological thought that began in that period. The system of Vedic astrology popular in India today is based on the writings of an ancient sage known as Parasara.

Vedic astrology is also known as Jyotish astrology which forms part of the Jyotish system of health and right living. Unlike Western astrology which is based on an empirical system of inquiry Jyotish ideas are said to be derived from a philosophy that could be described as "knowledge by cognition". According to legend Jyotish knowledge came into the world as a result of a mass meeting of *siddhas* or enlightened sages. Seventy thousand siddhas convened at the dawn of the world and entered a state of trance meditation. One siddha remained conscious and posed questions about the world, the answers provided by his meditating brothers formed the body of universal Jyotish knowledge.

This legend illustrates an idea fundamental to the Hindu philosophy; wisdom is not gained by outward inquiry but by focusing the awareness on a subject until knowledge about it is obtained from within. The meeting of the ancient siddhas is also said to have given rise to the goddess Indra, recognised in Hindu culture as the creative energy.

Jyotish astrology differs from Western astrology in two key areas – its mechanics and the emphasis of its insights. Jyotish horoscopes look different from Western horoscopes, they recognize different heavenly bodies and they interpret relationships between these bodies differently; these are the mechanics of the system. In emphasis Jyotish astrology interprets the notion of the interconnectedness of things central to all astrological systems in a different way.

In Western astrology the interconnectedness of things is represented by the idea that the heavens reflect specific details about who an individual is. Jyotish astrology is much less concerned with the character of the individual. In Hindu thought an individual is merely the current incarnation of a vast interaction of karmic forces that drive the soul through eternity. A Jyotish horoscope can be seen as a map tracking the currents of these karmic forces from the past into the future. By reading the karmic values that a soul has at the moment of its birth into a new incarnation the Jyotish astrologer believes that he or she can tell how that soul lived its last life and what effect this will have on its new life; the individual characteristics of the soul in its new life are relatively unimportant.

194

At first sight the mechanics of the Jyotish system and the Western system differ substantially. In fact they use very similar ideas under different names and the difference in their application is largely a matter of cultural divergence.

Modern Western astrology recognizes ten heavenly bodies – Sun, Moon, Mercury, Venus, Mars, Jupiter, Saturn, Uranus, Neptune and Pluto – although there is some controversy about the status of the last three which were discovered only within the last two centuries. Jyotish astrology recognizes the Sun and the Moon plus the planets up to Saturn, but does not include the recently discovered planets. In addition it has two more mysterious bodies known as Rahu and Ketu. These are sometimes described as imaginary planets but in fact are mathematical points in space that represent the two positions at which the Moon crosses the celestial equator.

These bodies are known as *grahas* and, as in the Western model, they each have an individual character. Rahu and Ketu are not usually counted as grahas since they are not physical bodies. Nevertheless they have character, they are the diametrically opposed and equal forces. Naturally the names of the heavenly bodies differ from the Western versions.

In both Western and Jyotish models the background to the relationship of the heavenly bodies is a system of twelve zodiac signs, or *rasis* in the Sanskrit. These signs are essentially the same in both systems, although of course they have different names.

Unfortunately it isn't possible to simply translate a Western sun sign into a Jyotish sign. This is because the Jyotish system takes account of the procession of

Western	Jyotish
Aries	Mesha
Taurus	Vrishabha
Gemini	Mithuna
Cancer	Kataka
Leo	Simha
Virgo	Kanya
Libra	Tula
Scorpio	Vrishika
Sagittarius	Dhanus
Capricorn	Makara
Aquarius	Kumbha
Pisces	Meena

the equinoxes. In about 285 AD the Western and Jyotish houses were aligned, because of the slight "wobble" of the Earth's axis the position of the houses in the West shifts by about one degree every seventy-two years. This is compensated for in the Jyotish system which means that today there is about a twenty-three-degree gap between the perceived position of the Western sign Aries and its Jyotish equivalent Mesha. This means that the heavenly bodies are read as being against entirely different signs at the same moment by the two systems.

The fact that the Jyotish system and the Western system were in line in 285 AD strongly suggests that this is the date at which the two systems diverged from a common root. The Babylonian system of astrology developed between 700 and 400 BC does not take account of the procession of the equinoxes and has been suggested as the basis of both Western and Jyotish systems. It is likely that Jyotish system broke away when Indian astrologers noted the effect of the procession.

This refinement is based on a the use of a sidereal system as opposed to the Western tropical system. In the tropical system the start of the first sign, Aries, is marked by the point at which the sun crosses the plane of the Earth's equator. In the sidereal system the zodiac is fixed in reference to the position of constellations. These constellations also drift over time but at a much slower rate than the procession of the equinox.

A good example of the different approach of the two systems is in the use of Western sun signs and Jyotish "houses" or *bhavas*. In Western tradition the most heavily emphasized meaning is the reading from the position of the Sun at the moment of birth, this gives the sun sign and is supposed to be the most basic predictor of character. In the Eastern tradition there is a system of twelve houses which relate to general currents on the life of the individual rather than in the individual's character. Although they are not directly equivalent it is interesting to compare the kind of things that sun signs stand for with those that houses stand for.

The final point of difference between the two systems is in their interpretation of what Western astrology calls "aspects" – the positions of the heavenly bodies relative to each other.

Although the Jyotish system of astrology is based on

Comparison of Western sun signs with Jyotish houses

Sun sign	House
Aries Hot-headed and impulsive character	Lagna Physical appearance, overall health.
Pisces Introverted, mystical, receptive character	Satru Challenges from competitors or enemies

---

ancient concepts unique to the land of its origin, specifically the philosophy of Hinduism, there is clearly a lot of cross-over with ideas from those which moulded the Western system. Undoubtedly the process also worked in the other direction as well, to what extent each influenced the other is impossible to fully unravel. In many ways the Jyotish system has stood the test of time better than its Western counter-part. It is rooted in a culture that places less emphasis on the linear progress of humanity and instead relies on a "bigger picture" of the cycles of the universe. It's an insight that is becoming increasingly pertinent to modern thought.

Chinese and Tibetan Astrology

Chinese astrology and its close cousin Tibetan astrology make up the third great system of divination from the heavens to have survived into the modern era. Very ancient Chinese practices of divination uncovered by archaeology involved the use of tortoise shells. Prehistoric peoples of the region cracked tortoise shells with fire or rock and read the future from the pattern of the fractures. The tortoise retained its place in the mythology of Chinese astronomy and it is said that ancient sages discovered the codes to unlock the messages of the heavens on the shells of sacred tortoises.

Chinese astrology uses very different methods from its Western and Vedic counterparts but elements of a common heritage can be discerned. As in other astrological systems the number twelve is of fundamental importance. In the West there are twelve sun signs ranging from Aries to Pisces, in the Chinese system the counterpart of these sun signs are the twelve animal years.

According to legend the years were assigned to various animals by the divine Buddha. One day Buddha invited all of the animals of the earth to visit him in his jade palace on New Year's Day. Only twelve of the animals turned up so Buddha honoured them by giving them power over a year each; the sequence is said to have been determined by the order in which the animals arrived at the palace. The first was the rat, then came the ox, the tiger, the rabbit, the dragon, the snake, the horse, the sheep or goat, the monkey, the rooster, the dog and finally the boar or pig. Ever since that time the people of China have recognized each successive year as being ruled by this sequence of animals.

Each of the animal years has its own character. As in Western astrology the twelve elements and their combinations are supposed to cover every possible aspect of the universe. The rat is outspoken and mischievous, the dog is watchful and thoughtful and the snake is logical and philosophical. The characteristics of the animal year that an individual is born into is the central feature of popular modern astrology. Because the Chinese New Year doesn't begin until 16 February in the Western calendar the year systems of the two cultures cannot be directly transposed.

Modern scholars have been able to trace the origins and development of Chinese astrology largely through its influence on Tibet. Chinese history is far more tumultuous than the history of its northern neighbour and many ancient Chinese texts survive only via Tibetan translation. Tibetan record-keeping is also extremely accurate and stretches back at least 2000 years.

According to Tibetan tradition Chinese astrology was first introduced to their kingdom in 635 AD by the Chinese wife of the thirty-third Tibetan monarch. The complete system that she imported was already very ancient in the seventh century. Tibetan texts state that its origins were first compiled by the legendary first ruler of China Fu Shi who reigned from 2852–2738 BC; if true this would make Chinese astrology by far the oldest uninterrupted system of divination.

The Tibetan narrative goes on to speak of a dragon that rose from the Yellow River that had the eight trigrams known as the "First Heavenly System". These were recorded in a work known as the *Lyan-Shan* and latter added to in one known as the *Ku-hi-Tsan*. The "Later Heavenly System" was compiled from the marks on the shell of a tortoise presented to the Chinese emperor in 2205 BC. Chinese scholars point out that the titles of these legendary Tibetan books translate into Chinese as *Lien Shan*, "Signs of Changes in the Mountains", and *Kuei Tsang*, "Journey and Return to Womb and Tomb". These are the two lost books of a trilogy, only the *I Ching* survives.

The original I Ching method of divination was based on eight trigrams or collections of three horizontal lines. Each trigram stands for aspects of nature, personal life and society. The lines that make them up in different combinations are Yin, feminine and receptive, or Yang, assertive and masculine. These are the lines that diviners sought to find in the cracked tortoise shells or in bundles of tossed yarrow stalks. The later development of the I Ching into a system of sixty-four hexagrams is said to have been carried out in the twelfth century BC. Later additions such as the ten stems and the twelve branches were also made. The assigning of Yin and Yang values to the five elements of ancient Chinese philosophy – wood, fire, earth, metal, water – completed the system.

Casting a horoscope using the Tibetan astrology involves examining the relationships between the date of an individual's birth with the eight trigrams, the nine magic square numbers, the twelve animals and the five elements. Results are expressed in terms of four areas of life; life energy, health, finance and success. An inharmonious balance of energy in any of these areas is taken to indicate that problems will arise. Drawing on practices that stretch back even further than the influences of Chinese astrology the horoscope caster may recommend that magical rites are carried out to placate or deceive the evil demons that the bad energy balance will give rise to. One of these rites includes the offering of a doll to the demons in the case of potential illness. To protect buildings or homes threatened by these forces the astrologer may recommend building a miniature replica of the structure and enticing the demons to inhabit it.

A further complication of an already labyrinthine system is the ancient Tibetan calendar which is based on the Moon rather than the Sun. The new moon appears on the fifteenth day of each month and the full moon on the last day. It is divided into twelve months of exactly thirty days each, which gives 360 days, and also includes five unlucky skip-days to keep it in line with the solar year of 365 days. As with the Chinese system the years are assigned to the twelve animals; every twelfth year of a person's life is thought to bring hardship and is termed the "obstacle year". Each year also has one of the five elements assigned to it which effect the way in which the character of the year is manifested.

The four main elements of Tibetan astrology are derived directly from Chinese traditions. The first element is the animal-year tradition, the second is the trigram tradition familiar from the I Ching, the third is the nine magic numbers which derive from the Lo and Ho maps which rotate each year through the animal houses. The final key is the cycle of the elements associated with the years and their relation to the birth and death cycle of the individual soul.

The details and procedures of Chinese-based systems of astrology are immensely difficult to understand without the cultural background that they emerged from. It is perhaps more instructive to examine the very basics of this philosophy rather than any particular manifestation of it such as Tibetan astrology or Vedic astrology.

Ancient thought was obsessed by the idea of fate. In life the thought inevitably occurs to the individual that certain things are out of his or her control. The elements are an obvious example but perhaps the most profound is the future; essentially we can do little to affect what will happen to us especially when we do not know what is around the next corner. The desire to know what is going to happen is the driving force behind all systems of divination including astrology.

The first philosophical step in quantifying fate is the recognition of what the ancients would have called the fate of heaven. This is the idea that ourselves and the world we are born into have been designed by a creator or some other superhuman force. It is the most fundamental aspect of fate – the heavenly sphere cannot be touched or influenced by the earthly sphere, all control goes in the other direction.

The second aspect of fate is the fate of birth. These are the broad brush-strokes of the design dictated by the heavenly sphere. It manifests itself in the circumstances of the birth of the individual; man or woman, rich or poor, talented or crippled. Basic sun sign and animal sign reading represent the attempt to read these broad strokes of a person's life.

The third aspect of fate is the fate of action or behaviour. It can be seen as the recognition that the way we act in life has an influence on the outcome of our life. This influence can deflect or subvert the basic fate of birth. For example, if a man is born with enormous musical talent but never bothers to undertake musical training his birth fate will be diverted. On the other hand if he practices tirelessly and makes sure that he studies under the best teachers his birth fate will be enhanced. In both cases the birth fate remains the same but the way it manifests itself differs. Astrologers believe that the fate of action depends on the character of the individual and can be read from such things as planetary aspects and ascendencies.

The fourth aspect of fate is the fate of the unexpected. These are the day-to-day events external to ourselves that can have a profound effect on the course of our lives. An example would be a car accident that robs a great pianist of the use of his hands. The pianist's birth fate gave him talent as a musician, his action fate or the form of his character reinforced that fate and then the fate of the unexpected subverted the whole pattern. To astrologers the fate of the unexpected is represented by the position of heavenly bodies in relation to the day-to-day life of the individual.

In Chinese and Vedic astrology these basic insights are channelled through concepts such as karma which provides an explanation of how these fates take their form in each individual's life. In the Western tradition the "will of God" plays the same part.

Much of the symbolism and mechanics of the world's systems of astrology are little more than cultural window dressing; the mystery of the four steps of fate lies behind them all. The continued popularity of astrology and other methods of divination can be attributed to the fact that science makes no attempt to provide a key to these mysteries, in fact it denies that these mysteries even exist. In one sense they are absolutely right. Science sees the world from outside the human perspective – there are unknowns but there are no mysteries from that point of view. As long as people are concerned about what the future holds they will always seek a way of finding out and since this concern is a basic part of the way the human mind works – from the past into the future – it is unlikely that this desire will ever go away.

The Great Mayan Count

The Mayan culture and the cities they left behind constitute one of the world's greatest mysteries. These extraordinary people carved more than a hundred cities out of the jungle and tamed a hard, inhospitable part of the world. Nobody is sure where they came from or exactly what function their huge pyramid-like temples served. When the first Europeans arrived on the Yucatan peninsula, Mayan civilization was already long gone. For reasons that we still don't understand their whole culture collapsed over the course of four or five generations in about 800 AD.

Very little evidence of Mayan customs survives. Large numbers of beautifully illustrated codices were burned by early Christian missionaries who believed they were the works of the devil. Only three codices survived this insane destruction and were taken to Europe. Scholars who have spent years studying these documents have shown that they contain elaborate and complex calculations of the rhythms of the planet Venus and other heavenly bodies. Gradually as more and more of the Mayan's temple cities were uncovered in the jungle which had reclaimed their land, scholars were also able to interpret the numerous symbolic carvings that the Mayans decorated their buildings with.

A picture emerged of a civilization that had been obsessed with the passage of time. The Mayans had not developed the wheel, the true arch or a system of weights and measures but they had developed such an advanced system of mathematics that they could calculate dates thousands of years into the future or the past and their astronomy had accurately mapped the stars.

The Mayans' cities were not true cities in the modern sense, they were essentially temple complexes with a large farming and support population living in primitive dwellings around the stone-built central precincts. One of the greatest mysteries of the Mayans has always been how they managed to make this system work. For centuries agriculture in the area has been based on a primitive slash-and-burn method known locally as *milpa.*

The Yucatan peninsula has poor soil spread thinly over a bed of limestone which rapidly soaks up and channels water away. Farmers traditionally cut down or burnt the vegetation from a manageable patch of virgin forest during the dry season. The land is then sown in time for the rainy season which brings forth a crop, if the farmer is lucky. After two years the poor soil is so exhausted and the re-encroachment of grasses and jungle so extensive that the land must be abandoned. The land must be left for at least three years and usually more like six to eight years before it can be planted again.

As long as the population remains small and widely dispersed this system is perfectly adequate for the primitive farmers' needs. Population density in the area of the Yucatan that used to be inhabited by the Maya is between twenty-five and one hundred people per square mile.

People who practise this form of agriculture do not

live in large cities, each farmer needs such a large area of land that the distance from home to the fields would be just too great. Archaeological evidence suggests that populations in Mayan times were sixteen times greater than can be supported by the milpa system today, and they had cities. Excavation of the Mayan city of Tikal indicates that up to 11,000 people must have lived closely packed around the temple complexes.

Not only were the Mayans able to feed large population concentrations, they were also able to leave a large work force free from the land to work on the construction of new temples. Mayan temples are huge, well-constructed buildings that must have taken millions of man-hours to erect, finish and decorate.

Exactly how the Mayans managed this is something of a mystery, but perhaps the greater mystery is why they wanted to live like this. What was going on in these cities that drew such a huge conglomeration of people?

All the evidence suggests that Mayan cities were strictly religious and ceremonial centres. The large associated populations that clamoured around them were probably there to support the lifestyle of the ruling class and an army of priests. When the Spanish arrived they reported that the Mayans had an infinite number of gods and that human sacrifice had been an almost daily occurrence. Both of these turn out to be unsurprising exaggerations, but not by much.

Human sacrifice was certainly practised by the Maya, as it was by other South and Central American cultures. Exactly when these sacrifices were carried out remains a matter of speculation. What we do know is that the dates of ceremonies were determined according to an extremely complex system of at least three calendars which interacted with each other.

The sacred calendar, know as the Sacred Round, was a cycle of 260 days made of two interlocking monthly cycles of twenty and thirteen sacred figures. The Mayans had a unique view of the relationship between the passing of time and the gods. Each day of the twenty-day cycle was a named god. These gods "carried" the day and were related to one of the thirteen sacred numbers of the second cycle.

The system of the Sacred Round can be visualized as two interlocking cogs, one with twenty teeth that correspond to the twenty day gods, and the other with thirteen cogs. Each day the wheels turn so that the next pair of cogs interlock. Because one wheel is smaller than the other it returns to its original position – i.e. completes one cycle – before the larger wheel. This means that by the time the twenty cog wheel has completed one rotation and the first day god in the sequence comes round again he is matched with a different number than the first time. After 260 days the large wheel has completed exactly thirteen complete rotations and the small wheel has completed twenty. The first god and the first number line up again for the first time in 260 days and the Sacred Round is complete.

In addition to the Sacred Round the Maya also had a secular year calendar based on the lunar cycle of approximately 360 days. Five extra days had to be added at the end of this year to keep it in line with the solar year. These five days were considered to be out of time and extremely unlucky. This calendar, known as the *tun*, and the Sacred Round interact in the same way as the two cycles of twenty and thirteen. In this interaction there are two wheels of 365 five and 260 days respectively. This cycle returns to its original position only after 52 years, the completion of this cycle was known as the Calendar Round.

As if this wasn't complicated enough the Maya also operated a system known as the Long Count. This was calculated in terms of the *katun*, a cycle of twenty tuns or 7200 days, and the *baktun*, a cycle of twenty katuns or 140,000 days. Other intermeshing cycles ranging in periods from centuries to millions of years were also used.

It's important to realize that the Mayans didn't see this as an invented system. The twenty gods the Sacred Round was based on were very real and inescapable figures and the 365-day secular year was enshrined in the cycles of the Sun and the Moon. The relationships between the calendars had very real implications in the Mayan religion. Each first day of the 52 years of the Calendar Round matched with a different god-day of the Sacred Round. If that day happened to be the god of the corn then the year's harvest could be expected to be good, if on the other hand it was the god of mischief a year of trouble could be expected.

Given the short life-spans of people in those times it's highly unlikely that people would have seen out an entire Calendar Round. The Mayans believed that history repeated itself during each Calendar Round. There was no real progress or change. A man could be safe in the knowledge that the men and women alive 52 years in the future, long after he was dead, would experience exactly the same events as himself.

In order to keep the gods happy with the correct ceremonies on the correct days the Mayans had to develop a highly complex counting system to keep track of the cycles. The highly advanced methods and concepts that they developed match anything developed by other civilizations but they were used strictly for sacred calculations.

The Mayan number system uses twenty as a base, the Arabic system used in most of the world today uses ten. Like the modern system it is also positional, in other words the value of figures is determined by its relation to other figures. For example the numbers 123 and 321 use the same figures but the difference in their position gives us information about the value of the number as a whole. Unlike the Romans, who were contemporaries of the early Mayans, they also developed the concept of zero. Mayan figures are represented by a series of lines and dots. The figures one to four are represented by the corresponding number of dots, five is a horizontal line and six is a line with a dot on top.

One of the most prominent features of any Mayan city are limestone columns carved or painted with figures that record the time of their erection in great detail. Known as *stelae* these features were clearly central to the Mayan faith and were erected all over the Mayan empire at the end of each twenty-year katun. In about 790 AD this practice reached a peak when nineteen cities erected stelae. Twenty years later only twelve cities erected these monuments and twenty years after that only three did. Mayan civilization had clearly taken a dramatic dive. Within a century only ten per cent of the Mayan population remained.

What happened to the Mayans? Since the discovery of the mystery everything from massacre to plague to mass migration have been suggested. There is little evidence that war or invasion from outside was to blame, the cities were left decrepit but largely intact. It is more likely that the agricultural system collapsed or that the cohesion of the largely independent cities broke down and a system of food distribution along with it. Perhaps the Mayans just exhausted the land and were forced to leave. In fact Mayan civilization did not disappear completely. In the highlands to the north a later culture grew up from its remnants, although it never reached the heights that the Mayans had.

The last generations of true Mayans must have been gravely perplexed by the events that were overtaking their culture. The great count of history as they knew it with its ever-repeating patterns was breaking down. For all their mathematical prowess the priests could not calculate how to placate the gods who were bringing destruction to the land. From the myth and folklore of the area terrible images of desperate mass sacrifices have come down to us. The last dark days of the Mayan count must have been terrible indeed.

The Great Wheel

The planet that we live on is, as far as we know, unique. When the first photographs of the Earth were taken from space they revealed a sphere of breath-taking, jewel-like beauty. Suddenly it became clear to a whole new generation why our ancestors regarded the world as a goddess. The sky above our heads and the earth beneath our feet have always been central elements in religious thought. These two elements are intimately related by the seasons which dictate the cycles of life everywhere on the planet. Consequently, observation of the seasonal cycles has been important to humans since the very earliest days.

The Earth has seasons because of a peculiarity of its cosmic orientation. The axis around which our planet rotates every twenty-four hours is tilted by a few degrees from the vertical. The practical upshot of this is that the northern and southern hemispheres receive less light and heat on one side of the Earth's yearly orbit of the sun than they do on the other, in other words the days and the nights vary in length. Less light and shorter days equals winter, more light and longer days equals summer.

Concentrating just on the northern hemisphere it is clear that there is a point in the year at which it receives the minimum sunlight and another at which it receives the maximum, these are the mid-winter and mid-summer points or winter and summer solstices. They fall on 21 December and 21 June respectively.

Two other dates are also significant, the two days of the year on which the length of the day and night are exactly equal, these are known as the equinoxes. The vernal or spring equinox falls on 21 March, the autumnal equinox on 21 September. These four dates have been celebrated by cultures all over the world for millennia. When human beings first began to adopt an agrarian lifestyle and abandoned their old hunter-gatherer ways the seasons suddenly took on a new and critical importance.

The cycles of birth, growth and death followed by new birth the next spring were so important to ancient agrarian cultures that they formed the frame-work of their religions. These earth and sky worship-

ping religions were centred around these four important dates that marked turning points in the year: the
lowest point of winter and the highest point of
summer – the solstices – and the moment when
winter turns to summer and summer turns to winter –
the equinoxes.

At some point in the hazy past four more dates also
became spiritually important. These were the
midpoints between the four original dates and eventually they became even more important than the
solstices and the equinoxes. Known as cross-quarter
days they mark the point at which each of the seasons
reaches its height.

In Europe these eight days have been celebrated
since well before recorded history began. There are
two main strands of evidence for this conclusion. The
first is archaeological. Sites such as Stonehenge are
clearly aligned with the sunrise points on the dates in
question. Stone circles can be seen as solar and lunar
observatories that not only indicated when the sacred
moments had arrived but also celebrated them in their
very structure.

Ancient burial mounds are commonly oriented with
their entrances towards the sunrise point of the winter
solstice. This has been interpreted as evidence of a
faith in some kind of reincarnation. The winter solstice
is the moment when the cycle of the year is reborn,
our ancient ancestors doubtless connected this with
hopes of human rebirth into an afterlife. As the
centuries passed and the specifics of the old faiths
were forgotten, the instinct to orientate religious
buildings towards a significant point remained. The
clearest example of this is the traditional eastern
orientation of Christian churches. This tradition is

directly descended from ancient practices: the sun rises in the east and the rising of the sun is the moment of the day's rebirth.

The second strand of evidence is cultural. In ancient pagan religions of which we have written records, such as the religions of the Romans and the Greeks, there is abundant evidence that these dates were celebrated and associated with specific fertility gods.

Even though the religions that originally recognized these dates have long since disappeared, the dates themselves have remained culturally important. In Europe and North America this is largely due to the influence of Christianity. In the very early days of the Christian Church, missionaries found that the pagan beliefs of the peoples they were attempting to convert could be readily adapted to Christian concepts. Over time the old pagan dates became dates in the Christian calendar and many of the rituals associated with those dates were also incorporated. The most obvious of these survivals are Christmas, Easter and All Hallows Eve, or Halloween.

The importance of these annual moments can also be traced through the traditions of astrology. The twelve sun signs of the zodiac divide neatly into the four quarters of the ancient year. The first sign, Aries, begins on the date of the vernal equinox, 21 March. The fourth sign, Cancer, begins on the date of the summer solstice. The sun enters the seventh, Libra, at the autumnal equinox and the tenth, Capricorn, at the winter solstice. These four cardinal points of the Western zodiac were in place during the reign of the Egyptian pharaoh Rameses II more than 3000 years ago.

In the nineteenth and twentieth centuries scholars

devoted a lot of attention to tracing the origins and cultural descent of the eight great ancient calendar divisions. They revealed a rich and fascinating history that tells us a lot about the development of our civilization and culture.

The First Quarter

Since the ancient vision of the year is of an endless cycle or rotating wheel, an interpretation of it can begin at any point. Spring is as good a place as any to start and provides the most satisfying opening to the story. There are three main characters in the drama; the earth goddess, the sky father and the child. The earth goddess has three guises; the maid or virgin, the mother and the hag or crone. The sky father is a dual god with a light and a dark face known variously as the Oak King and the Holly King or the light god and the dark god. Their child is the year itself and the youthful incarnation of either the light god or the dark god. They have many different names and guises in many different cultural traditions but they all represent the same fundamental idea. In Christian myth they are the Virgin Mary – the earth goddess, God – the sky father, and Christ – the child.

Imbolc or Candlemas – 2 February; Cross-quarter day

This is the midpoint between the winter solstice, the lowest point of the year's rotation, and the vernal equinox. It is celebrated as the very beginning of spring and the end of the dark quarter or winter. In northern Europe it is often a season of harsh weather when the very first signs of the Earth's rebirth are beginning to emerge; buds are forming, the very first flowers are beginning to sprout and hibernating animals begin to emerge. It is also the beginning of the lambing season. Although there may be several more weeks of wintry weather, the year has turned the corner from death and decay to the first signs of rebirth.

The word *Imbolc* literally means "in the belly" and refers to the belief that the earth mother is showing the first signs of her pregnancy – the child that will be the bounty of the new year is showing its first signs of life. Imbolc is also known as *Oimelc* which means "the milk of ewes" and celebrates the start of lambing.

In Ireland the ancient Celtic earth mother *Brighid* or Brigit was honoured at this time of year by priestesses who kept a flame burning in her name all year round. Christianity appropriated this figure and made her Saint Brigit, patron saint of poetry, healing and, significantly, midwifery. In Christian myth Saint Brigit is also supposed to have been the foster mother or wet nurse of Christ. Another form of the name Brigit is *bride* and the goddess is supposed to have given her blessing of fertility to all human brides. To be married on Brigit's day had special significance.

Rituals associated with this celebration include the making of straw dolls which are carried from door to door in baskets by young girls. Each household bestows a gift on the Brigit doll to ensure that she will smile on them in the coming year and that she has the strength to give birth. Brigit crosses are woven from straw and exchanged as gifts to give protection and luck in the coming year.

A key element of Imbolc rituals is the idea of rekindling and preparation. Fires in people's homes were put out and then re-lit once the hearth had been swept.

Bonfires were lit out in the open and candles placed in every window or doorway of every home to symbolize the return of the Sun. The blessing of agricultural tools was also a common element of rituals at this time, especially the plough. In some areas Imbolc was the day of the first ploughing to prepare the land for sowing the first seeds of the year. In others the plough was decorated and processed through the village accompanied by children begging for gifts.

In the Christian calendar the day is known as Candlemas, the time at which all the candles to be used in the coming year are blessed. The tradition of placing lighted candles in all windows was also preserved by the Church. It is also known as the Feast of the Purification of the Virgin Mary. In medieval times women were considered to be "impure" for four to six weeks after giving birth and were traditionally housed in the church during this period. According to the Christian calendar Mary gave birth on Christmas Day so Imbolc marks the end of the period of her confinement. For pagans this is the moment when the earth mother transforms from her guise as the crone of winter to the virgin of spring.

In many places this date is also associated with weather prediction, a tradition that survives in North American culture as Groundhog Day. On this date the hibernating groundhog emerges from his burrow and checks to see if he has a shadow. If he does, he returns to his burrow and goes back to sleep because there will be six more weeks of winter weather, until the next significant date, the vernal equinox. This custom is also found in an old English saying "If Candlemas Day be bright and clear, there will be two winters in the year". In Celtic myth this is the day that Brigit's snake emerges from the earth and tests the air to tell if spring will come early or late.

In the ancient Roman calendar a fertility festival known as *Lupercalia* was held at this time of year. Priests dressed as the mischievous god Pan would run through the streets whipping young women with goatskin thongs to make them fertile. The date we know today as Valentine's Day, 14 February, is also connected to Imbolc. Over the centuries the reorganization of calendars and the addition and subtraction of days has led to the two festivals being separated by twelve days but it's clear that the emphasis on love and the heart are intimately connected to the concepts of Imbolc.

Modern Wiccans who attempt to recreate and honour the pagan rituals of the past regard Imbolc as one of the most significant of the eight sabbats. Candles for the year's ceremonies are prepared on this day and the custom of putting candles in windows is also followed.

In terms of the great drama of the year the period between Imbolc and the next festival of the vernal equinox is a time of preparation for the earth mother. At its beginning she is transformed into the maiden and by its end she is mature and ready to be implanted with the seed of the sky father. At this stage the sky father is represented only by his incarnation as the weather and Imbolc is the day on which to divine his mood or intentions for the next six weeks. The child is no more than a potential at this stage.

Ostara or Lady Day – 21 March; Vernal Equinox
On this day the balance of the day and the night shifts in favour of the day; darkness is defeated and light

becomes ascendant. It is the true arrival of spring when every living thing is blooming and bursting with new life. In the great drama the earth mother has reached maturity and is married to the sky father; later she gives birth to the fruit of this union – the harvest.

In Saxon mythology the first full moon after this date is sacred to the fertility goddess *Ostara*, whose symbols are the egg and the rabbit. With the introduction of Christianity into these regions the date became connected with the death and resurrection of Christ, Easter. In many ancient traditions the vernal equinox is the moment of the rebirth of the sky father or the beginning of the year. The date of the equinox itself is known as Lady Day or the Feast of the Annunciation. In pagan myth this is the time when the goddess becomes pregnant, it is the time for sowing seeds, in Christian myth it is the time when the Virgin Mary is visited by an angel who tells her that she will have a child – Christ is born nine months later in the last quarter of December.

The sky father comes into his own at this time of year. For the first time in six months his power triumphs over the power of the darkness and his strength waxes from this point until its greatest potency at the summer solstice. In some traditions this is seen as the moment that the sky father is born, his death and resurrection are celebrated just as Christians celebrate the death and resurrection of Christ.

In ancient times the vernal equinox was more important to southern European cultures than those in the north, who tended to delay their celebrations until the cross-quarter festival six weeks later known as *Beltane*. In Italy the death and resurrection of the vegetable god *Attis* was celebrated at this time. In Rome the rituals associated with this celebration took place on the very spot where the Vatican stands today. In the early days of the Christian Church's establishment in Rome local pagans accused the priests of the new religion of stealing their festival.

In the north the vernal equinox is the time for planting and hope. As a solar festival it is strongly associated with fire and light. Huge bonfires were lit on hilltops and were said to bring fertility to all the land on which their light fell. For luck people jumped over the dying embers of these fires or drove their cattle through them.

The Second Quarter
The first quarter of the year is a time of worry and hope – will the earth mother be strong enough, will the sky father return from the dead? The second quarter is one of growing confidence and hope. The marriage of the sky and the earth grows more profound. The power of the sun increases every day and the fertility and growth of the earth matches it. The earth mother begins to take on her full majesty and beauty until she reaches a high point at midsummer.

Beltane or May Day – 1 May; Cross-quarter day
Beltane was one of the two most important festivals of the ancient faiths, the other being *Samhain* or Halloween. It marks the beginning of summer and is essentially a celebration of the fertility of the land and the people.

Unlike other pagan festivals it was never successfully replaced by a Christian equivalent but eventually adopted wholesale by the Church. The Christian calendar has this date as Roodmas, the consecration of the cross which the Church tried to put up in place of the sexually charged image of the Maypole. The celebration of May Day has never been wholly subsumed by Christian theology, in fact for centuries it was seen as a day when the strict observation of the commandments was abandoned – particularly those associated with sexual morality.

In ancient times marriages of a year and a day were made on May Day and until very recently many rural communities remembered this practice in the custom of pairing up young men and women for the night. Married couples were allowed to remove their wedding rings and the vows that they symbolized for a day.

Other folk rituals associated with the day include walking or beating the boundaries. It was traditional for landowners or feudal lords to walk around the boundaries of the territory they controlled to check on the state of fences and hedges. Priests also used to tour the boundaries of their parishes, sometimes accompanied by bands of children who would beat the ground with bundles of budding willow.

In Celtic Europe the celebration of Beltane began at sunset on the preceding day – the Celts measured days from sunset to sunset rather than from midnight to midnight. Great fires were lit at sacred sites and ceremonies performed by their light. As at the vernal equinox, which was not celebrated by the Celts, people would jump the flames and cattle would be driven through the embers or between a pair of fires before being taken to their summer pastures the next day. In the Roman calendar this period was marked by a three-day festival known as the Feast of Flowers which was notorious for its orgies and drunken excesses.

The encouragement of human fertility was a central element of Beltane celebrations in northern Europe and often involved the use of explicit sexual symbolism that the Christian Church later did its best to stamp out. Urban Puritans in seventeenth-century England were particularly appalled at the May Day practices that they uncovered in rural communities.

In many places there was a tradition of "greenwood" marriages. The young men and women of the village would spend the night before May Day chasing and, often catching, each other among the fields and woods. In the morning they would gather branches of blossom and bring them back to decorate the village. Later in the day a feast would be topped off with dancing around a Maypole. In 1644 the Puritans banned Maypoles and May Day celebrations in England. One writer remarked of the outrageous festivities:

> *Men do use commonly to run into woods in the night time, amongst maidens, to set bowes, in so much as I have heard of ten maidens that went to set May, and nine of them came home with child.*

The tradition of the May queen and king is also descended from these sexually charged rituals. The folk tale of Lady Godiva, a noble lady who rode naked through the streets of Coventry, is thought to be based on memories of a festival in which a May queen selected for her beauty was paraded through the city in ancient times. In the modern folk tale nobody was allowed to look at the lady and the man who broke the rule was immediately struck blind by God – a clear cultural echo of the suppression of this ritual by the Church.

The month of May is named after a Greek nymph deity who was also called the most beautiful of the Seven Sisters of the Pleiades. Beltane comes from the Irish Gealic *Bealtaine* meaning the fire of the Celtic god of light Bel or Beli. In Irish mythology it is a day that holds special significance beyond its ceremonial role. The first settler was said to have arrived in Ireland on May Day and his people were said to have been destroyed by a plague on the same date. In Wales the eve of May Day was thought to be marked by a terrible scream that could be heard throughout the land.

In the great drama of the year the sky father or sun god now reaches manhood and this is the time of his coronation. The growing beauty of the earth maiden draws him nearer and their child enters the season of his quickening.

Litha or Mid-summer – 21 June; Summer Solstice
The longest day of the year and the mid-point of its cycle has long been one of the most significant ancient festivals. The sun or sky god reaches the apex of his power and majesty and the earth mother reaches the peak of her beauty. In many traditions this peak of life is also seen as the moment of death. This is probably the most ancient aspect of mid-summer ceremonies and is represented in the duality of the Oak King and the Holly King.

The Oak King is the ruler of the waxing year, his dark twin, the Holly King, is regent of the waning year. In many traditions mid-summer and Yule or mid-winter are the times at which the one slays the other and takes his throne only to be usurped in turn by his

reborn brother six months later. In later, more sophisticated versions the brothers grow up alongside each
other. As the Oak King reaches the peak of his maturity
at mid-summer the Holly King is still a youth. As the
power of the dark twin grows that of his light brother
diminishes until, at the autumn equinox, the dark twin
overthrows him.

This never-ending war of the light and dark brothers
is fought for the love of the earth maiden who is at her
most beautiful in this season. The union of the Holly
King and the earth maiden leads simultaneously to his
death and the rebirth of his dark brother who takes his
place.

In this way the celebration of the summer solstice
when the world is full of life becomes a celebration of
death and its twin, the winter solstice, which takes
place when the world is devoid of life, becomes a celebration of birth. Rituals to mark this event commonly
centred around a fire sacrifice of a effigy of the Oak
King and perhaps a real human. Legend and folklore
hints that in some places a king was chosen to rule for
a year on this date and that when the end of his rule
came he would fulfil his role as the Oak King and be
consigned to the flames of the mid-summer bonfire.

The fire aspect of the mid-summer took many and
varied forms. A widespread practice involved rolling a
flaming wheel down a hill. This clearly stands for the
descent of the disk of the sun in the second half of the
year and the ritual funeral burning of the Oak God at
the moment of his peak. Divination was also widely
connected with these rituals. In places it was said that
if the fire burnt out before the wheel reached the
bottom of the hill the autumn would be harsh and the
harvest poor. In Scandinavia the great mid-summer

bonfire was also used to predict the weather for the second half of the year; if the flames blew to the south the weather would be good, if they blew to the north it would be a hard winter.

The ashes of the mid-summer fire also had many uses. They were spread in the fields to increase the harvest yield, fed to cows or hens to make them produce more or rubbed on the body as a protective charm.

In Russia and eastern Europe a straw figure is placed near a felled tree which is named death or winter. The figure is carried by the villagers as they leap over the mid-summer fire and then thrown into the flames or into a river the next day. The figure is the sky father, the felled tree is the shadow of his dark twin and his sacrifice is necessary to keep the great wheel turning.

The death and sacrifice theme is still played out in folk customs all over Europe. Men or boys dressed in green are chased and led to the great fire which they have to dance around. In some places the ancient custom of the wicker man has been revived. Giant effigies of the sun god which once would have contained animal sacrifices are constructed and burned. The Burning Man festival held annually in California is perhaps the most spectacular modern interpretation of this ancient idea.

In Britain the custom of the mid-summer bonfire has survived only in a radically altered form: Bonfire or Guy Fawkes night. The burning of a straw man, the communal bonfire and even the wheel are represented but have been subverted. In the seventeenth century the Church associated this custom with the attempted bombing of Parliament by Guy Fawkes, a Catholic activist. The date was also moved to 5

November which brought it into close association with the autumn festival of *Samhain*. Essentially the church killed two birds with one stone. Both fire festivals were merged and their original meaning hidden behind anti-Catholic propaganda.

The figure of the Green Man is extremely prominent right through the medieval period in Europe. The Green Man is of course the Oak or the Holly King and may well be connected to even more ancient, pre-agrarian, deities such as the hunter god or the stag god. He is represented in carvings in countless rural churches and survives to this day in the names of old inns and pubs. The legend of Robin Hood is also thought to be associated with this powerful cultural icon. In Christian myth he is the rustic John the Baptist and the church replaced Litha with his feast day.

At this point in the story of the year the earth mother becomes the dominant figure, the sky father has served his purpose, he has impregnated her and protected her until the moment that their child is born. In a sense the child is both the fruit of the year and the sun king's dark brother who will rule in his place. The earth maiden becomes the earth mother and her child matures in the next quarter until he is cut down and consumed as the crops and the fruits of the harvest.

The Third Quarter

As the mid-point of summer passes, the year begins its long, slow decline to the depths of winter. The dead god of the sun sinks slowly into his western tomb where his wounds will heal and he will be regenerated. Although this is a time of dying it is also one of celebration as all the preparations of humans and nature reach fruition in the harvest. Themes of death and resurrection reach their peak in the festivals celebrated at this time.

Lughnasadh or Lammas – 1 August;
Cross-quarter day

In parts of Europe this date marked the beginning of the early harvest. The Christian tradition celebrates *Lammas* or "loaf mass" on this day as the first loaves of the grain harvest are baked and set on the church altar. The Celtic name *Lughnasadh* refers to the funeral games and celebrations of Lugh, the Irish sun god whose death occurred at the summer solstice six weeks earlier. In some ancient traditions the sun god will not die until the autumnal equinox and the festival becomes a premonition of his death or a celebration of the passing of his mother, who is also his wife, the earth mother.

Like the spring festivals Lammas was a date for "trial" marriages. Couples would be joined for a year and a day. If at the end of that period they decided not to continue the arrangement they would stand back to back before the assembled village and walk away from each other. If the arrangement was to their satisfaction they would be formally married from that day, later this meant having the marriage solemnized by a Christian priest. This practice is said to have survived in rural areas into the sixteenth century and is represented today by the tradition of engagement.

In medieval times Lammas was traditionally a time for craft and guild fairs. In cities and market towns the local guilds would put on displays of their wares and the streets became a riot of colour and fun. This was probably the remnant of a very ancient practice of thanking the gods not just for the harvest but for the tools that would be used to bring it in.

The tradition of rolling the burning wheel was also carried out at this time in certain parts. At this date the tradition is connected with Saint Catherine who was said by the Church to have been martyred on a wheel, although in fact her origins are pre-Christian. Even today the burning wheel is known as a Catherine Wheel. The confusion about the date of Catherine's feast day was due to the fact that it was frequently moved by the Church who were never really comfortable with the pagan symbolism she invoked.

Some interpretations of the year cycle see this as the moment when the sun god enters his old age and his dark twin leaves his childhood and becomes an adult. The struggle for the throne of the sky begins in earnest. This is also the time of the birth pangs of the earth mother. She is beginning to bear the fruit of the year, a process that will continue until the great autumn festival of Samhain. As she produces the food that will keep people alive through the dark reign of the winter sun she weakens.

Mabon or Michaelmas – 21–25 September; Autumnal Equinox

Like the vernal equinox this day was seen as a day of balance. Once again the power of light and dark are exactly equal but this time it is the darkness that is strengthening and the light which is failing. It is the date for celebrating the fruits of the harvest and the good works of the year.

An extremely popular and well-known folklore figure connected with this time of the year is John Barleycorn. In medieval times the story of his birth, growth and death was the inspiration for songs, poems and plays. He represents the folk memory of the pagan gods of the sun and of vegetation. John Barleycorn grows up strong and tall in the fields. Then he is cut down and murdered and his life blood is drunk by his killers. For six long months he lies in his tomb until he begins to come to life again and returns to the fields. In later traditions the life blood of John Barleycorn was identified with whiskey, originally it would have been all the good things of the harvest.

The gathering of seeds as well as fruits is an important aspect of this time of year. In order for the vegetation god to be reborn the following year his body – his seeds – must be carefully stored away for the winter. Grain stores were effectively the tombs of the vegetable god and there are many folk customs connecting the two. Protecting the grain store from the elements and from wild animals was just as important as protecting the dead from these things. Charms and rituals designed to do one job also served to do the other. In Christian times the priest would bless the grain store just as fervently as he would bless the dead – the survival of the whole community depended on it.

Certain Celtic myths tie this date in with the eternal struggle between the light and the dark sky gods. This is the date on which the light god is vulnerable. His twin now equals him in strength and, on the following day, defeats him in battle and takes his throne. The dark or horned god now takes his brother's wife, the earth mother, and impregnates her. His son, who is really another incarnation of himself, will be born nine months later on the summer solstice and will grow to maturity in time to defeat the light god once again at the next autumnal equinox.

The death of the light king was sometimes commemorated using the last sheaf of wheat to be cut in the fields. The stalks were woven into a human shape and then processed through the village before being cast onto a fire or thrown into a river that would carry the god to the underworld in the west. These mock sacrifices were probably the origin of the myth that the Celts of northern Europe made real human sacrifices. The only evidence for this comes from Roman accounts written during the conquests of Julius Caesar. Almost certainly these were propaganda and tall tales woven around the sacrifice of the wicker or straw man at the end of the harvest.

Medieval troupes of travelling players often put on performances of miracle plays known as *Rise up Jack's* at this time of year. Closely connected with the John Barleycorn legend they told the story of a strong young man who is murdered and then brought back to life by a mysterious doctor who has travelled in foreign lands. The murdered Jack is clearly an amalgam of the old sun god and Christ, the doctor can be seen as a priest or even as the ancient figure of the shaman who mediated between the world of the gods and the world of the human.

The Fourth Quarter

The last quarter of the year was a struggle for survival in the ancient world. The days were short and dark, the only food available was that which had been stored from the harvest. The dark lord's reign grew stronger and more bitter by the day and the beautiful mother earth was transformed into the withered crone. Unsurprisingly this is the season of the greatest festivals of the pagan calendar; above all people craved joy and light in the season of darkness and dreariness.

Samhain or Halloween – 31 October;
Cross-quarter day

Perhaps the greatest of the ancient feast days, *Samhain* is the only one that has retained much of its pagan flavour into the modern era. Not only is it regarded as the night on which spirits and ghosts of all kinds walk the earth, it has even retained the memory that the festival should be held on the night before the cross-quarter day – the Celts measured days from sunset to sunset.

Samhain marked not just the end of autumn and the beginning of winters: it was also the Celtic new year. Just as ancient tradition saw the day beginning with darkness and moving into light it saw the year in the same way. It is partly the significance of this event, the resetting of the great wheel of the year, that made the festival so important.

The tradition of the dark king and light king myth marks this day as the day on which the light king is buried and the dark king ascends his throne. But before power is transferred there is a day of chaos and misrule. At the opposite end of the year, Beltane, there is a relaxation of moral rules, at Samhain there is a relaxation of the rules regarding the dead. The veil between the living world and the world of the dead is drawn aside for one night and the denizens of each can intermingle.

In the Christian calendar this tradition is recognized by the festival of All Hallows Eve, from which we get the modern word Halloween. This was a festival to commemorate the dead of the parish and the martyrdom of the saints. The Church certainly didn't admit that the dead could return on this night but, by keeping the significance of the date alive, they unwittingly preserved this aspect of the festival as well.

Gods associated with this date tend to be two-faced. One face looks towards the departing year and commemorates what is dead, the other face looks to the coming year and celebrates what is to come. No doubt these idols were set up in doorways and at boundaries to amplify the symbolism. These two themes of celebrating the dead and peering into the future are entwined in both ancient and modern customs.

In many cultures it was believed that the dead were free to revisit their families on this night, a prospect of mixed trepidation and joy. Extra places were traditionally laid at the feast for people who had died in the past year but care was also taken to ensure that the dead returned to their realm when the night was over. In many places candles or avenues of lanterns were placed leading to the graveyards so that the dead would be drawn back there after their night of freedom.

The modern custom of the Jack o' Lantern is a direct descendent of this practice. Lanterns were used to greet and guide dead family members who might be returning and to entice them back to their graves. The tradition of carving a frightening face into the lantern is thought to have been a form of protection against less friendly spirits who might be abroad on Samhain night.

The Celts of Ireland traditionally opened the tombs of the dead and lit them with lanterns on this date. Their mythology is full of tales of brave heroes who ventured into the underworld on this night to learn its secrets or to plunder the wealth of the dead. In all such stories it was essential that they return to the world of the living before the first cockerel crowed the following dawn. The crowing of the cockerel was regarded in many places as a force that evil spirits and the dead could not oppose. Its sound would drive them back to the underworld.

The nature of Samhain as a night somehow outside of time made it the perfect moment for divination of the future. Folklore from the Middle Ages clearly retains elements of this ancient tradition. Most popular forms of divination concern love and marriage. On this night young girls would carry out all kinds of rituals to divine the name of their future husbands. Apple peel taken from the apple in one strip and cast over the shoulder was expected to spell the initial of the future suitor. Nuts placed on the stove could also reveal his identity or intentions depending on whether they exploded and flew off or simply cracked and burned. Other methods commonly involved mirrors and the ashes of the hearth fire.

Although clearly the product of a much later age these frivolous folk myths preserved the ancient notion that divination carried out on this night was more powerful than at any other time. Other modern customs of the period such as bobbing for apples and dressing up in costume probably also have very ancient roots.

The tradition of bobbing for apples in which a person has to try and retrieve apples from a bowl full of water using only his or her mouth has striking similarities with Celtic initiation rites which may have taken place at this time of year. Like the Christians after them the Celts used immersion in water to symbolize the spirit of the god entering the body. The bowl of water itself is also packed with symbolism. Celtic myths mention sacred cauldrons of regeneration that symbolized the womb of the earth mother, the apples are symbolic autumn fruits and the fact that somebody playing this game has to hold their breath can be seen as symbolic of going into the world of the dead and then re-emerging fighting for air.

The custom of trick-or-treating also has a long history. Villagers dressed themselves up to resemble the spirits of the dead and went from door to door. If they were not given a treat, usually of the alcoholic variety, they would do some mischief to the household. This practice can be traced from the days when it was believed that the dead really walked abroad on this night. Offerings of food or drink could prevent them from bringing harm to the household. In many places dressing up meant cross-dressing, the men would dress as women and the women as men, another aspect of the chaos or misrule of the day.

In terms of the great drama of the year Samhain is almost the closing act. The lord of darkness is firmly established in his throne after this day and the sun god weakens as he retreats towards the west. This is also the moment when the earth goddess takes on her third aspect, the hag or the crone. Her fertility is all used up and she nurtures only the dark child that will be next year's lord of the dark. Crops not gathered in from the fields before Samhain were considered tainted and taboo. They would be left to rot where they stood as an offering to the dark lord. Even if the harvest had been small, to try and gather these poisoned crops would have been inviting ill fortune and the wrath of the dark one.

Yule or Christmas – 21–25 December;
Winter Solstice

Although of lesser importance than Samhain in the ancient calendar Yule has become the dominant festival of the Christian year. As such it has taken over not only the meanings of the pagan festival held at the lowest point of the year but has also come to incorporate important elements of other ancient festivals. Because it is the season that marks the end of one year and the beginning of the new it has attracted much of the symbolism that used to belong to Samhain, the Celtic new year.

To the Christian the most important aspect of Christmas is of course that it celebrated the birth of Christ. There is no historical evidence that Christ was born at this time of year, if he existed at all, but by placing his birth date on top of the ancient festival of the winter solstice the Christian Church associated their saviour with the saviour of the pagan faith – the reborn sun god. Like the traditional dates of other festivals, Christmas Day has slipped from its astronomical basis by a few days. In some Christian countries celebrations are held on the 24th, in others it's the 25th.

Ancient and Christian traditions are very difficult to unravel at this time of year. The connection between the birth of Christ and the rebirth of the light twin aspect of the sun god is clearly central to the story. The solstice marks the lowest point that the sun reaches in the sky. The day is at its shortest and the night at its longest; in northern parts of Scandinavia the sun almost disappears altogether and there is a full day of darkness. This was such a powerful experience for northern Europeans that it became embodied in their myth of the end of the world when the sky wolf would finally catch and swallow the sun forever.

The solstice is the moment when the power of the dark god reaches its peak and, just as the summer solstice was for the light god, it also contains the seed of his eventual downfall. At the moment his power reaches the point where it seems that the day will be banished forever, the sun god is reborn and begins to grow a little in strength with every passing day. In three months' time he will be equal in strength to his dark twin and will take the throne again.

The word *Yule* comes from the Anglo Saxon *iul* meaning wheel. This is the great wheel that symbolizes the turning of the year. For the Celts the year had already begun six weeks before but the solstice was an appropriate moment to recognize the great wheel for them as well. For Celtic priests the midwinter solstice was the time to gather sacred mistletoe which had many magical uses and was a symbol of fertility lying dormant in the land.

The tradition survived in the custom of decorating houses with holly, ivy and mistletoe. It was considered bad luck for these decorations to be still in place by Candlemas, the cross-quarter festival of Imbolc, which was the time for cleaning out the old and preparing for the new. As with most festivals a bonfire was of central importance. Not only did it cheer people up in the midwinter season it invited the return of the sun and showed defiance to the dark lord whose power was broken on this night.

Another custom that owes its origins to pagan ways is that of wassailing. In certain parts of Europe, particularly those that grow fruit, the trees are serenaded on the winter solstice by the rowdy shouts and songs of drunken villagers. Cider or ale may also be poured over the roots. The idea is to wake the tree up and let it know that the sun is on its way back.

Bonfire tradition survives in the shape of the Yule log which was traditionally burnt in Christian households right up until the twentieth century. Often a piece of the log would be kept over to kindle the next year's Yule fire.

The earth mother takes on her most terrifying form in this season. She is the wicked snow queen of a thousand fairy tales, the hag with withered limbs and the bringer of death cloaked in a white mantle. Nevertheless, it is at this moment that she gives birth to the sun king.

Much of the modern customs of overeating and drinking during the Christmas and New Year season can be traced to the influence of Roman culture. *Saturnalia* was the Roman festival held for twelve days in honour of the god Saturn. In the early days of the Roman religion Saturn was a dark and forbidding god, the southern European equivalent of the northern dark sun twin. By the time of the early Empire when Roman culture began to spread across Europe, Saturn was seen more as a god of decadence and misrule.

Perhaps the oddest figure to have been adopted by Christianity is the old man known variously as Santa Claus, Father Christmas or Saint Nicholas. He is the embodiment of the spirit of jollity and the dark god of the woods rolled into one – his cloak is red because it is soaked in blood. Yet he is also the spirit of giving and sharing. In the harsh mid-winter when survival was a struggle, sharing food and making sure that everyone had enough to eat was vital to the survival of the tribe as a whole.

From this point the wheel of the year begins its cycle all over again. Surviving symbols of the old ways remain in surprising abundance in modern culture. On New Year's Eve the image of an old man as the old year and a baby as the new can be seen in everything from newspaper cartoons to greetings cards. The Christmas tree is a combination of the Yule log tradition and a recognition of the dark god of the woods. Years ago people placed the figure of a witch at the top of the tree – the earth mother in her guise as the hag. The tradition of placing a star or a candle at the top of the tree is clearly symbolic of the young sun king who is born on this day.

Mythic Quests and Stories

Mythology

Many of the themes that have emerged in the course of this book can be found enshrined in myths and legends. Every culture in the history of the world has produced myths and legends, our own included. In the days before written languages were invented cultures relied on a tradition of oral storytelling to pass knowledge from one generation to the next. An important part of this knowledge was the role of the gods in the history and future of the world.

For millennia, stories have been a crucial element in holding cultures together. A group of people who do not share the same myths and stories are not a culture at all, stories are one of the defining features of any civilization. For most of the Christian era this tradition of oral storytelling remained vital since the vast majority of people could not read. For the best part of 2000 years Christians have only known the central myths of their faith second-hand.

Even today when literacy is almost universal in the Western world few people have read the original versions of the stories that lie at the heart of the

Christian rooted culture, and yet everybody knows them. The story of the life of Christ, his miraculous birth, his miracles and his death are common currency in the West.

Stories have two amazing qualities. They make things much easier to remember and they can convey subtle meanings that are beyond the reach of mere lists. For example any medieval peasant could easily have recited Christ's family tree and listed his disciples. This wasn't because they had learned them by rote but because since the moment they were old enough to attend church they had been hearing stories about them. Placed in the context of human interactions and narrative drama, events and names become a whole lot easier to recall. Every British school child knows the date 1066 because it is connected to a memorable story.

The ancients used exactly the same methods to ensure that knowledge of the doings and origins of the gods was kept alive down the centuries. The stories differ wildly in their details from age to age but they all have common elements and deal with the same perennial themes. The most prominent of these themes are the journey of the soul, the origin of the world and humans, the ending of the world and the aspects of the universal god of the sky and the universal goddess of the earth.

The Death of the Sun God

Probably the clearest and most satisfying myth about the death of the sun god whose aspects were celebrated at the winter and summer solstices is the ancient Nordic myth of Balder the beautiful.

The Tale of Balder the Beautiful

Balder, god of the sun, was the son of the Nordic over-lord of the gods Odin and his wife the all-seeing Frigg. He had a twin brother named Höd who was blind and a beautiful wife named Nanna, goddess of the moon. Since the moment of his birth Balder had been the delight of Asgard, the realm of the Norse gods. His beauty and his radiant smile gladdened the hearts of everyone. It was said that he had runes carved into his tongue that enabled him to charm anyone and that he sang wonderfully. Not only was he beautiful and cheerful he was also strong and brave, the perfect warrior.

One day the gods were distressed to find Balder sitting silently with a frowning aspect. His mother, Frigg, asked what the matter was and he told her that he had been having terrible dreams in which he saw himself murdered and banished to Hel, the cheerless realm of the dead. The gods were horrified, they knew that dreams of this kind could only mean that sadness was ahead. So beloved was Balder that a great council was held to decide what should be done to protect him from the evil fate that apparently awaited him.

Before Odin took his seat at the head of the council he climbed to his throne in his mighty watchtower that looked out across the whole world to look for evil omens. In every realm of the earth Odin observed calm and nothing out of place. Finally he turned his gaze to the subterranean halls of the Kingdom of Hel and saw that they had been swept, and decorated with terrible and dark symbols. The tables had been cleared for a feast and two thrones had been set at the right and left

The Norse god, Odin.

hand of the throne of Hel herself. Odin could see that important guests were expected in the underworld and very much feared that one of them might be his favourite son.

Odin kept his dark forbodings to himself and convened the council of the gods. After days and nights of debate it was decided that a promise would be demanded from everything in the world that it would never harm Balder. Frigg sent her messengers forth to every corner of creation to gather the promises. Everything loved Balder so the promises were easy to gather. Fire and water promised never to harm the god, every animal on the land, every bird in the air and every fish in the sea promised not to harm him. The trees, the plants and the flowers, the sicknesses and the plagues and even every stone, metal and clod of earth promised that no harm would come to Balder through their action.

Within a short time the messengers returned and Asgard rejoiced to hear that everything in the world had made the promise. Frigg, Balder's mother, was particularly relieved. Although she had the power to see into the future the one thing she was not allowed to see was the fate of her son. Even Odin allowed himself to believe that disaster had been diverted, despite the preparations he had seen in the halls of Hel. One god, who had not been present at the council and who habitually kept apart from the others did not rejoice at the news. He was Loki, god of mischief and evil deeds.

Loki had always been jealous of Balder and longed for his death. As one of his aspects was the god of fire he was necessary and tolerated but men and gods had always loved Balder, the sun god, more. Loki's sister was Hel of the underworld and he had told her to prepare for the arrival of Balder. He had evil plans to finally do away with his bright rival.

Once the promises had been received the gods decided to test their efficacy. First Balder's wife pricked him gently with the finest of needles to see if he would be harmed; the needle refused to enter the sun god's glowing skin no matter how hard she tried to force it in. Next the gods tossed tiny pebbles at Balder to see if he would be bruised; the pebbles turned aside and fell harmlessly at his feet. Next they tried to tie a rope around his neck to see if he could be strangled; the rope refused to knot and frayed into pieces. Finally the warlike god of thunder Thor tried to strike Balder with his death-dealing hammer; it turned aside despite his best attempts.

Soon this became a sport among the gods. All manner of weapons and deadly influences were hurled at the god who stood and laughed as they clattered to the ground without even touching the lightest hair on his skin. Loki, who had the power to take on any shape, saw his chance and approached Frigg in the guise of a bent old woman.

Loki asked the goddess why the other gods were attempting to harm her son while she sat by and did nothing. Frigg explained about the promises that had been obtained from everything on the earth. Loki pressed her further "Was nothing forgotten?" he asked. Frigg replied that indeed nothing had been forgotten but that one thing had not been asked to swear. "What would that one thing be?" inquired Loki. The goddess explained that she herself had gone to ask the promise of the mistletoe that grew on the oak tree in the courtyard of Asgard. When she saw how frail and tender it was, however, and noticed that it had to cling to the strength of the tree for its very survival she felt that there was no need to demand the promise and she left it in peace.

Loki crept out of the hall, reassumed his own shape and hurried to the courtyard. He plucked the tender shoot of mistletoe from the tree and took it to his secret den where, using magic, he fashioned it into the head of an arrow. Always one to get others to do his dirty work Loki settled on a cruel plan. He returned to the court where the gods were still engaged in the sport of trying to harm Balder and approached Höd, the sun god's blind brother. Disguising his voice he whispered in his ear "Why do you not take part in the sport? You should honour your brother's gift as the other gods do". Höd replied bitterly that he longed to take part but that since he was blind he could not. Loki handed him a bow fitted with the deadly arrow and whispered that he would help him take aim.

Enthusiastically Höd took the bow and all the gods stood back to watch. Loki guided his elbow as he drew the bow and let the arrow fly. It pierced Balder through the heart and his laughter ceased. The company of gods fell into silence as Balder sank to the floor and his blood flowed across the floor. Höd wondered at the silence and called out to know what had happened. The only reply was the sound of swords being drawn as the company advanced towards him. Realizing what he had done Höd brought down a darkness to hide himself and fled from Asgard never to return. Wrung with regret and fear he took to hiding in the great forest ever listening for the sound of his pursuers.

Loki was triumphant, his laughter was the only

sound that could be heard above the weeping and wailing of Frigg and Nanna. Frigg cried out for a messenger to go to the halls of Hel and ask for the return of her son. Helmod the messenger stepped forward and said that he would make the perilous journey. For nine days he rode across a world in darkness filled with the lamentation of every living thing until he reached the land of Niflheim and the halls of Hel.

Meanwhile Balder's body was taken to the sea and placed in a great boat stacked with firewood. All the gods and representatives of every living thing placed gifts and offerings on the boat until it glittered with gold and precious gems. Nanna could bear the heartache no longer and she collapsed in a death swoon. Her body was placed beside that of her husband. Odin was the last to present his gift, he placed a magical ring on his son's finger and knelt down to whisper in his ear. It is said that only at the last moment before the world is destroyed will it be known what Odin said to his dead son.

The boat was so laden with gifts that the gods couldn't push it into the sea and a host of giants had to be fetched to perform the task. As the sad cargo drifted out towards the West, Odin cast a burning torch into the vessel and the bodies of Balder and his wife were consumed by the flames.

In Neflheim the messenger Helmod finally approached the dread throne of the queen of the underworld. Even here the weeping of the world could be heard and the shade spirits of Balder and Nanna sat pale and motionless at the great feast table. Helmod begged Hel to allow Balder and his wife to return to the world of life. Hel replied that she would allow

Balder to return if every living thing on earth would mourn him. Helmod was overjoyed since he knew that every living thing had loved Balder and he had heard their weeping as he had crossed the earth. Before he left, Helmod took the magical ring from Balder's lifeless finger so that Odin could present it to his son again when he returned to life.

Once again Frigg's messengers were sent out across the world, Helmod chief among them. Within a short time they had questioned every living thing and heard that all wished for Balder to return. As the last messenger was returning to Asgard he passed a cave that he did not recognize and decided to check that no one was living inside who may have been missed. Inside the cave the messenger found an old and hideous giantess named Thökk who had never seen the light of day. "Weep for Balder. Why should I weep for Balder?" she cried "He has done nothing for me – let Hel keep what is hers".

With a heavy heart the messenger had to return to Asgard and tell the gods that this one unnatural creature alone among every living thing on the earth had refused to mourn Balder. Hel refused to release Balder and the gods were distraught. Odin became suspicious when he heard that the old giantess had never seen the light of day since he knew that all living things need the sunshine. He descended to the lair of Loki and caught him in the act of transforming from the shape of Thökk back into his own form. The final treachery was revealed.

The gods finally lost patience with Loki for his double deception and he was taken to a cavern deep in the earth and bound to a rock. A giant snake was coiled around his body that dripped agonizing venom onto his face. It is said that Loki will remain in his horrible prison until the end of the world when great convulsions of the earth will finally free him and he will lead the forces of darkness in the final battle, Ragnarok.

Time passed and the death of Balder went unavenged. Then, one day, a bold and beautiful youth arrived at Asgard and demanded to see Odin. He was admitted to the chambers where all celebration and joy had long since ceased and his fairness and cheer caused amazement. Approaching Odin he kneeled and said simply "I am awaited". A strange smile came over the old god's face and he replied, "Go with my blessing, you know your task".

The mysterious youth rose and strode out of the hall. After days and nights of tireless walking he reached the forest where Balder's blind brother Höd was still hiding. Höd heard the youth coming and guessed his purpose but he had become tired of his miserable life and did not attempt to run away. Instead he stood his ground and the youth struck him dead with one blow.

When Höd arrived in the land of the dead Hel was astonished at his resemblance to his twin brother and questioned him. Höd explained Loki's treachery and the misery that now presided on the earth and even Hel was moved by the tale. Recognizing that Höd was as much a victim as his brother she decreed that each one of them would be allowed to return to the world of the living for half of the year in turn. While Balder was on earth the world would enjoy pleasure and warmth. While Höd was on earth all living things would endure cold and hardship that would remind them of the death of Balder. All the gods and the living things of the world rejoiced, although they knew that things would never be as they had before. The twilight of the gods had begun.

The myth of Balder is one of the most powerful and meaningful of all Norse tales, it is central to their view of the universe. The symbolism of Balder and his blind brother is clear. Balder is the sun of summer who was celebrated by ancient peoples at the festival of the midsummer solstice. Höd, his blind and melancholy twin, is the dark god who reigns in the winter season. As in the symbolism of the festivals the dark god kills the light. The youth who appears mysteriously in Asgard is of course Balder himself reborn. He in turn slays the dark god and Balder is returned to the earth for six months. The word that Odin whispered in his ear? "Reincarnation".

Balder was just one of many incarnations of the sun god found in ancient cultures. Another tale that has a lot of similarities with the Balder myth is the classical Roman and Greek story of the death of Adonis. The mythologies of this period were far more sophisticated than those of the Norse peoples. The original symbolism of many of its figures had largely been lost under layers of soap-opera about the daily lives and loves of the gods and goddesses. The youth Adonis is in fact an aspect of the sun god Apollo who probably originally played his part in the drama.

The Legend of Adonis
Aphrodite the fairest of the goddesses and the champion of love and desire was walking through a wood one day when she came upon tree that had been split in half by a bolt of lightning. Lying between in the

middle of its split trunk was a beautiful baby boy whom she decided to rescue and raise.

Unfortunately Aphrodite was too busy meddling in the affairs of mortals to have time for the child so she left it with her sister Persephone, who ruled the under-world alongside the dark god Hades.

Time passed in the world of the gods and many years in terms of the world of men so that when Aphrodite returned to see the child he had grown into a young man. Adonis, as he had been named, was the most beautiful mortal male that had ever been born. He was also the most skilled hunter among mortals and cared much more for chasing boar than for chasing girls. Aphrodite fell in love with him the moment she saw him and demanded that her sister return him. Unfortunately Persephone loved the boy as her son by this time and refused to hand him over.

Aphrodite was forced to retreat but she lost her will to live and took to pining in dark wooded glades. The world of men soon began to notice her absence as love went out of the world and men and women turned against each other. Aphrodite pursued Adonis and begged him to love her but even her supernatural beauty could not turn his head from the hunt.

One day as the goddess was sitting at the feet of Adonis who was resting after a hunt she asked him what he intended to do the next day. Adonis became tremendously excited and told her that he had heard about the largest, oldest and fiercest boar in the world and that he intended to set out in pursuit. Aphrodite knew full well that this boar was the aspect of a dark forest god that had already slain countless hunters and she begged Adonis not to go. Adonis became angry and told her that her beauty and love were nothing beside the thrill of the chase.

The next day, before dawn, Adonis set out with his spear in his hand. Just as the sun was rising Aphrodite was awoken by a dreadful baying of hounds and the cry of voices. She rushed into the forest fearing that the worst had already happened.

Adonis had travelled far with his swift stride and it took Aphrodite a long time to reach the hunt. As she got closer she observed the bodies of hounds that had been torn apart by the mighty boar and strewn around the forest floor. She hurried on and soon came across the mangled bodies of men, Adonis's companions, who had met the same fate. Now frantic she rushed into a forest clearing and saw the huge boar and Adonis facing each other. The boar leapt at the hunter who cast his spear deep into its belly, but the blow came too late. As the boar fell its mighty tusk pierced Adonis's side and he fell to the ground dead.

Aphrodite's cries of anguish were so loud that they awoke Zeus, king of the gods and Aphrodite's father, who rushed to find out what ailed his daughter. Aphrodite begged her father to return Adonis to life but the old god could not meddle in the fate of a mortal so directly. Next she begged that she be allowed to live with him in the dark realm of Hades but Zeus could not allow love and beauty to go out of the world.

Zeus consulted Persephone, who was overjoyed that her adopted son had returned to her realm. When she heard about her sister's anguish she was moved and proclaimed that Adonis would be free to roam the world of the living, but only for six months of the year. The other half of the year he must spend in the underworld. Zeus told Aphrodite about the arrangement and the goddess was consoled.

The next spring Adonis was reborn and love and beauty returned to the world until he was called back to the underworld. In the season that he was away Aphrodite would return to her pining and beauty would fade.

The theme of the death of the sun god is less easy to trace in the Adonis legend but it is discernible. Adonis's beauty and virility are clearly symbolic of his status as the ancient god of light, even though he is represented as a mortal. The dread boar that lives in the dark forests plays the role of his dark nemesis; both kill each other simultaneously, although in some versions the boar is not killed until Adonis returns from the underworld to hunt it with renewed vigour the following year.

Another element that is introduced in this tale is the close connection between the sun god and the earth goddess – Aphrodite was originally a fertility goddess above all else. This theme is much more explicit in the earlier Babylonian myth of Ishtar and Tammuz which was clearly the original template for the tale.

Ishtar and Tammuz

Ishtar was the queen of the earth in the Babylonian version and Tammuz, her husband was the brightest and most beautiful god of the fields. Tammuz is murdered by jealous peasants who hacked his body to pieces with scythes and ground his bones to make bread. Hearing of the death of her beloved husband, Ishtar is distraught and decides to travel to Irkalla, the land of the dead, to retrieve him.

As she approaches Irkalla her sister Erishkigal, who

rules over the underworld, notices her and fears that she has come to take her throne. As a precaution she instructs the demons that guarded the seven gates of her realm not to let Ishtar in.

As Ishtar approaches the first gate her way is barred by a huge and fierce demon. She removes the crown from her head and gives it to the demon as a bribe and he lets her pass safe in the knowledge that the six other demons beyond him will keep her out. At the next gate she hands over the rings from her fingers and is allowed to pass once again.

By the time Ishtar reaches the last gate she has given away all of her fabulous jewels and had nothing but her finely embroidered gown. The seventh demon is unwilling to accept it as a bribe because he knows that his mistress will be angry if he lets her in. But, as Ishtar removes her gown, the demon is blinded by her unveiled beauty and she is able to slip past him.

Naked and powerless before her sister, Ishtar begs for the return of her husband. Seeing her powerlessness the wicked Erishkigal imprisons her and impales her on a stake. The world sinks into melancholy and life begins to fade with the mother goddess absent. Eventually the other gods, fearing that the world will come to an end, manage to rescue her – but at a price. The old deal is made, Tammuz can return to the earth, but only for six months of the year.

The Mourning of the Earth Mother

Tales about the seasons fall into two broad categories. We have already seen how the mythical death and annual resurrection of the sun god is represented by a duel between a light and a dark twin. The fertility of the earth is clearly linked to this cycle. The bareness of the winter months is seen as the earth goddess in mourning for her dead consort, the sun. She takes the form of Aphrodite in the Greek myth and of Ishtar in the Babylonian.

The second strand of such myths puts the earth mother in a more central role. In the Greek myth of Demeter and Persephone winter is the time when the earth goddess mourns for the death of her daughter, the goddess of the spring. These myths tend also to be connected with the origins of agricultural knowledge among mortals. Once winter makes its entrance into the world, the gods feel it is their duty to provide people with a means of survival. This can be seen clearly in the North American Native myth of Wunzh and the god of the corn.

The Abduction of Persephone

Once, when the human race was young and the gods spent much of their time on the fair earth, there were no seasons and no hardships. Demeter, the earth goddess who brought life to all things, worked tirelessly and the world bloomed and was blessed with prodigious cereal and fruit crops that grew without the need for human intervention.

Demeter gave birth to a daughter whom she named Persephone. This child was the fairest and freshest of young women. She resembled her mother in beauty but had also the lightness and paleness of youth. Demeter saw her daughter growing into a fine young woman and saw how much she loved the earth and especially the fairest and tenderest flowers. Demeter decided to give the care of these plants over to her daughter who was delighted to receive it.

One day, being young and not yet fully aware of her responsibilities, Persephone grew bored of the constant work and decided to take a rest in the flower meadows of her favourite place, the island of Sicily. With her troupe of nymphs she spent many happy hours wandering through the meadows and picking the brightest flowers to wind into her hair. Lying down to rest in the grass Persephone saw the most beautiful lily that she had ever set eyes on and reached out to pick it. The very instant that her fingers touched its petals, however, there was a terrible rending roar and the earth split open beneath her.

The lily slipped from Persephone's grasp as she plummeted into the gaping chasm that had opened up beneath her. The terrified goddess let out a cry as she saw the rend closing above her head and she continued to fall in darkness. Eventually, after what seemed an eternity of falling, she perceived a dim light and was caught by the massive, strong arms of a figure who stood waiting at the bottom of the immense chasm. Looking into his dark face and his cold eyes she knew that he could be no other than Hades, lord of the underworld and that there could be no escape from his grasp.

Hades was mightily pleased with his prize. For a long time he had wanted a wife to relieve the darkness of his realm but he had been rebuffed by all the goddesses who had no wish to be taken from the bright realms of the earth above. Since the day Persephone had been born Hades had picked her out and waited until she was away from the protection of her powerful mother. Tired of being turned down, the dread god of death and darkness had decided to kidnap her by force. As he had seen her reach for the most beautiful lily in the field the temptation had become too much and Hades had split open the earth to bring her to him.

The cry of dismay that Persephone had uttered as she fell into the earth eventually reached the ears of her mother who rushed to find out what was the matter. Demeter searched the island but could see no trace of her daughter. Eventually she came to the spot where her daughter had been abducted. The chasm had long since been closed but Demeter saw the same lily that Persephone had seen and knelt down to look at it more closely. When she saw how tender and perfect it was she feared that her daughter had been transformed into the exquisite blossom by some malign entity.

For days and nights Demeter stayed kneeling beside the lily. All her love and attention was focused on it and every other plant and flower on the world began to wither and die without her care. Eventually her tears flowed into the waters of a little stream that ran through the meadow and woke the spirit of its guardian nymph who emerged from the waters and spoke to Demeter. "Why do you neglect the earth and allow all the flowers and plants to die?" asked the nymph. Demeter told her that she feared her daughter had been transformed into a lily and that she no longer cared for anything else but this one blossom.

The nymph of the stream, whose course took her beneath the earth and through the kingdom of Hades, was able to tell Demeter what had really happened to her daughter. She told Demeter that she had seen Persephone sitting beside Hades in his underworld caverns and had wondered why she was there so far from the fields that she loved.

Demeter flew into a towering rage when she learned what had happened and rushed straight to the throne of Zeus himself, ruler of the gods. There she explained her story and demanded that Persephone be returned to her. Zeus was unwilling to help since he knew that the abduction of Persephone by his brother Hades had been fated since the beginning of time. Demeter was persistent and eventually extracted a promise from Zeus that her daughter would be returned as long as no morsel of food had passed her lips during her stay in the underworld. Demeter was overjoyed since she was sure that Persephone would have been too sad to eat and she set off on the long journey to the under-world to reclaim her daughter.

In the meantime Zeus sent his swiftest messenger to inform his brother Hades of the deal he had just made with Demeter. Hades had long expected that Demeter would come for her daughter and was prepared. Persephone had not touched a morsel of food, just as her mother had thought she would not, but now Hades offered her a sweet and juicy pomegranate. The luscious ripe fruit reminded Persephone sorely of her mother and she longed to take a bite, but she knew that accepting food from Hades would tie her to his kingdom forever. Hades went away and left the fruit and Persephone could resist it no longer since she had lost hope that she would see the sunny world again. Taking one delicate bite she swallowed four seeds of the sweet fruit.

When Demeter triumphantly stormed into Hades' hall she was dismayed to find the dark lord holding the pomegranate with the tiny bite taken out of it.

Demeter knew that bite out of the sacred fruit, the symbol of love and fertility, meant that a part of Persephone's heart belonged forever to the dark lord. Nevertheless she pleaded for the return of her daughter and appealed to Zeus saying that she could no longer care for the plants of the earth as long as her daughter remained in the underworld. Zeus, seeing that this was true, decreed that Persephone should spend four months of the year with Hades, one month for every seed she had swallowed, and the rest of the year with her mother.

Seeing that this was just and that her daughter had clearly developed a love for Hades, Demeter had no choice but to accept. From that time onwards Demeter went into mourning for the four months that her daughter was away with her dark husband and all the plants died in that time only to be reborn when Persephone returned to the earth as the radiant spring.

In one version of this tale Demeter spends many years searching for Persephone before Apollo, god of the sun who sees all things that happen in the daylight, tells her where she is. During this time Demeter wanders the world in the guise of an old crone, the withered and wasted aspect of the earth mother familiar from winter festivals. During her travels she visits Eleusis, which is ruled over by the wise king Celeus.

In the king's palace she is greeted kindly, although she appears to be no more than a poor old woman, and grows to love a sickly little child whom she is charged with caring for. Through this child, the son of the king whom nobody expects to live, Demeter grows to love humanity and takes pity on them for the hard-ships they are enduring now that the plants of the earth are withered and the trees bear no fruit.

Under her care the child becomes hearty and strong and grows into a fine young boy whom the king names Triptolemus. Demeter grows to love the boy so much that she decides to bestow immortality on him. She anoints him with sacred oils and lowers him into the flames of the hearth so that the mortal parts of his being will be burnt away.

At that moment the boy's mother comes in and is horrified to see the old woman lowering her son into the fire. She wrenches him away and turns on the old nurse with fury. Suddenly Demeter takes on her godly form and the mother knows who she is. Unfortunately the spell of immortality is broken and Demeter cannot rework it. Instead she decides to teach Triptolemus some of her secrets so that he will know how to culti-vate the food-bearing plants and will never starve. She gives him the first plough and teaches him the secret of the seed. She also gives him a flying chariot so that he can travel the world and teach his knowledge to all peoples.

It's a powerful evocation of the relationship between humans and the mother earth. Demeter is willing to bestow immortality on the son of man but is foiled at the last minute. Since the moment is past and humanity will now always be mortal and suffer hunger she taught him instead how to sustain himself through the winter. A very similar tale comes from the Ojibwe tribe of the Great Lakes region of North America, although here the gods tend to have male personas.

Wunzh and Mondamin, Spirit of the Corn

Once there was a poor man who lived with his wife and his five sons and five daughters in a beautiful land of lakes and mountains and forests. In the spring, the summer and the autumn the old man and his oldest sons would hunt in the forest, his younger sons would fish in the lakes and his wife and his daughters would gather fruits in the forests. In this way they had plenty to eat and lived happy lives for most of the year.

In the winter, however, the animals that the old man and his sons hunted hid beneath the mountains and could not be caught. The lakes where his younger sons fished became frozen into sheets of milky ice and the fish could not be caught. The forests where his wife and daughters gathered fruits were covered in a blanket of snow and the berries were hidden from them so that they could not be gathered. The family became sick and went hungry.

One day the old man's youngest son, whom he had named Wunzh, came to the age where he would be accepted as a man. Before this could happen Wunzh had to undertake Ke-ig-nish-im-o-win, the fast during which his spirit guide would come to him. All men must have a spirit guide who will lead them through life and protect them.

On the appointed day Wunzh set out into the woods and built a lodge in a lonely place where he would spend seven days without food and away from the company of his family. On the first day of his fast Wunzh was still full of energy and curious about the world and he set out to explore. As he walked down a forest path he was startled by a deer that leapt out of the trees in front of him. This was followed by a rabbit that ran across the path and a pigeon that flew from the branches. High above his head Wunzh heard the call of the wild goose, whom his people call Wawa, and he was struck by the bounty of the animals in the forest and was about to give thanks to the Great Spirit when he remembered how the animals hid away during the winter and his family went hungry. He prayed out loud "Why must it always be so Great Spirit, why must it always be so?"

On the second day of his fast Wunzh walked in the green valleys and along the edges of the water meadows. He noticed the berries on the bushes and the fruits on the trees and was about to give thanks for their abundance when he remembered how they were hidden by the winter snows and how his family went hungry. "Why must it always be so Great Spirit, why must it always be so?" he cried out.

On the third day of his fast Wunzh walked along the streams and beside the lakes. Suddenly a sturgeon leapt in the lake with a great splash and Wunzh paused to look into the waters. There he saw the perch and the herring and the great snapping jaws of the pike whom his people called Meskenozha. Wunzh was about to give thanks for their abundance when he remembered how the waters were frozen with milky ice in the winter and how his family went hungry. For the third time he prayed "Why must it be so Great Spirit, why must it be so?"

On the fourth day of his fast Wunzh was too tired and weak to walk so he stayed in his lodge waiting for his spirit guide to visit him. As evening came and the sun sank in the west Wunzh saw a figure coming out of the sky cloaked in the magic and mystery of the sunset. The figure came closer and Wunzh saw that he was like a man except that he had golden hair and he wore silver feathers and clothes of brightest green. The man stood before him and spoke. "The Great Spirit has heard your prayers and sent me to answer them. But first you must wrestle me to the ground to show that you are a worthy man."

Although he was faint with hunger Wunzh got to his feet and accepted the challenge. He fought well but could not overcome the spirit who seemed to have the suppleness and flexibility of a young, green branch. Finally Wunzh was cast to the ground and the visitor said "I will return tomorrow to test you again". With that the green-clad figure departed the way he came.

All the next day Wunzh rested in his lodge but nevertheless grew weaker through lack of food. At sunset the spirit from the sky returned and challenged Wunzh again. This time the spirit had the strength and solidity of the bough of a mighty tree and Wunzh could not overcome him. Although he fought well Wunzh was thrown to the ground and the stranger departed.

On the sixth day everything happened as before. This time the stranger was as elusive as the breeze in the grass and Wunzh could not lay a hand on him. As he collapsed exhausted from his labour the spirit knelt beside Wunzh and said. "Know that my name is Mondamin, the corn, and that tomorrow you will defeat me. When I am dead, strip away my garments and bury me in a place where the roots and weeds have been cleared away. After you have done that return to my grave every month and keep it cleared of weeds and grass."

On the seventh day Wunzh's father came to his son with milk and food and begged him to eat for he could see how weak the boy had become. Wunzh refused, he knew that he must wait until sundown when the stranger from the sky would come for the last time. That evening, as the sun set, Wunzh saw Mondamin approaching on the golden rays from the west and stood up to meet him. They wrestled and Mondamin was as supple as a young green branch, as strong as a mighty bough and as elusive as the breeze in the grass. Wunzh felt a mysterious new courage spring up in his heart and, with a last effort, he rushed at his foe and wrestled him to the ground.

Mondamin lay dead at Wunzh's feet and the young man was very sad since he had loved and admired his friend. Nevertheless he did as Mondamin had instructed. He stripped him of his clothes and buried him in ground that had been cleared of all roots and weeds. Then Wunzh returned to his family who held a great feast in his honour.

Wunzh did not tell his family about Mondamin but every month he returned to his grave and kept it clear of weeds and grass. The spring rains came and watered the grave and the summer sun grew stronger and stronger and beat down on the soil. The men hunted in the forest, the boys fished in the lake and the women gathered fruits in the forest and still Wunzh said nothing of his friend who lay under the earth.

Then, one day when the sun was at its strongest, Wunzh went to tend the grave of Mondamin and found a tall and green plant had sprung up from the centre of the plot. The plant had long green leaves in place of the green garments, silvery tassells in place of the silver feathers and, at its heart, a wonderful golden fruit in place of the golden hair. Wunzh recognized his friend enthusiastically and Mondamin whispered to him the secrets of how he could be made to multiply in great abundance.

Wunzh ran and fetched his father and brought him to the place. "This is my friend Mondamin whom I buried and who has been born again" he cried. "Because of him we will never be hungry again."

The Human Condition

Tales of gods and goddesses are all very well for explaining the cycles of life and death that overtake the earth, but what of the people on the earth? We are like the animals and the plants in that we too are born and die and yet, in some indefinable way, we are unlike them too. Touched by a divine spark, where did this strange creature called the human being come from and why are the fates so interested in its progress?

These questions and hints at their answers are raised in the tradition of storytelling that tells of the adventures of human heroes. The journeys of Perseus and Jason and the Argonauts, or the epic adventures of Gilgamesh or Odysseus are about the passage of the human being through life; the struggles, the triumphs, the tragedies and, above all, the inescapable fates.

One of the world's oldest and most admirable pieces of literature comes from the ancient kingdom of Babylon and is known as the *Epic of Gilgamesh*. The best-known version of this incredible tale comes from the seventh century BC, but fragments of an even older version, perhaps 4000 years old, have also been uncovered.

Gilgamesh is a superhero and a mighty king, but he is also a kind of everyman. During the course of his long life and his many adventures he faces the same dilemmas and makes the same mistakes of any mortal. Despite his power he is subject to disaster visited on him by the gods and, when he reaches for immortality, it slips out of his grasp as it must always slip out of the grasp of mortals.

The Life of Gilgamesh

Long ago in the land of Sumer there lived a great a mighty king named Gilgamesh. He was a lion of a man, stronger than any warrior, braver than any other and more handsome too. From the great and sacred city of Uruk the young Gilgamesh ruled his kingdom but, despite his beauty and courage and strength, he was not a wise man and he ruled badly. He used his power shamelessly to get wealth and he took any woman he desired.

Eventually the people grew tired of his misrule and called out to the gods, "You who made Gilgamesh, make another like him so that they may fight each other and leave us in peace". The gods heard this prayer and, seeing the opportunity for some excellent sport, went to the Great Mother Aruru and asked her to make a match for the king of Uruk.

Aruru made a man unlike any other. She made a man of equally mighty frame as Gilgamesh and of equally brave heart, but she made him more of a wild beast than a man. She named her creation Enkidu and covered him with thick hair like a beast and sent him to live in the wild places with the animals. Enkidu became the champion of the animals. He hunted with the wolves and the lions, he drank with the deer at the water holes and he guarded them on the plains.

Enkidu knew nothing of the ways of humans and despised them because they trapped the animals that he loved. When hunters dug pits he filled them in and when they spread nets he cut them so that his kindred could not be caught. So busy was Enkidu that it became impossible to hunt and the people appealed to Gilgamesh to rid them of this wild-man menace since none of them could hope to match his prodigious strength.

Gilgamesh thought of a plan to trap Enkidu. He told the people to take the most beautiful woman they could find and bring her to the water-hole where the wild man came to drink with the herds. He instructed them to strip the woman of her clothes when Enkidu arrived and to watch what happened.

The hunters were sceptical but they found a woman and took her into the barren plains where Enkidu was known to roam. They came to the watering hole and hid themselves amongst the reeds to wait for his arrival. Towards sundown the beasts began to arrive at the water-hole and among them, running on all fours, was the wild man Enkidu. Just as he was about to lower his head into the water the hunters stripped the woman naked and thrust her out into the open. Enkidu caught sight of her reflection in the water and looked up to see what manner of creature this was. When his eyes fell on her naked beauty he was immediately filled with lust and he leapt on her.

For six days and nights Enkidu satisfied his new-found hunger with the woman and at the end of that time she had complete power over him. The wild beast had become a man and was enslaved to woman. When Enkidu tried to approach his beast friends they shied away in fear as they would from any human and Enkidu was filled with fear and loneliness. Like a wounded dog he crept back to his mistress and she commanded him to go with her to the city and to think of the wilds no more. This was how Enkidu was tamed and came to the royal city of Uruk.

In the city the tamed beast-man was wondered at by the citizens. His mighty frame and prodigiously hairy body prompted many to say that he would be a match for Gilgamesh himself. When word of this reached the king's ears he proclaimed that a wrestling match would take place and that he would surely vanquish the uncouth and uncivilized wild man.

On the night before the contest Gilgamesh had a dream in which he was endlessly struggling with a man of enormous strength whom he could not vanquish but only keep at arm's length. In the morning he consulted his mother, who was a gifted seer, and she told him that the opponent he had fought in his dream was Enkidu and that he would not be able to vanquish him but that they would become as close as brothers.

The contest went just as had been foreseen. Gilgamesh and Enkidu struggled with each other from dawn to dusk and then all through the night until dawn came again but neither could master the other. Eventually both collapsed with exhaustion and embraced. The regal might of the king had not been able to overcome the raw animal strength of the wild man and each recognized themselves as half of an eternal partnership. From that day onwards Enkidu and Gilgamesh were inseparable. They fought wild animals together and travelled far and wide across the land.

One day Enkidu had a dream of his own in which a mighty eagle carried him off into the sky and then cast him into the underworld of the shades from where he would never return. Gilgamesh was afraid for his brother and asked the goddess Shamash what it meant. The question was answered with a challenge. To discover the meaning of the dream Gilgamesh would have to travel to near the ends of the world and do battle with a terrible monster known as Khumbala.

Gilgamesh set out on the journey that would take nearly two and a half years and would bring him eventually to the Cedar Mountain where Khumbala lived; by his side went Enkidu. When the pair finally arrived at the mountain they were appalled at the size of the giant Khumbala and shook with fear when they heard his roar, which was like thunder. Nevertheless Gilgamesh made his preparations for battle and asked the gods to aid him. With the help of the elements, which the gods turned against the giant, Gilgamesh triumphed and made the long journey home.

Older and wiser now Gilgamesh was greeted like the conquering hero he was and a great feast was prepared in his honour. Once his wounds had been cleaned and his hair and his beard trimmed, Gilgamesh emerged from his palace glowing like a god in the glory of his triumph. At this moment the great goddess Ishtar happened to be looking down at the earth and saw Gilgamesh shining like a god. She was immediately smitten and called out for him to become her lover.

Gilgamesh was sorely tempted by the beauty and radiance of the goddess who was all the beauty of the earth rolled into one, but he remembered what had happened to Ishtar's husband Tammuz and he refused her. The goddess was enraged to have been turned down by a mere mortal, even one as radiant with power as Gilgamesh, and she swore her revenge.

From that moment of his greatest triumph there was no escaping the evil fate that the goddess had planned for him.

First, Ishtar asked her father Anu to send the bull of heaven against Gilgamesh, which he did. The bull was a mighty and deadly beast with horns as sharp as daggers and the strength of an army. Gilgamesh was unafraid and came out to meet the bull but it soon looked as if he would be destroyed by the irresistible beast. Suddenly Enkidu leapt over the wall of the city and threw himself on the beast that was about to end the life of his brother. Summoning every ounce of his animal strength Enkidu pulled the bull of heaven apart with his bare hands and flung its skin in the face of the goddess Ishtar.

Now Ishtar was in a fury greater than ever before and she sent a plague to kill Enkidu. For twelve days and nights Enkidu clung on to life as the malady sapped his strength and wasted him away. Gilgamesh, the unconquered warrior, stayed by his side day and night but could do nothing to defend his brother against this enemy. Finally, on the twelfth night, Enkidu died and Gilgamesh fled screaming from the palace like a madman.

With the passing of Enkidu the fear of death entered Gilgamesh's heart for the first time and he longed to find an escape from its clutches. He threw aside his kingly robes, wrapped himself in animal skins and set out into the wilderness to find the secret of eternal life.

Gilgamesh resolved to travel to the Island of Paradise that lay on the other side of the great Ocean of Oblivion. There he would seek the council of Uta-Napishtim, the ancestor of all men who had survived the great flood in which the world had been drowned aeons ago. After many years of wandering he came to the very edge of the world at the Mountain of Mashu where the sun sleeps at the end of the day.

The scorpion men who guarded the entrance to the Ocean of Oblivion were so vast that their bodies spanned the gap between the heavens and the earth, but they let Gilgamesh pass, perceiving that he was nearer to a god than a man. For two days Gilgamesh travelled through the heart of the mountain and never saw the sun in all that time. Finally he emerged from beneath Mashu to find himself in a wonderful garden by the shore of the Ocean of Oblivion.

This was the paradise garden of the goddess Siduri Sabutis, known as the Guardian of the Inn. Her realm was full of earthly delights and she tempted Gilgamesh to stay with her so that he could enjoy the luxuries and pleasures that only she could provide. Once again Gilgamesh was sorely tempted. The women of the garden were the most beautiful he had ever seen, the wine was the most delicious and the fruits were the most succulent. But he knew he could never be at peace until the threat of death that hung over him was lifted and he reluctantly tore himself away to continue his quest.

Following the advice of Siduri Sabuti, Gilgamesh found the boatman Urshanabi who was the only one who knew how to cross the Ocean of Oblivion safely. To touch the waters of the ocean was to bring instant death and oblivion of the memory of life, but Gilgamesh was willing to undergo even this peril so that the threat of death might be lifted from him for eternity. The boatman told him to go into the forest and to cut down 120 trees so that he could use them as oars.

Gilgamesh gathered the tree trunks and set out across

the ocean. With every stroke he threw an oar away so that none of the water should accidentally touch his hands. In this manner he reached the Island of Paradise in safety after 120 mighty strokes. There he sought out Uta-Napishtim, who was amazed to see a living mortal in his realm.

Uta-Napishtim questioned Gilgamesh closely when he heard of his mission and said "Does a house stand forever? Does the corn in the fields grow forever? To everything there is a beginning and an end, and so it is with the life of a man". But Gilgamesh persisted and so the immortal proposed a test. "Sleep is the twin of death. If you can resist the one for six days, then perhaps there is a chance that you can resist the other." Even as he spoke Gilgamesh, exhausted after his journey across the Ocean of Oblivion, felt his eyelids growing heavy and fell into a profound sleep.

When he awoke Uta-Napishtim was gone but his wife took pity on Gilgamesh and told him about a plant that grew at the bottom of the Ocean of Oblivion. Known as Old-Man-Grows-Young this plant had the power to twist fate by restoring youth to anyone who ate its fragrant leaves. Eagerly Gilgamesh set off again. When he reached the centre of the ocean he tied rocks to his feet and plunged into its waters, which did not harm him. Gilgamesh sank to the bottom of the ocean and there he saw the plant that the immortal woman had spoken of. He tore it from the ocean bed, untied the rocks from his feet, and rose to the surface in triumph.

Gilgamesh resolved to return to his kingdom, where he had not been heard of for many years, and share this miracle with his people. During the journey he stopped by a clear spring to quench his thirst and to wash the dust from his body. Laying the magical plant on the ground he dipped his head to the water just as Enkidu had done so many years before and gulped at the pure, cool water.

As he drank a snake happened to come past and was drawn by the fragrance of the plant Old-Man-Grows-Young which she had never tasted before. Hungrily the snake chewed the plant and swallowed the whole thing. Immediately she sloughed off her skin and became reborn, an ability she passed on to all her children from that day forward. Gilgamesh looked up and saw what had happened. He grabbed for the snake, meaning to slice it open and retrieve the plant, but she was too quick and slipped out of his grasp and disappeared into a hole in the earth.

Gilgamesh had lost the prize he had sought for so long. A moment's carelessness and the greatest secret in the world was gone, all of his efforts and his trials had been for nothing. Just like his brother Enkidu, Gilgamesh knew that he too must die.

Everywhere in this tale there are compelling echoes of the human condition. Enkidu is a man born into a state of primitive innocence and happiness. When he sees the woman he is filled with lust and loses his paradise forever, just like the biblical Adam who was tempted by Eve.

Enkidu and Gilgamesh wrestle but neither can defeat the other. This is clearly because they are both aspects of the same thing, the human soul. Gilgamesh represents the finer instincts and the drive towards civilization and Enkidu is the primitive heart that cannot help but crave conflict and excitement despite their ruinous effects on peace and harmony in the world. The two become as inseparable as brothers because they are inseparable in the makeup of a human being.

In the revenge of Ishtar we see the irrevocable power of fate. Although Enkidu triumphs over the physical threat of the mighty bull of heaven both he and Gilgamesh are powerless to fend off the attack of the plague that Ishtar sends in its place. All the strength and majesty of the greatest heroes cannot stand against the will of the gods.

When death enters into the world of Gilgamesh the fear of death comes with it. The king's quest to find immortality is an inevitable consequence, as is its ultimate failure. The goddess in the garden, who represents all the good things of life, cannot persuade Gilgamesh to give up his quest and be happy with the pleasures of the earth. He cannot sit back and accept the fact of his death, fear drives him on to ever greater perils and, ultimately, disappointment.

The immortal Uta-Napishtim offers the best advice of all; if a man cannot even resist sleep when he is tired how can he hope to resist death when he lives. Some scholars interpret the last section of the epic, in which Gilgamesh dives into the Ocean of Oblivion and retrieves the plant that will give him immortality, as a dream that he has during the sleep that he cannot resist.

The Epic of Gilgamesh is a tale with many messages. It is a glimpse into the understanding of a people who lived 4000 years ago and it is striking how similar their obsessions were with our own. Above all the legend is a great story and we should not forget that great stories are one of the finer pleasures of the earthly realm. Even if Gilgamesh did not win us immortality, he left us a great story that has echoed down the millennia.

While mortal men rarely fared well at the hands of the gods mortal women often fared even worse. Greek mythology is full of tales of beautiful young maidens who are abducted and ravished by lusty gods or who become the victims of the jealousy of goddesses. The life of Gilgamesh was a tragic trial, but at least he was an active protagonist and he brought a large part of his troubles on his own head. The tale of Psyche is about the victimisation of a complete innocent.

The best known version of this myth comes from *The Golden Ass*, the second century AD Roman work by Lucius Apuleius. In the earlier Greek version Cupid, the god of sexual love, would have been known as Eros and his mother, Venus, as Aphrodite. It is interesting to note the many elements in this story that can also be found in Northern European folk tales such as "Cinderella" and "Beauty and the Beast"; the wicked sisters, the husband that cannot be looked at and the impossible tasks are perhaps the most strikingly familiar.

The Trials of Psyche

Once there was a rich and powerful king who had three daughters. All were beautiful and charming but by far the most beautiful and charming was Psyche, the youngest. Her name meant soul and she was indeed the soul of the royal palace. Her beauty delighted everybody and her wit and good humour enchanted even the animals. Her two sisters were a little jealous of their younger sibling, but Psyche was such a delightful creature that they couldn't bring themselves to bear her any malice.

As time went by Psyche grew into the fairest of all

mortal maidens and the goddess Venus came to hear of her. One night Venus parted the clouds and looked down with curiosity on the sleeping form of Psyche. Venus perceived that the girl rivalled even her own supernatural beauty and became fearful and jealous. Determining to punish the unwitting Psyche for having the impudence to outshine her, Venus sent her son Cupid on a mission of vengeance.

Cupid was ordered to wound Psyche with one of his arrows of love so that she would fall helplessly in love with the first unworthy stranger who came along and have a miserable life. Cupid descended to the earth and entered Psyche's chamber. When he perceived her beauty Cupid let out a sigh. Psyche was awoken by the sound and sat up startled. Fearfully her gaze darted around the room, but Cupid was invisible to her. Cupid was so surprised that he wounded himself with his arrow and instantly fell in love with the girl. The god determined that Psyche should be his bride but knew that if he revealed himself to her she would worship him as a god rather than love him as a man. Leaving Psyche's chamber with reluctant steps Cupid flew away to secret places to hatch a plan.

A year passed and Psyche's eldest sister was married. In another year the next sister was married, but when a third year had passed and no suitors had come forward for Psyche the king began to fear that the gods were meddling. The king decided to consult a famous oracle who had bitter news for him. The oracle told the king that the gods had ordained that Psyche would never have a human husband. She advised that the girl should be dressed in the finest bridal finery, taken to the top of a high mountain and left there to receive her supernatural suitor.

The king knew that it was pointless to ignore the word of the oracle and had no choice but to act on her advice. Psyche was dressed in the finest bridal gown that the world had ever seen, and a huge torch-lit procession was organised to escort her to the top of the mountain. The procession was magnificent but more like a funeral march than a bridal parade. Everybody feared that the gods would send a hideous monster to devour Psyche and none doubted that they would never see her again. After many tearful farewells Psyche was left alone on the mountain top.

For many hours Psyche sat alone. The torches burned out and a cold wind began to blow. Although she had hidden her fear from her father, Psyche was now terrified and expected a winged monster to swoop down on her at any second. Suddenly a warm wind sprang up and drove the cold away. The wind grew stronger and stronger until Psyche began to fear that she would be blown off her precarious perch. With a final mighty blast the wind lifted her high into the air and carried her far out into the darkness.

After what seemed like an age Psyche was gently deposited in a field of fragrant flowers, just as dawn was breaking. Exhausted by the perils of her night-time flight and lulled by the scent of the waking flowers, Psyche fell into a deep and enchanted sleep. When she awoke the day was well advanced and she could see her surroundings a little better. She found herself in a beautiful but unfamiliar valley far away from her homeland. Through a copse of silvery trees she glimpsed a fabulous palace and decided to make her way there.

Inside the palace all was silent and deserted. She was about to leave, thinking it must be the home of a powerful king who might be angry to find her there, when she heard whispering voices. Following the sounds she came to the most glorious room she had ever seen. A clear and bright fire was burning in the hearth and its light played on the gold and silver plates of a feast that had been set out on a table before it. Psyche was hungry and the cheery room made her loose her fear so she set about the glorious food with an appetite. By the time she had finished the sun had set and the palace was growing dark.

Psyche threw herself on the bed and lapsed into deep thought about all that had befallen her. She remembered the sigh that had awoken her from her sleep three years before and wondered about that most of all. Soon she was fast asleep. When the night was at its darkest Psyche was awoken by the sound of rustling wings and padding feet. She sat up, terrified that the winged monster had finally come for her, but then she heard a soothing voice. "Don't be afraid sweetest Psyche. Live with me as my bride in this palace and I will love and care for you forever. Only one thing I must ask; you must never try to look at me, for if you do we will be parted forever."

Psyche was comforted and she fell asleep again easily. The next morning she wondered if it had all been a dream, but everything was exactly as she remembered it. Since there was nowhere for her to go Psyche spent the day exploring the palace and the valley and found them to be delightful. That evening she found the fire miraculously alight and a sumptuous meal laid out just as before. When the night was at its darkest Psyche heard the rustling of wings and her mysterious husband came to her.

Life soon settled into a pattern. Psyche lived in the palace and enjoyed all manner of amusements and every night her husband would come to her. But, when she awoke in the morning, he was always gone and she could find no sign of him anywhere in the palace or the valley.

Psyche was very happy in her new life, but after a while she began to miss her sisters. One night she persuaded her husband to bring them to the valley for a visit. Although he was very against the idea he kept his word, and the very next day Psyche's sisters found themselves deposited in the valley by the same mysterious means the Psyche had arrived there. The sisters were overjoyed to see Psyche, who they thought was dead, and the three of them spent a wonderful day in the valley and exploring the fabulous palace.

As evening approached and it was almost time for them to leave the sisters asked Psyche when they would be meeting the husband who provided all this luxury. Sheepishly Psyche had to admit that even she had never seen her husband. The sisters were disappointed and advised Psyche that this was a less than satisfactory state of affairs. They even suggested that the mystery husband was a gross monster after all who was just fattening her up to be eaten.

Although Psyche didn't believe that her husband had any cruel intentions her sisters' admonishments aroused a sense of injustice in her and she suddenly became intensely curious to see her husband's face. That night she secreted an oil lamp under her bed and, when she was sure her husband was fast asleep by her side, she lit it and looked over at him. The glorious and beautiful form of Cupid, god of love, was revealed to her instead of the deformed monster she had feared. She was so startled that her hand shook and a little burning oil fell on the sleeping god's shoulder.

Cupid awoke and saw Psyche staring at him. He knew the spell had been broken and that they could never be together as long as she knew him to be a god. Sadly he stood up and walked out of the palace without saying a word. As he did so the palace and the valley vanished and Psyche found herself back on the bare mountain top where her adventure had begun. Cupid fled to his secret place to mourn his loss and Psyche wandered out into the world to look for him, although she knew that she could never find her husband unless he allowed it.

For months and years Psyche wandered in the wilderness until finally she came to the place where Venus herself lived. The heartbroken girl did not know that the goddess had been the chief architect of her sorrows and decided to beg her for help to find Cupid. The goddess's thirst for revenge had not yet been satisfied and she saw the ideal opportunity for further cruel sport at Psyche's expense. Venus promised to help Psyche if she could perform a simple task for her, and the girl readily agreed.

Venus asked Psyche to go into the cellar of her palace and to sort the grain that was kept there for her doves into its different kinds. If she could do this before the sun set, promised Venus, the goddess would help her find Cupid. Thinking little of the task Psyche descended to the grain store and there realised that she had been tricked. In vast piles were grains of every sort mixed up together. By the end of the day Psyche had only managed to make a few small piles of sorted grains – it seemed certain that she would fail. Just as she was about to give up, Psyche spied an ant advancing towards the grain piles. Suddenly a huge column of ants flowed into the chamber like a river and began sorting the grains. Within minutes the impossible task was completed and the ants had disappeared the way they had come.

When Venus returned she was extremely angry and realised that some god had intervened to help Psyche. She set the girl a second task even harder than the first – to collect the golden wool from the rams that lived on the other side of a river near her palace. Psyche went to the river and looked across at the rams. Immediately it was clear that she would never be able to collect their glittering wool. The animals were huge and fierce with razor sharp horns and venomous teeth.

Psyche sat down on the bank in despair, but as she wept she heard a voice in the reeds whispering to her. The voice advised her to wait until the evening when the rams laid down to sleep and to gather the wool that had been caught on the branches and bushes. Psyche followed the advice and returned to Venus with her arms full of the glittering fleece. Once again Venus perceived that she had been helped and set the hapless girl a third task even harder than the other two. Psyche was to draw a pitcher of water from the Fountain of Forgetfulness.

With a heavy heart Psyche travelled to the place where the fountain was to be found and, as she had suspected, saw that it was an impossible task. The fountain was at the top of a sheer mountain and the only path to the top was guarded by two fierce dragons who never slept. Just then a mighty eagle swooped down, picked Psyche up and flew her to the top of the mountain over the heads of the guardian dragons. Psyche was able to draw the water and return with it to Venus.

The goddess was now enraged and decided to set a final task that the girl couldn't possible accomplish even if she had the help of a god. Psyche was commanded to descend to the underworld with a message for Persephone, Venus's sister, asking her for a piece of her beauty. In despair Psyche climbed a tall tower and was about to leap to her death when the very stones of the tower spoke to her.

Following the advice she had been given Psyche took two coins and two pieces of bread and set off on the long road to the underworld. When she came to the river that separated the underworld from the world of the living she gave Charon the boatman one of the coins so that he would ferry her across. When she came to the great dog Cerberus, who guards the entrance to the underworld, she gave it a piece of bread and it let her pass.

Before the dark throne of Persephone, queen of the underworld, Psyche made the request she had been ordered to make explaining that Venus had lost some of her beauty while tending her sick son who had been injured by burning oil. Persephone handed Psyche a small box containing a fragment of her beauty and warned her strictly against opening it. Psyche returned the way she had come. With the second piece of bread she distracted Cerberus so that she could leave the underworld, and with the second coin she paid Charon to take her back across the river.

Once she was safely back in the land of the living Psyche began the long journey back to the palace of Venus. As she walked she began thinking how badly the goddess had treated her and despaired that she would ever relent and tell her where Cupid was hiding. Eventually the foolish girl decided that she would not take the box back to Venus but that she would use it on herself so that Cupid would be sure to come back to her. As she opened the box, however, she fell into a deathly swoon and collapsed on the road. It was another trick. Venus had known that Psyche would not be able to resist looking in the box just as she had been unable to resist looking at her husband.

By this time Cupid had recovered from his wound and, despite his fears, was unable to resist looking for Psyche. When he found her apparently dead by the side of the road he knew instantly that he had been wrong to abandon her. As he kissed her for one last time Jove, the great father of the gods, moved his hand and Psyche recovered from her swoon. The wings of a butterfly grew from her back and the couple ascended to Olympus, the home of the gods, where Jove himself gave Psyche the sacred nectar that bestowed immortality.

The associations and metaphors in this ancient tale are manifold. On one level it is simply another tale of the mortal at the mercy of the gods, who can be both cruel and kind. Another reading becomes obvious when you know that the word "psyche" is Greek for "soul". The perils and trials of Psyche are the perils and trials of the human soul. From innocence it passes through wonder, immature love that lacks faith, hardships and finally peace and sleep. The transformation of Psyche from mortal to immortal is symbolised by the butterfly wings – the emergence of the butterfly from the apparently dead husk of its cocoon has long been a symbol of rebirth. In one sense the tale of Psyche can be seen as one of the earliest stirrings of the idea of the immortal soul that is able to transcend the world and share the realm of the gods.

In the Beginning

To the human mind all things must have a beginning, even if that beginning is ever so far in the past, and the world itself is not exempted from this rule. Almost all creation myths start with a state of formlessness and chaos that is often represented as a churning ocean – and so it is with the Christian myth.

Human beings are, obviously, land-based creatures so it becomes necessary that one of the first acts of a creation that will culminate in the birth of humans must be a separation of the land from the sea. Also vital is the separation of the earthly realm from the heavenly realm, a distinction that we have already seen was central to ancient peoples' world-views.

Once these two miracles have been accomplished it only remains to place the heavenly bodies in their orbits, the creation of the sun and the moon, and the stage is set for the birth of the natural world with humans at its pinnacle. It's refreshing to look at less well-known creation myths to demonstrate the universality of these themes. The tale of the spider and the clam shell is from the Polynesian island of Naura.

The Spider and the Clam Shell

One day the old spider who had spun her web in the sky since the beginning of time looked down on the vast and never-changing ocean and saw a strange object floating on the endless waves. Descending on a thread the old spider discovered that it was a huge clam shell and she was greatly amazed.

Wanting to see inside the spider tried to prize the shell open but she did not have the strength. Next she tapped on the shell with her spindly legs and was amazed to discover that it was hollow. Now her curiosity was fully aroused and she used every ounce of her magic to part the two halves of the shell just enough so that she could squeeze inside.

Inside the clam shell it was very dark and cramped and the old spider could not even stretch out her legs. With her sensitive feet the spider began to explore the interior of the shell by touch since she could not see anything. Eventually she felt a smooth, rounded object that was coiled and reasoned that it must be a snail. As was her way the spider bound the snail under one of her legs and slept with it there for three days and nights. In this way she gained power over the snail and she set it free to wander about inside the shell.

The spider continued her exploration and soon found a second snail, larger than the first, which she treated in the same way. When she awoke she noticed that the first snail had not gone very far and said to it "This shell is very cramped, can you make it a little larger so that we can stand up at least". The snail replied that it could and immediately the clam shell grew larger so that the spider could stretch out her legs. With this accomplished she picked up the little snail and set it on the roof of the shell as the moon.

Now that she had a little light to see by the spider noticed a large worm coiled in the bottom of the shell. She asked the spider "Can you make this shell a little larger so that we can stand up?" The worm replied that it could and stretched out its mighty body between the two halves of the shell and pushed with all its strength. The worm pushed and heaved until he unhinged the sockets of the shell and opened them wide apart. The upper half become the realm of the heavens and the lower half the realm of the earth.

The labour of the worm caused sweat to pour from his body, which settled in the bottom of the shell and became the salty sea. With his task accomplished and all his strength used up the mighty worm lay down and died and his body became the mountains. Finally the old spider took the larger snail and set it against the roof of the shell as the sun. From that day to this the spider has controlled everything in the shell and her body and her legs stretch from one edge of the world to the other.

The spider in this Polynesian tale can be seen as fate, the one god who stands outside creation and controls even the gods. The connection between weaving and fate is very ancient – in this case it is the weaving of the web of the spider, but in other traditions it is weaving in the sense of making cloth. The Greek myth of Arachne is a good example of this.

Arachne

Arachne was a mortal woman who boasted that her skill in weaving surpassed that of Athena the goddess. Athena came to hear of this boast and decided to teach Arachne a lesson. She came down to the earth in the guise of an old woman and challenged the haughty girl to a weaving competition. Once Arachne was committed the goddess revealed herself, but it was too late for Arachne to back out.

Athena set to work weaving a beautiful tapestry with scenes that showed the folly of mortals who tried to evade the fate set down for them by the gods. Arachne responded by making a tapestry that showed the follies of the gods. Athena was so enraged that she turned Arachne into a spider. The message is clear: both gods and humans may lay plans for the future but the human attempt to weave its own web of fate will always fail.

The Egyptian Heaven and Earth

Before the beginning of all things there was only the great and formless sea Nun, and from it was born Atum-Ra who held the seed of all life that was to come. From his mighty body Atum-Ra created Shu, the air, and Tefnut, the dew and the rain. The air and the rain, who were brother and sister, came together as husband and wife and produced Geb and Nut, who also became husband and wife in turn.

Creation would have continued like this but, seeing Nut and Geb lying together, Atum-Ra stepped in and let it be known that he wanted them separated. This task he gave to Shu who went to where the young lovers lay and roughly forced them apart. Shu lifted the body of Nut high above her so that her body was arched high above Geb, only her toes and her fingertips touched the toes and fingertips of her husband.

Atum-Ra commanded Shu to keep the couple apart so Shu, the air, placed her body forever between Nut and Geb. In this way Nut became the vault of the heavens and Geb became the land. Atum-Ra also put a curse on Nut so that she could not bear children and all of the days of the year swore to uphold the curse.

Creation would have remained like this if another god, the compassionate Thoth, hadn't stepped in and thought of a plan to relieve the suffering of Nut and Geb. Thoth challenged the moon to a game of draughts and won for himself control of a fraction of her light. From this light he fashioned five extra days and added them to the 360 days of the year. Because these days were new they were beyond the control of Atum-Ra and Nut and Geb could be together for this brief period. It was enough, and Nut gave birth to five children, one on each day.

On the first day she gave birth to Osiris who was to become the lord of life and eternity. On the second day she gave birth to falcon-headed Horus, on the third she produced red-haired Set who would challenge Osiris for rule of Egypt one day. On the fourth day came Isis, giver of life and future wife of Osiris, and on the last day Nephthys, Queen of the Dead and future wife of Set was born. The children of Nut and Geb became the founding dynasty of Egypt and their history became the history of the gods of men and women who would come later.

Another brother and sister who were also husband and wife and who gave the world its form come from Japanese myth. In this tale there are also connections with the distinction between the world of the living and the world of the dead; two opposite realms inextricably linked. To this day Izanagi and Izanami are remembered in the form of two rocks found in Isa Bay. For as long as anyone can remember these two rocks have been linked by a massive coiled rope that bridges the narrow stretch of water that separates them.

Izanagi and Izanami

One of the last generations of gods to be born was the brother and sister Izanagi and Izanami. At that time the world was no more than a formless bed of reeds that floated on an endless ocean. The gods decided that it was time that the world was given form and they chose Izanagi and Izanami to carry out the task.

The brother and sister descended from the plain of heaven and became husband and wife. Izanagi had been given a magical jewelled spear with which to carve form into the world and this he dipped into the sea and began to stir.

In the place where the spear stirred the water crystals began to form in the churning water and when Izanagi withdrew the blade a few of these fell back into the water and formed the first land, which was named Onokoko. Izanagi and Izanami stepped off the Floating Bridge from heaven and onto the land and began to create the islands of Japan. Izanami gave birth to nature and its gods.

The god of the wind, the god of the mountains, the god of the trees and the god of fire were born in this way. When the god of fire was conceived he was so hot and fiery that he killed his mother Izanami and she descended to Yomi, the land of the dead. The tears of her husband were so copious that they formed the goddess of the Moaning-river and he decided to retrieve his bride.

Izanami met Izanagi at the dark and shadowy entrance to Yomi, but she would not step out and would not allow him to step in. She explained that she could not return because she had already eaten the food of the dead. Izanagi would not listen to her and was determined to enter Yomi and drag her out. Lighting a torch he strode through the entrance and was horrified by what he saw.

Izanami, his beautiful wife, had become a hideous decaying corpse seething with worms and maggots. Izanami was humiliated to be revealed to her husband in this state and from her shame came a terrible anger. She loosed all the demons of hell to chase her husband away and Izanagi had to flee in terror as he saw them advancing on him.

With the demons snapping at his heals Izanagi just made it back into the world of light. Exhausted he threw himself into the sea to wash away the contamination of the dead. He washed his left eye and from it came the goddess of the sun, whom he placed on the plain of heaven. He washed his right eye and from it came the god of the moon, whom he set to rule the kingdom of the night. He washed his nose and from it came the god of storms, whom he gave the seas to rule over.

Izanagi stayed in the realm of the living while Izanami became the queen of the dead and remained in Yomi. From that day until the end of time they have agreed to be apart.

In this tale we begin to see the elements of strife and gory bloodshed that characterize many ancient creation myths. In the Greek, Nordic and Babylonian creation myths the world is born out of inter-generational conflict between the gods.

The chief gods of these pagan religions were not the first born but the sons and daughters of the first born who turned on their parents and took their place as the rulers of the universe. In many cases these first-born gods are brutal and elemental forces with dangerous appetites and no morality. It falls to their children to control these primordial forces and to create the ordered world that humans will eventually inhabit.

The Babylonian Creation

Before the beginning of things there were only two beings: Apsu the ocean and Tiamat the sea. Together they filled the universe and they mingled with each other and gave birth to three generations of gods. The last of these generations included Anu and Ea and the gods of the sky, the earth and the underworld.

Soon Apsu began to regret producing these children. Mummu, spirit of the waves, disturbed his rest during the day, and the serpents Lahkmu and Lahakmu kept him awake at night. These were the gods of the first generation born to Apsu and Tiamat and Apsu determined to be rid of them so that he could get some peace.

Apsu made an alliance with Mummu and plotted to kill the later generations but Ea, who saw all things, divined their intentions and imprisoned them with a magical spell before they could carry them out. Ea stole Apsu's crown, killed him and built a palace on the back of his vast corpse.

Tiamat, the first mother, was enraged at the murder of her husband and prepared to do battle with the wayward Ea. From her body, which produced all things, she produced eleven armies of demons, each one more terrible than the one before. She made a legion of serpents with poisoned fangs, a legion of dragons with glittering scales, a legion of giant scorpion men, fish men, storm demons and hell hounds. With her army assembled, Tiamat advanced on Ea's palace where all the gods were hiding in fear.

Anshar, of the second generation after Apsu and Tiamat, sent his son Anu to face the goddess, but he turned back in terror when he saw her. Anu's brother Ea, who had slain Apsu and taken his crown, also lacked the courage to face the rage of Tiamat. Finally Marduk, son of Ea, stepped forward and offered to face the demon army. In return he demanded dominion over all the gods, control of the fates and responsibility for creation.

The other gods were loath to concede such prizes but

it looked as if none of them would survive anyway so they agreed to Marduk's terms. Marduk received the sceptre, the throne and the royal ring and he gathered his weapons together to go into battle.

Mounting his storm chariot, which was drawn by the steeds Killer, Pitiless, Trampler and Flier, he took to the skies and rushed towards the advancing demon army. When Tiamat saw Marduk she laughed at his small size and opened her mouth to swallow him and his chariot whole. Marduk released an evil wind which filled Tiamat's mouth and bloated her belly. Then he loosed an arrow of lightning that pierced her body and split the goddess mother's heart.

When they saw that Tiamat was dead the demon army lost courage and turned to run, but Marduk caught them in a giant net and they became his servants. Next he dismembered Tiamat. He smashed her skull and slit her arteries so that her blood flowed all over the world. Then he split her body in half and made one half the sky and the other half the land. On the sky half of her body he fixed the sun and the moon and the stars and on the land half of her body he created humans. As the gods had all agreed, creation remained the way Marduk had made it from that day forth.

The Nordic Creation
In the beginning there was the realm of ice, Niflheim, and the realm of fire, Muspell. Both of these regions were impossible to live in but, where they met and mingled, there was a region where the fire melted the ice and the ice quenched the fire and it was as warm and pleasant as a summer's day.

Here the melted snow and ice ran together into a huge pool which began to take form and move as life was born within it. Eventually the giant Ymir took shape and he was the first living thing in creation. Ymir stood up and stretched his mighty frame and looked out at the emptiness of the world. He saw the emptiness of the land of ice, where nothing could live, and he saw the emptiness and fury of the land of fire.

One night, as Ymir lay sleeping, he broke into a sweat because he was having a dream that we cannot know, and from this sweat was born a male and a female giant who were to be the father and mother of the race of giants.

Also born from the ice, as Ymir had been, was a giant cow known as Audumla. The cow licked the salt from the ice and four rivers of milk flowed from her udders, which Ymir drank from to sustain himself. As Audumla licked at the ice the hair of a man emerged. She licked some more and the head of a man was uncovered. The cow kept licking and eventually the whole body of a man was set free from the ice – his name was Buri and he was the first man.

Buri had a son named Bor who married one of the daughters of the ice giants. This pair had three sons: Odin, Vili and Ve who were half-men and half-giants. When these sons grew up they came to hate the frost giants who were cruel and barbarous and a great conflict took place. At the climax of this war Ymir, the father of the giants, was killed by Odin and his blood gushed across the world like a tidal wave. All but two of Ymir's race were engulfed and drowned by this gory flood. These two escaped in a boat and went on to found a new race of giants but, for the time being, the world was left to the victorious Odin and his brothers.

Odin carried the body of Ymir to the centre of the realm and from it he fashioned the world as we know it.

From the giant's flesh he made the soil, from his unbroken bones he made the mountains and from his shattered bones he made the rocks and the pebbles. From his blood he made the oceans which he poured in a great ring around his creation. Finally Odin took Ymir's skull and fashioned the vault of the heavens.

Once this work was done Odin took sparks and embers from the land of fire and fixed them to the roof of Ymir's skull to form the stars. In the sky he also placed the Sun and the Moon but as he did so two terrible and ferocious wolves leapt into the sky to consume them. The Sun and the Moon fled from the wolves and they will be chased across the sky until the day of the final battle when they will be caught and consumed.

From the maggots that were feeding on the corpse of Ymir, Odin made the races of dwarves and placed them at the four corners of the world where they live to this day in dark, underground places. Finally Odin placed the mighty serpent Jormungand in the ocean and the snake was so vast that it could loop all around the world and hold its tail in its mouth.

Perseus and the Myth of the Journey

Perhaps the most sophisticated and all encompassing myth from the pantheon of the ancient world's stories is that of the hero Perseus. Embroidered over many centuries the tale came to include elements of almost all of the themes that are represented in the other myths examined here. Perseus the hero, part mortal and part god, is a kind of Gilgamesh, Psyche and Hercules all rolled into one. His adventures take him to the ends of the earth and the edges of the heavenly realm.

With gifts bestowed on him by the gods, Perseus is near invincible and capable of tackling the ultimate evil in the world – the heart-slaying gaze of the gorgon. But he is also a hapless mortal playing a part on the stage directed by the gods. In the end even his purity and moral righteousness cannot save him from becoming the pawn of cruel fate. The triumphs of his life are no more than steps on the road to a futile and absurd tragedy.

The Tragedy of Perseus

Acrisius was a good and proud king who, like many other men, believed he could cheat the fates. The greatest pride of Acrisius's life was his beautiful daughter Danae, so it was with heartbroken disbelief that he received the prophecy of the Delphic oracle that she would give birth to a son who would kill him. Although great was his love for his daughter, Acrisius's fear of death was greater and he resolved to make sure that his daughter could never have a son. Accordingly he had a vast and strong tower made of brass constructed, and there, at its summit, he imprisoned Danae in a chamber without doors or windows.

Danae could not understand why her loving father had turned against her so cruelly and spent her lonely days weeping in the high tower that had become her prison. One day the great god Zeus looked down and saw the maiden sighing her youth away in her lofty cell. Filled with desire for her beauty and pity for her situation the father of the gods decided to go to her. Taking on the form of a golden shower of light Zeus passed effortlessly through the thick brass walls that would have been impenetrable to any mortal and comforted the girl in his customary lusty manner.

As a result of this brief visit Danae conceived a child and the boy was named Perseus. When Acrisius heard that his daughter had given birth despite all his precautions he became very afraid and determined that he must rid himself of both of them before the prophecy could come to pass. The king could not bring himself to murder his daughter and his grandson directly so instead he had them locked in a wooden chest which was then thrown out to sea. As far as the king knew the chest had sunk to the bottom of the sea or been devoured by a sea monster, but in fact it was borne safely across the waves until it was caught in the nets of a fisherman named Dictys off the island of Seriphos.

Dictys was related to the king of the island, Polydectes, who invited the miraculous voyagers to stay with him in his palace. As the years passed Perseus grew into the fine young man he would be expected to be as the son of Zeus. Polydectes, a lascivious and cruel king, developed a passion for Danae but, as long as Perseus was around, he didn't dare act on it. Eventually he conceived a plan to rid him of the young man for good. Polydectes announced, falsely, that he intended to marry a princess from a neighbouring kingdom and held a great feast to celebrate the fact. Guests arrived from far and wide with fabulous gifts, but Perseus, who distrusted and disliked the king, brought nothing.

Noticing this slight Polydectes demanded that the youth should bring him a gift worthy of his divine parentage – the head of the dreaded gorgon Medusa. The gorgons were the most feared creatures in existence. They were three terrible sisters who had once been beautiful but who pride and greed had turned into monsters. Their faces were disfigured with the tusks of boars and their hair had been replaced by a loathsome nest of snakes. Worst of all their despair and anger had turned their hearts to stone so that any mortal meeting their gaze would immediately die and be transformed into rock. Only one of the sisters, Medusa, was mortal, but it would surely be an impossible task to kill her. Perseus had the pride of youth, however, and could not bear to decline the challenge and be humiliated by the king, so he accepted. Polydectes had always known that he would, and next morning as Perseus set off on his quest he chuckled heartily to himself, eyeing the fair Danae hungrily.

Perseus came to the shoreline and sat down to think. He had set out in such a hurry that he had brought no weapons for the task ahead, and neither had he thought to inquire where exactly the gorgons were to be found. It seemed as if his quest was doomed to failure before it had even begun, but the young hero could by no means bring himself to return to the palace and admit defeat. As he sat brooding on his foolishness the great goddess Athena, who loved to aid handsome young warriors, came down to him.

Athena gave him certain gifts to help him in his quest. She gave him a scimitar, which was the only weapon in the world capable of penetrating Medusa's tough skin. She gave him a bright shield and advised him to fight the creature by looking only at her reflection in the shield's mirror-like surface. Finally she gave him Hermes's sandals, which would allow him to fly and to cover seven days' journey in one day. The goddess blessed her hero and advised him to travel to the island where the horrible Graeae lived, three sisters of the gorgons.

Using his magical, winged sandals Perseus soared into the air and soon came to the realm of perpetual dusk where the icy and fog-choked isle of the Graeae was to be found. As Perseus alighted on that benighted piece of earth he could hear the voices of the three hags arguing amongst themselves. "Give it to me now sister, it is my turn to have it" came the first voice. "No, you had it last, it is mine now" came the second. "You both lie, it is mine, give it to me now" came the third voice. Perseus was amazed by this strange argument and wondered what it could mean. Stealthily he crept through the mist until he could see the Graeae and perceived what it was that they were arguing about.

The Graeae, or the Grey Ones, were so old and haggard that they had only one eye remaining between them, which they used in turn to peer peevishly at the world. When Perseus saw this he immediately realized how he could gain power over the sisters, who were said to be powerful witches. As one sister passed the horrid watery eye to her sister Perseus dashed forward and grabbed it from her withered hand. Realising that they had been robbed the three blind sisters flailed about to find the thief, but Perseus used his sandals to hover in the air and kept out of their reach.

In a strong clear voice that amazed the Graeae Perseus demanded to know where he could find the gorgons and threatened to smash the eye if he did not receive a truthful answer. There was much grinding of toothless gums and curses uttered, but the sisters realised that Perseus had them. "Go to the island of the garden of the Hesperides" the ghastly trio chorused "they will tell you where to find the gorgons. But it will do you no good, even one as cunning and brazen as you cannot hope to overcome our sisters".

Perseus was glad to be away from the place and was soon winging his way to the paradise garden of the Hesperides where the apples that bestowed immortality on the gods grew. The nymphs who tended the garden were happy to greet the handsome hero but regretted that they could not tell him where the gorgons lived. Perseus was about to return to the island of the Graeae and carry out his threat when the nymphs told him that they would take him to meet the giant Atlas, who supported the heavens on his shoulders. Such an ancient and far-seeing being was sure to know where the Gorgons could be found.

After a long journey to the edge of the world Perseus stood before the ancient colossus Atlas. The mighty giant looked him up and down with his vast and infinitely experienced eye as he considered the hero's request. Finally he said that he had indeed seen the dwelling place of the gorgons and promised to tell Perseus if he would agree to one condition. "I am old and tired," said Atlas, "when you have the head of the gorgon Medusa, bring it here so that I can look at it and be turned to stone. I cannot let the heavens slip, but I can no longer bear the pain of keeping them aloft. If my body was stone I could bear the weight without discomfort and finally have some rest." Perseus agreed and the sad old giant stretched his vast arm across the sky and pointed to the cave where the gorgons were to be found. Before he left, the nymphs of the garden gave Perseus a helmet that they had stolen from Hades, lord of the dead, and which rendered its wearer invisible.

Even with his magical sandals it took Perseus a long time to travel the length of Atlas's vast arm, but eventually he came to the dark and terrible cave where the gorgons were to be found. Slipping on the helmet of invisibility Perseus crept into the cave and saw the three sisters for the first time. Two of them were asleep but the third and youngest, Medusa, was pacing the cave and bemoaning her fate. Although her body was still young and beautiful her hands had claws of brass and her face was horribly disfigured. The writhing snakes that had replaced her hair made Medusa shudder every time they touched her soft white shoulders and Perseus saw that it would be a mercy to kill her.

All around the entrance of the cave were the frozen forms of other heroes and travellers who had dared to come to that place and who had been turned to stone for their troubles. Remembering to use the bright shield as a mirror. Perseus approached his prey and struck off her head with a single blow. Instantly he put the writhing head in a goatskin bag and took to the air to make his escape. Medusa's scream had awoken her sisters, who set out in crazed pursuit, but as long as Perseus wore his helmet they could not see him.

As he flew, some drops of Medusa's blood dripped on to the sands of the deserts below and, where they fell, become the deadly snakes that still plague those regions to this day. On and on flew Perseus until the blood-curdling screams of Medusa's sisters had been left far behind. Just then the hero saw the figure of a beautiful young maiden chained to a rock on the shore far below. Instantly smitten by her, Perseus descended and alighted beside her.

Seeing her cruelly chained he demanded to know who could have done such a thing to one so innocent. The girl, whose name was Andromeda, explained that her mother, the Queen of Ethiopia, had offended the gods by claiming to be more beautiful than any immortal. As a punishment Poseidon had sent a mighty sea beast to ravage the coast of the kingdom and an oracle had revealed that this beast could only be satisfied by the sacrifice of the haughty queen's daughter. After a mighty battle with the sea monster Perseus defeated it and claimed Andromeda as his bride.

Not forgetting to visit the titan Atlas, who he turned into a mighty mountain range that stands to this day on the borders of the North African desert, Perseus made his way home with his new bride. Arriving at the palace of Polydectes, who had tricked him into undertaking the dangerous quest and who never expected to see the young man alive again, he learned that the king had been cruelly treating his mother. Striding into the king's hall, Perseus, resplendent with the gifts given him by Athena, approached the dumbfounded king and presented him with his gift. As soon as Polydectes glanced at the face of the gorgon he was turned to stone and his body was left where it sat on the throne as a warning to future kings.

Perseus's fame spread throughout the world and even his grandfather, Acrisius, came to hear of him. Learning that his daughter and her son were still alive and had not drowned in the chest so many years before, Acrisius was filled with remorse and longed for a reconciliation with his lost family. At that time the old king was attending the games being held in memory of the king of Thessaly and could not leave to seek out his grandson until they were over. Unknown to Acrisius, Perseus had already set out to visit him at his home in Argos but a storm had blown his vessel of course and the young hero was at that moment also in Thessaly.

Inevitably Perseus was invited to honour the kingdom by taking part in the funeral games, an invitation he readily agreed to. On the next morning Perseus took his place on the field for the discus-throwing event. The crowd marvelled at this young warrior who seemed to bear the mark of the gods on his brow, and everybody waited breathlessly for his first throw. Among them was Acrisius, who also admired the young athlete but had no idea that he was in fact his own grandson.

As Perseus made his throw the fates stepped in and played their cards. A gust of wind deflected the powerful throw and the discus plunged into the crowd where it struck Acrisius on the forehead, killing him instantly. The prophecy had been fulfilled. Acrisius had been struck dead by his own grandson. For the rest of his long life Perseus had to live with the knowledge that all his adventures and triumphs had led to no more than that single, meaningless twist of fate.

A Modern Legend

October 1959 saw an event that was to change the way we looked at the heavenly bodies that have been familiar to our ancestors for thousands of years. In that month an unmanned Russian spacecraft, named Luna 3, travelled to the far side of the moon and sent back photographs of the lunar surface. For the first time in history we saw close-up views of a sphere other than our own familiar earth.

Until that point the sun, the moon and the other planets had existed in our consciousness only as remote and unchanging lights in the sky. Even the moon, the closest celestial body to us, was essentially no more than a bright disc to everyone other than the tiny minority of professional and amateur astronomers who had studied it through telescopes. Suddenly it was possible to open your newspaper in the morning and see photographs that showed the surface detail of the moon as if it were no more remote than an Arabian desert or some other exotic part of the world.

Within thirty years every major body in the solar system, except for distant Pluto, had been visited and photographed from close quarters. During that period a series of deep space probes carried out the most incredible voyages of discovery that humanity has ever witnessed. They extended the compass of the known universe by millions of times and brought us into direct contact with the true faces of the ancient gods of our ancestors.

Since the earliest astronomical observations had been made the brightest objects in the sky apart from the sun and the moon, those we now know to be the other planets of our solar system, were named and regarded as gods. In modern English this tradition is preserved absolutely. Western civilisation, with its roots in the ancient Greek and Roman worlds, refers to the planets according to the names of the Greek and Roman gods they were thought to embody. Taking the innermost of the planets first, we can trace these ancient identities and compare them to what the modern creed of science says about their personalities.

Mercury, known as Hermes to the Greeks, was the messenger of the gods. He plays little direct part in the ancient myths beyond carrying messages from the gods to each other or down to some mortal who has had the misfortune to get mixed up in their affairs. One of the few stories about Mercury's deeds has him stealing cattle from his brother Apollo while still a child and then denying that he even knows what a cow is when accused of the theft. He takes the role of the patron of travellers and thieves in the ancient mythology and is also connected with dreamers and visionaries.

Between 24 March 1974 and 16 March 1975 the American probe Mariner 10 made three passes of the planet Mercury and sent back the first, and to this date the last, close-up pictures of this small world. As the ancients had said, Mercury is a swift and decidedly eccentric body. Its year is only eight-seven earth days long, but each of Mercury's days is the equivalent of fifty-eight earth days – in other words more than half a year passes between dawn and dusk on the surface of this strange world. Not only that but Mercury's orbit around the sun is highly erratic. Its distance from the sun varies by more than fourteen million miles during each eighty-seven-day-long year – the equivalent variation of the earth's orbit is only three million miles.

Next in line is Venus, known as Aphrodite by the Greeks. The great beauty of the gods she is variously the goddess of love and loveliness. When she first came into the world, born from the foam of the sea, she caused consternation among the older goddesses and sent pulses races among the gods. For all her beauty Venus was notoriously flighty and capricious. These characteristics led her to annoy Zeus on many occasions until he decided that she should be married to Vulcan, god of the forge, who was the ugliest and least favoured of the gods on Olympus.

Not surprisingly Vulcan suffered more from the match than his wife who was endlessly unfaithful to him. Her first lover was Ares, god of war, with whom she had several children including Cupid the god of sexual love. It was Venus who became jealous of the mortal Psyche, the most beautiful woman who ever lived, and her son Cupid who fell in love with the girl and indirectly brought her much hardship. The tale of Pygmalion shows Venus in her typical role. The sculptor Pygmalion had always kept himself away from people and scorned love in favour of art. When one day he created a sculpture of a woman so beautiful that he fell in love with her Venus turned the statue into flesh and blood and Pygmalion was won over to the ways of the heart.

The true nature of the planet Venus had long been the subject of controversy among astronomers and remained so right up until 21 October 1975 when the Russian spacecraft Venera 9 landed on the surface and sent back the first photograph. For years attempts to glimpse the surface of Venus had been hampered by the planet's dense and all-encompassing cloud cover. Venus is very similar in mass and volume to the earth and many scientists hoped that its cloud cover might conceal a surface that supported abundant life and an atmosphere similar to that which would have been found on earth in the age of the first amphibians.

Apart from the sun and the moon, Venus is by far the brightest object in the sky. This is due to its proximity and the highly reflective quality of its clouds. Its shining, mysterious radiance in the night sky is the primary reason for its association with the ancient goddesses of love and beauty. Like the Venus of myth, however, its heart holds surprises of a not always pleasant nature.

The first Russian landers that attempted to set down on the planet were fried by extremely high temperatures and crushed by massive atmospheric forces before they could even penetrate the clouds. It turns out that Venus's dense and heavy atmosphere traps heat on the surface so that, during the Venusian day, the mean temperature reaches more than 350 degrees centigrade – hot enough to melt lead. Its surface is hotter even than that of Mercury, which is many millions of miles closer to the sun. It's nice to think that the ancients got something right when they conjoined the cool beauty of Venus and Aphrodite with the sweaty heat of Vulcan's forge.

Mars was a much more significant god to the Romans than his counterpart Ares had been to the Greeks. Romulus and Remus, the central figures of the myth of the founding of the city of Rome, were his sons. Hot-headed and heedless of danger few ancients dared to offer prayed to this god since his interventions could be so unpredictable and disastrous. Mercury was a close ally of Mars's, ever since the god of thieves had rescued the war god from a pair of giants. Venus was his lover. Two of Mars's sons, Phobos, or Alarm, and Deimos, or Dread, have given their names to the two small moons of the red planet.

The exploration of Mars by unmanned probes has been one of the most extensive of the space age so far. This is partly due to its proximity and partly to long held beliefs that it was the most likely place in the solar system, apart from the earth, that life might be found. The American probes Viking I and Viking II were the first to successfully land on the planet and send back significant amounts of data, including the first surface pictures, in 1975.

Flybys and orbiters had already revealed that there were some incredible surface features. The largest known volcano in the solar system, appropriately named Mount Olympus, stands three times taller than

Everest and has a base almost 400 miles on diameter. Evidence of a violent heart within the planet of the war god seemed indisputable – although the volcanoes of Mars are thought to be long extinct.

Hopes of finding life have all but vanished. The thin atmosphere and harsh solar radiation have persuaded most scientists that nothing could be living there now, although there may have been life in some earlier, gentler epoch of the planet's history. Perhaps the home of the god of war and destruction was never a good place to expect to find fragile life.

Way out beyond the orbits of the four inner planets we find the gas giants Uranus, Neptune, Saturn and mighty Jupiter. Larger than all the other planets put together and with a vastly powerful magnetic field that extends its influence for millions of miles through interplanetary space, Jupiter is appropriately named after the father and king of the Roman gods – known as Zeus by the Greeks.

This outer domain of the solar system has been explored by four extraordinarily successful American probes; Pioneer 10 and 11 and Voyager 1 and 2. Launched in March of 1972 the Pioneer 10 probe is currently the furthest man-made object from the earth. It has long since passed out of the solar system and is now making the first journey into the near total mystery of interstellar space. This little robot has truly travelled to the ends of the world.

All four of these probes have sent us images of Jupiter, and the Voyager probes in particular have vastly increased our knowledge of the place. As is fitting for the king of the gods Jupiter is a place of incredible power and majesty. The first thing the probes encountered was Jupiter's vast radiation belts. These were detected at a range of more than twelve and a half million miles, and by the time Pioneer 10 made its closest approach the radiation was so intense that it almost killed the probe. The great red spot had long been a feature studied through telescopes and scientists were eager for a close up view of this phenomenon. It turns out to be a vast and permanent storm in the atmosphere with winds circulating at hundreds of miles an hour. The storm is big enough to swallow the earth several times.

Associated with Jupiter are a myriad of moons, at least sixteen, varying in size from a few miles in diameter to several thousand. Unsurprisingly they have largely been named after the numerous mortal women that Jupiter pursued and seduced in the mythological tales. Europa was pursued by Jupiter in the form of a white bull from the sea. Io was herself transformed into a white heifer so that Jupiter's wife would not guess that she was his lover. Europa, a strange and mysterious world that may conceal a warm ocean beneath its cracked ice surface, is considered by many to be the last best hope for finding life in our solar system.

Beyond Jupiter we begin to enter dark realms of the solar system where old and forgotten gods reign supreme. Saturn, surely the most mysterious and awe-inspiring object in our family of planets, is named after one of the monstrous predecessors of the Olympian gods, the Titan known to the Greeks as Chronos – Time, the devourer of all things. In the early chapters of Greek mythology Chronos is defeated by his son, Zeus, and sent into exile. Zeus, or Jupiter, only survived into adulthood because of the cunning of his mother Rhea.

The story goes that Saturn heard a prophecy that one of his children would unseat him from his throne, and so whenever his wife gave birth he would swallow the infant whole. When Jupiter was born Rhea handed her husband a large boulder wrapped in swaddling cloth which he swallowed in the belief that it was his son. In this way Rhea was able to keep the existence of Jupiter hidden until her son was old enough to defeat his father.

Once Saturn had been defeated, Jupiter, the new king of the gods, freed his brothers and sisters from the belly of their omnivorous father and allowed them to choose their own part of the universe to rule. Among them were Neptune and Pluto, brothers of Jupiter who chose to rule over the oceans and the underworld respectively. Neptune, also known as Poseidon, was visited by only one probe – Voyager 2. Pictures revealed a planet of incredibly calm beauty. The deep, ocean-blue colour of the atmosphere is unlike anything else in the solar system. Pluto, dark lord of the underworld, has never been visited and remains a mystery lurking at the very edges of our solar system. At its furthest point from the sun Pluto is so far out that the star that is the source of all life on our planet is barely more than a bright speck in the sky – truly an appropriate state of affairs for the bringer of death.